Inventing Entertainment

Inventing Entertainment

The Player Piano and the Origins of an American Musical Industry

Brian Dolan

ROWMAN & LITTLEFIELD PUBLISHERS, INC.
Lanham • Boulder • New York • Toronto • Plymouth, UK

ROWMAN & LITTLEFIELD PUBLISHERS, INC.

Published in the United States of America
by Rowman & Littlefield Publishers, Inc.
A wholly owned subsidary of The Rowman & Littlefield Publishing Group, Inc.
4501 Forbes Boulevard, Suite 200, Lanham, Maryland 20706
www.rowmanlittlefield.com

Estover Road
Plymouth PL6 7PY
United Kingdom

British Library Cataloguing in Publication Information Available

Library of Congress Cataloging-in-Publication Data:

Dolan, Brian.
  Inventing entertainment : the player piano and the origins of an American
musical industry / Brian Dolan.
    p. cm.
  Includes bibliographical references.
  ISBN-13: 978-0-7425-6127-4 (cloth : alk. paper)
  ISBN-10: 0-7425-6127-5 (cloth : alk. paper)
  ISBN-13: 978-0-7425-6461-9 (electronic)
  ISBN-10: 0-7425-6461-4 (electronic)
  1. Player piano—United States—History. I. Title.
ML1070.D66 2009
786.6′6—dc22   2008031587

Printed in the United States of America

♾ ™ The paper used in this publication meets the minimum requirements of
American National Standard for Information Sciences—Permanence of Paper for
Printed Library Materials, ANSI/NISO Z39.48-1992.

For Richard A. Dolan
Temporary steward of an American institution

Contents

Acknowledgments ix

Preface xi

1. Soundscape and Memory 1

2. Missionaries and Museums 7

3. Chronic Mechanitis 31

4. Every Collector's Dream 55

5. A Musical Morse Code 71

6. A Search for Identity 87

7. Possession 103

8. Expression 117

9. A Race for the Rolls 135

10. Music for the Masses? 153

Epilogue 165

Notes 175

Selected Bibliography 193

Index 197

Acknowledgments

IRST OF ALL, I'd like to thank Richard A. Dolan for prompting me to explore this history and helping me get to a number of archives for research. The rest of the Dolan clan and the extended family of employees at Story & Clark Pianos and QRS were very helpful, directing my attention to various people to talk to and places to seek information about the history of player pianos. Thanks also to Tom, Don, Terry, Ann Jones, and Bob Berkman for continuing the tradition of entertainment.

A number of people have fielded questions and been very helpful en route: Bob Berkman, CEO of QRS Music Technologies, for his hospitality and insight into the dynamics of QRS music roll history and his personal recollections; Bob and Ginny Billings, for their correspondence and their comprehensive *Rollography*; Mike Montgomery (who has shared his own interest in QRS); Robbie Rhodes, editor of *Mechanical Music Digest*; Tim Trager ("dealer, historian, lecturer, consultant, collector" extraordinaire in Chicago), and Ann Jones. A special thanks to Richard Reutlinger for hosting magnificent concerts, sharing his wonderful collection of automated mechanical musical instruments, and for being a conduit to the world of AMICAns.

My friends in England spent much time e-mailing me: Malcolm Cole of the Player Piano Group; Julian Dyer, who read some early chapters; Lisa Fagg (granddaughter of J. Lawrence Cook); John Farrell; Patrick Handscombe, Chairman of the Player Piano Group, U.K. (for explaining the complexities of Aeolian's Duo-Art recording system); and Mike Meddings (kudos to his doctorjazz website).

Much of the research for this book took place in the living rooms of single-family homes across America—only glimpses of which could be recounted in the pages here, but I thank all the members of the Automatic Musical Instrument Collectors' Association for their enthusiasm and hospitality.

As always, my immediate family showed their interest and support for my investigations and helped me to articulate the story along the way: Janet, Nancy, Daniel, Kathy, Sandy, Gale, and David. I thank my friends and colleagues at the University of California in the history of science, technology, and medicine for reading early proposals for this project and helping me to clarify some issues that I probably muddled again: Cathy Carson, Roger Hahn, Dan Hayes, Tom Laqueur, Cynthia Lee, Jack Lesch, Justin Suran, John Tercier, Charis Thompson, and Liz Watkins. I also thank Trevor Pinch, Emily Thompson, and David Suisman for their interest and support. As always, my wife, Dorothy Porter, was most encouraging and enthusiastic about helping me track down the sounds of history.

For access to manuscripts and other primary research materials, and for permission to quote from the materials in their collections, I thank John Shanahan from Lowrey Organ Company (which purchased Story & Clark Pianos in 1962); the archivist and staff at Syracuse University Archive (Melville Clark music archive); Bonnie Jo Dopp at the University of Maryland, who was most helpful in providing materials from the Howe Collection of Musical Instrument Literature; the library at Northern Illinois University, De Kalb (Melville Clark Piano Company [Wurlitzer] archive); and the National Museum of American History, Music & Musical Instruments Collections.

Preface

I HAVE SOME sort of inexplicable attraction to flea markets and garage sales. I long ago gave up on the idea that I was actually going to find a rare treasure—that diamond in the rough—in a dusty box labeled "Everything $1." But I remain drawn to the exploration of what people have finally decided to identify as their own junk. Perhaps it is not even their junk. Maybe it was inherited from their parents, filtered through a filial generation. But while perusing all sundry items displayed along folding tables, I am often struck by the idea that at some point, this stuff was probably important to someone. That thought alone suddenly gives more meaning—a sort of melancholy value—to the objects in front of me. The sellers are letting go of not only a material artifact but also of a memory. For them, it is time to let go, to offer it to others. They are at the spring cleaning stage of life. But for potential buyers like myself, sometimes such objects and memories are considered to be worth preserving.

My thoughts about preserving the past have turned into a professional bias. I received a degree in history, and for years I have pored through boxes of old manuscripts and turned the delicate pages of rare books, researching different aspects of the history of science, medicine, and technology. It is with some irony, however, that I learned a profound lesson about the meaning of history from an American expat biologist, Lisa Fagg, who lived a few streets away from me in Cambridge, that esteemed medieval market town. She also has an affinity for flea markets, it turns out. One day in the early 1990s during a trip to New England, she and a friend were strolling through a market when she heard music emanating from a piano in the distance. Something about it captured her attention. At that point, she turned to her friend and exclaimed: "That's Grandpa!" Because her grandfather, whose name was J. Lawrence Cook, had died some fifteen years earlier, it was a comment that needed some explanation. As Lisa set off "following her ears" in search of the piano, she recalled distinct childhood memories of listening to her grandfather—a professional African American musician and recording artist—at work at the piano. She learned, in her words, to recognize "the unmistakable musical 'voice' of Grandpa."[1]

Upon reaching the corner of the flea market, she approached a huge van with a player piano in it. The perforated music roll that was running through this automated instrument was one of the rolls her grandfather had made. "I was thrilled," said Lisa, and when she introduced herself as one of Cook's granddaughters to the vendors, they were honored. Lisa watched as the piano keys danced around to the music that her grandfather had performed long ago. It was as if he was sitting at the vacant spot in front of the piano. She learned from that chance encounter that there was a "J. Lawrence Cook special interest group" in America, and that they collect, sell, and trade "JLC" piano rolls. They are connected to an international network of aficionados of mechanical musical instruments who not only enjoy listening to such rare recordings of America's musical past, but whose efforts to preserve these historical "records" keep the opportunity alive for others to enjoy them. If it was not for the people whom Lisa had met at the flea market, she would not have had the chance to feel the closest to her grandfather that she had felt in the decades since his death.

When I met with Lisa a few years ago, she shared with me her thoughts about what it was like to rekindle old family memories with the aid of the sounds of history. It so happened that by this time, I too had an encounter with a player piano that brought back memories of my childhood. As a result, I decided to embark on a pursuit to explore the world of the collectors and dealers who preserve this past, and to learn more about the invention of the technology that allowed for the reproduction of piano music. I discovered that J. Lawrence Cook had an interesting role to play in this history, but Lisa's reminiscences brought it all alive in new ways.

Lisa grew up in Brooklyn and has vivid memories of visiting her grandparents in the Bronx when she and her grandpa sang the lyrics of new songs he had "reproduced" on piano rolls. He had been in the player piano business since its early days, since the 1910s, and over the decades had turned all types of new musical genres into "mechanical" music—from stride and jazz to Paderewski to the Beatles. "I remember the first time I heard 'Penny Lane,' 'Michelle,' and 'Eleanor Rigby'—and it wasn't coming from Liverpool," said Lisa. "I was sitting at the player piano beside Grandpa in my grandparents' house in the Bronx." I told Lisa that player piano rolls had a long history of spreading music around, before the gramophone or radio were used to popularize music. It was also an international trade. But what was intriguing about Lisa's story was that she was recollecting a moment in her grandfather's career and in the player piano industry that was struggling to survive compared to its heyday of the 1910s and '20s. By the 1930s, the industry had already fallen as a result of the Great Depression, witnessed a revival in the 1950s, and was about to face new challenges with jukeboxes, electronic synthesizers, and the apathy of the inheritors of an older generation's technology. Yet the business survived. The company that J. Lawrence Cook worked for—QRS, which was founded at the dawn of the twentieth century—had been purchased by a mechanical music enthusiast who vowed to keep it alive. It was "an American institution," he said. It is an institution that exists to this day, both as a contemporary company and as a legacy maintained largely through the efforts of collectors and enthusiasts of musical history.

What I learned when meeting people like Lisa or the "special interest groups" that she encountered at the flea market is that this history—about the sounds of history—is not merely a record of facts about the past. What I discovered in researching this book is that history can be kept alive in different ways. "I can still hear it all in my mind's ear," says Lisa. "Grandpa's gruff bass-baritone and my child's voice. He never seemed to grow weary of hearing—and singing—the same songs over and over again. It was incredible fun then, and listening to Grandpa's recorded music today takes me back to those wonderful times." For Lisa, a chance encounter with an old technology that is still in use has kept the spirit of the past alive and audible.

This is a book about such connections between the past and the present, about the technology through which history is preserved and the love and money it takes to preserve it. This is also a story of an American musical institution set within the context of business entrepreneurship and popular entertainment in America's Progressive Era and early Jazz Age. It reveals an overlooked chapter in the social history of the American entertainment industry—the development of mass-mechanized or "recorded" piano music and the social relations of businessmen and a diverse community of artists involved with it. The story revolves around the player piano, the binary digital encoding of its rolls, the first mass production of machine music, and the impact these technologies made on the lives of entertainers and audiences, past and present.

The player piano is both a visual entertainer and musical instrument. The absence of a performer in front of a playing piano is unusual. So is the presence of a dilettante pumping pneumatic pedals rather than playing keys to produce the sounds of a virtuoso. This anomaly intrigues in ways that can transcend the impact of the musical score. In the first decades of the twentieth century, this made the player piano's presence in parlors, saloons, fairgrounds, and family rooms enticing. As Kurt Vonnegut later wrote: "Makes you feel kind of creepy, don't it, Doctor, watching them keys go up and down? You can almost see a ghost sitting there playing his heart out."[2] When one watches the player piano, the invisibility of the entertainer is conspicuous, even mysterious, especially for those who see it for the first time.

A musical machine of extraordinary popularity before the advent of an improved gramophone or radio, the player piano introduced quality recorded music and popularized new kinds of music in the early twentieth century. When the player piano made its debut in Manhattan showrooms and at concerts at Carnegie Hall, audiences were captivated. Sales soon soared. The player piano—often known by the trade name of one manufacturer, Pianola—began to outsell regular pianos, and by the roaring '20s, "the player" had created an industry that in annual sales was second only to those of automobiles.

Its success was owed largely to the absence of the person who performed its "live" music, particularly given the prominence of pianos and the respect that pianists commanded in an era when musicians' careers were fraught with social and ethnic prejudices.

"In the years before World War I," remembered James P. Johnson, the famous stride pianist and avatar of African American jazz music, "there was a piano in almost every home, black or white. . . . Most people couldn't play them, so a piano player was important socially."[3] It was so important, in fact, that a new social hierarchy was created in cities such as New Orleans, Chicago, and New York, where the black entertainer attained a new, privileged identity by becoming an accomplished pianist. With the help of the sale of music rolls, recording for which earned some pianists a living, their musical compositions spread across the world. Perhaps because automation rendered the pianist invisible, the player piano was that much more agreeable to its mesmerized audiences. This is only part of the story of this phenomenon, however.

The chapters that follow explore the relationship between business, art, and technology concurrent with the success of the radio and phonograph, revealing how the foundation was laid for the cultural reception of later recording and broadcasting technologies. Examining the collaboration between engineers, entrepreneurs, and entertainers illuminates diverse themes, including the aesthetics of mechanized musical expression, strategies for the commercialization of talent, patterns of consumption of new musical genres (foxtrot, stride, and ragtime), and the changing cultural values associated with musical performance and evolving critiques of mass culture. By drawing on private manuscripts, material artifacts, and interviews, this book provides a composite portrait of innovative musical technologies in America from 1900 to 1930, thus contributing to our understanding of the history of Americana, technology, unique musical genres, and the social history of entertainment.

The book develops along two main areas of inquiry. The first investigates how a new musical technology affected the lives of those who helped to create it and use it. We learn that it created new opportunities for employment as recorders, editors, and arrangers of popular piano music, but what were entertainers' feelings about the mechanization of music? How did it affect the aesthetics of expression? Historians have revealed that some musicians felt threatened by the recorded music flowing into people's homes through radio waves and phonograph discs in the 1920s and '30s.[4] Some artists felt that the quality of the music being reproduced was not true to their talent, while others worried that the commercialization of music in the production of records and radio time might create unwelcome competition for an audience's patronage. These concerns would later play out in industry debates regarding copyright laws and royalties.[5]

However, this book demonstrates that there was a different attitude about the function of player piano recordings.[6] Contemporary advertisements proclaimed that the music on the rolls "captured" the artists' individuality and expression. While critics debated the extent to which a machine could embody human touch, many artists themselves embraced the player piano as a means of visually and audibly studying the compositions of others to *enhance* their skills. Nearly all the leading pianists in the world made piano rolls in the first three decades of the 20th century.[7] While historians of music have noted the breadth of individuals involved with recording rolls, no history has attempted to see this in a broader context, and to question the impact this technology had on the transformation of entertainers' lives or the degree to which the formation of a new musical industry transformed the business of Tin Pan Alley.[8]

As the historian of music David Suisman has recently shown, Tin Pan Alley in the late nineteenth and early twentieth centuries was an entrepreneurial hodgepodge of small companies competing for each customer's business. Built on the publication and sale of sheet music, Tin Pan Alley—originally referring to West 28th Street between Broadway and Sixth Avenue in Manhattan, where a number of music publishing houses were located—was noted for the public performances of the "pluggers" hired to publicize the latest songs and scores. It was largely owned by a German Jewish immigrant community, who promoted music as a tool of cultural and spiritual uplift.[9] While many other historical accounts have traced the ways that the phonograph transformed the music business—creating an industry driven by firms governed by a mentality of standardization and mass production—this book illustrates that another model of business practice developed just before the big bang of the record industry. Similar to the way that Tin Pan Alley forged new artistic and commercial relationships between different ethic groups, the early player piano industry—which arguably helped rather than hindered the traditional piano sheet music sales—also saw new career opportunities and collaborations emerge for African American entertainers.[10] As Suisman says of Tin Pan Alley, "at every stage, the industry also benefited from African Americans' own participation, for they too contributed to the production of blackface minstrelsy, coon songs, and ragtime. Yet they did so in ways marked by uneven economic power and control."[11] While an uneven distribution of economic power and control also applies to the business relations of the early player piano industry, we also learn that it afforded new opportunities for creative expression and artistic independence. This is what allowed J. Lawrence Cook, for example, to develop his own unique "musical voice" that his granddaughter recognized.

Each chapter that follows looks at a different dimension of the business of entertainment, the player piano technology, and the social reception of what was the early twentieth-century equivalent to the iPod phenomenon. Subtle themes run throughout, exploring how the player piano transgressed boundaries of art and science, live and recorded performance, stylistic conventions, notions of embodied skill, but how entertainers themselves moved between roles as artists, recorders, editors, arrangers, and engineers in the production of this unique form of music. By considering multiple facets to the story, I follow leads developed by other interdisciplinary historians who see music as embedded in a broader history of social relations, technology, taste, and popular culture.[12]

My second avenue of inquiry examines the impact of this technology on the "cultural consumption" of music.[13] How did the audience react to the new musical genres performed "live" in their homes, saloons, theaters, and concert halls across America? Many people to this day marvel at how a roll of paper with myriad tiny holes in it could be made to play music. These same coded rolls would later be adapted to creating guided missile codes in World War II, the "auto-typewriter," the first flight simulator, and binary coded computer cards.

In the heyday of the production of player pianos between 1900 and 1930, over two hundred thousand of them were sold a year, along with a staggering five million rolls a year, generating revenues for the industry of over a hundred million dollars a year. Their curious technical design introduced new ways of experiencing, appreciating, and studying music. They generated new ideas about what it meant to capture sound and soul. The player piano sparked dialogue between the realms of artistic expression and industrial creation. Was it an instrument or a technology? In the second half of the century, it infiltrated the literary imagination, becoming a symbol of industrial conquest over individual talent.

While the technology provided an opportunity to instruct aspiring musicians through demonstrable performance, the player piano also helped people engage with music by *de-skilling* the work involved in playing an instrument. A prominent marketing focus in this respect was white middle-class women in whose parlors sat "that shining monument to past girlhood—a silent piano" (in the words of a 1905 advert) who could now reach "perfection without practice" and entertain guests at home with a repertoire from Rachmaninoff to ragtime.[14] "What a leveler of distinctions" the instrument was, cheered the music critic Gustav Kobbé in 1912. The gendering of piano music also played on the masculinity of mechanization: men could now be interested in music through their interest in machines. By inviting middle-class consumers to effortlessly participate in, rather than passively listen to, musical performance, piano manufacturers forged a new way to pursue "a revolutionary musical democracy in America."[15] In short, the player piano was marketed and purchased as an instrument that made entertainers out of consumers. The technology to de-skill music performance invigorated popular imagination and stimulated much debate about what constituted real as opposed to artificial performance.

How did the emergence of a distinct style of player piano performance affect the way that other forms of music were appreciated by the public? How did the manipulation of mechanically reproduced music affect the way that new genres of music were understood and received by the public? Attention to the various ways that the public interacted with the player piano points to a key moment in the history of mechanical music: the invention of the "reproducing piano" at this time enabled the piano itself to recreate the dynamics, tempo, and other features of the way it was performed by the person who recorded it. Earlier player piano technology was based on the recording and playback only of notes—devoid of "expression." Reproducing pianos offered greater fidelity than acoustically recorded phonographs, and many pianists were therefore reluctant to record for phonographs.[16]

Within all the details and anecdotes about how these instruments were engineered, marketed, and used, another theme emerges: disappearance. The amount of time needed for practice to play a piano disappears in this story; the old Victorian pianos that did not play "by themselves" disappear from the marketplace; sheet music momentarily disappears in the abundance of player piano rolls; and finally, the human entertainer disappears. They become the invisible entertainers whose actions are only seen by the movement of the keys dancing around. What this book sets out to do is make these things reappear by looking at the rhetorical strategies, mechanics, and life of those behind the curtain who made the instruments appear to have a life of their own.

It is a life that is nearly extinct, save for the efforts of committed collectors, repairers, and the surviving legacy of the original American musical institutions whose history is here discussed. In contrast to the phenomenal international popularity of player pianos in the decades from 1900 to 1930, antique player pianos themselves virtually disappeared—eclipsed in history books by the rise of the radio and phonograph, and sent to landfills by families needing room for new kinds of entertainment centers. However, the 1950s saw a revival, and player pianos and all the music rolls once again found a market, fueled a growing community of aficionados and collectors of these now rare items. They set up associations and societies, hold annual meetings, and raise funds to repair, preserve, and enjoy these artifacts of Americana. They have prevented old sounds of history from disappearing. This book therefore takes this community as an entrée into this musical and cultural history, developing a narrative that follows the author's travels to meet collectors and historic collections that preserve the material culture of the past. What results is a book that not only explores history but reveals how history is maintained by contemporary society.

Chapter 1

Soundscape and Memory

$\int$ WAS ABOUT ten years old and just tall enough to reach the pedals of the piano. Sitting in my grandfather's living room in Florida during school breaks, I would entertain the family, and no doubt the neighbors, for hours with perfectly played scores. Stacked next to me on the bench was grandpa's prized collection of *New Yorker* magazines. In front of me was the upright Apollo player piano, which we simply called "the ol' player," where I watched the keys dance around while I pretended to be a virtuoso. On top of the player was a messy stack of long, narrow boxes containing all of the different music rolls he had collected in the 1950s. At the time, I didn't recognize the names of the artists or the titles of the songs. But I was a huge fan of ragtime.

As I pumped the pedals, watching the keys dance around below my fingertips, it never occurred to me that this music was anything but an expression of the capabilities of this magical instrument. I never thought about all of the musicians whose works I was replaying, nor did I wonder about how they managed to embed their talents into this machine. When I sat at the player, *I* was the musician. All of those entertainers of the past were invisible.

I did not think about that player piano for many years. In 2003, I went to Las Vegas to visit my uncle, Richard Dolan, whom I had not seen for many years. I had heard that he had gone into "semiretirement" and moved to Henderson.

Uncle Dick was a man of charisma perfectly suited to Las Vegas. He became wealthy by selling analytic chemistry supplies internationally. He was also notable for having an exceptional sense of humor. At business meetings he was known to hand out vinyl ear covers called "B.S. Protectors" (Blatant Statement Protector is printed in small type). He would often have a pocketful of red foam clown's noses, which he would often distribute to everyone at his restaurant table before the waitress arrived. When he picked me up from my hotel on the Strip, he pulled up in one of Liberace's rhinestone-covered convertibles, with blinking candelabra attached to the front for turn signals. "He rolled it out during his final performances at Radio City Music Hall in the '80s," said Uncle Dick, with a grin. "It matched his grand piano."

Uncle Dick had acquired this automobile at an auction as an addition to his "collection of Americana," which included many musical items. As we drove toward the Henderson foothills, Uncle Dick was telling me about his collection of pianos made by Story & Clark, founded in 1896.

"We put them on display in some of the casinos now and then, they sound great," he said.
"Who plays them?" I asked.
"Well, no one. They play themselves."
"You have a collection of player pianos? I remember those. I used to pump the pedals."
"We've retrofitted them. They are now completely automated, and they play music from a CD. It's all digital."
"It's all digital, huh?"

I had a vague grasp of how information could be encoded to send and record digital signals, as in digital cable TV or digital cameras, and I understood that music was digitized for storage on my iPod. However, I didn't understand how a digital CD could make a piano play, or what advantage this provided since one was hearing real keys hitting real piano strings. I was silent for a few minutes trying to picture what an all-digital player piano might look like. I figured I would explore these questions further when I had the chance to examine one of these retrofitted pianos in person.

"What do you mean?" I said. "Who's 'we'?"

Uncle Dick told me that some years back, in the mid 1980s, he had purchased a struggling company based in Buffalo, New York, called QRS Music Rolls. When he mentioned the letters, I remembered the Western-style, ornate, red printed label found on the end of every box of music rolls stacked atop grandpa's player.

"You make piano rolls? I thought you were retired."

He smiled, as one who loves surprising people does.

"The company doesn't make that many rolls any more," he said. "We still have the old equipment, but we've invented a new system. You'll see."

We arrived at his house overlooking the valley. His living room resembled a showroom of pianos: two old uprights and two shiny baby grands. Under each keyboard was a device resembling a portable CD player. He picked up a remote control and pointed it at the white baby grand. "You'll like this," he promised. A moment later, the keys became animated, background music kicked in, and Tony Bennett began singing "I Left my Heart in San Francisco." I could have anticipated it. Ever since I moved to San Francisco the year before, I had noticed that people like to demonstrate their fondness for the city.

"This doesn't remind me of the player piano of my childhood," I confessed. "Maybe it's this . . . modern music."
"You know what our best-selling music is, besides the Christmas CDs that people stuff stockings with? All the popular movies—the 'Titanic' song is huge. So is 'The Lion King' and 'Phantom.'"
"I always associate player pianos with ragtime," I said.
"Ragtime was *the* player piano music, when ragtime was hit music. But popular music changes. Tastes change."

"So," I wondered, "there's nothing different between this player piano and the old players except the kind of music that's played?"

The difference, he explained, was that the old system was built around holes punched in paper that operated the piano keys through pneumatic bellows. It was a system invented to capture the pianist's performance and then reproduce it. The digital system has the same capability but is synchronized with the audio track of all of the other instruments (and vocals) in the band. The hammers strike the strings, adding a "live" presence that entertains the audience.

The music played on while we sat next to the pool watching the shadows from the mountains creep across the valley. The sound of the piano in the background gave me the guilty feeling that we should be paying more attention to the entertainment, as if I should slip a few bucks into the tip jar for the hardworking piano man on my way out. Looking over the glowing green, blue, and red buildings that were the huge casinos along the Strip in the distance, I saw how very "Las Vegas" this impromptu concert had been. It had something to do with its being mechanical and impersonal. Like Las Vegas itself, the entertainment could go on all night, uninterrupted.

"You know," I said, "there are people who prefer playing scratchy old 78s to CDs. They say it sounds better. You think there are people who prefer the old roll pianos to the piano performance controlled by a CD?"

"Sure," he answered, "but it's a love/hate relationship—the whole 'automated' music enterprise. The old players opened the doors to the modern recording industry. They changed the face of music. For a while they fought off competition from radios and the phonograph, but society's tastes changed."

"I'll bet there's a taste for history," said I, ever optimistic.

"Try looking around San Francisco," he suggested. "There's a group there who love historical rolls. They say the rolls reveal stories about the people who made them, of the craft of making music reproducible. They write to us all the time wanting more rolls."

As we headed back to the Strip, a moment of silence emerged between the mechanized concert I had just heard and the cacophony of bleeps and dings from the slot machines. At that moment I thought about grandfather's old Apollo that was built eighty-five years before those in my uncle's living room, wondering what had happened to it after he had passed away in 1998. I could see the ivory-covered keys: two were chipped and some were more yellow than others. Above all, I recalled the sound of the ol' player, right down to the creak of the wooden bench. I wondered what others found in what seemed to be the forgotten music of a previous era. There was a history that I was now eager to explore. What better place to start than my hometown?

Chapter 2

Missionaries and Museums

A WEB SEARCH at home revealed a nationwide group of "AMICAns," members of the Automated Musical Instrument Collector's Association. The founding chapter of this association was established in 1963 in San Francisco. Its aim is not only to bring together people who have shared interests in antique mechanical instruments but to preserve our musical past. "With almost missionary zeal," its call for membership applications says, "AMICA has prevented the destruction of many fine rare instruments that have been restored to their former glory." A press release mentioned that they had recently raised funds to help refurbish antique player pianos on display in Virginia City, Montana. This Victorian gold mining town is a tourist attraction, a "very much alive ghost town . . . frozen in time." The player pianos help recreate an Old Western ambience. Apparently many members of AMICA first encountered them on vacations there. These were the kind of people who would help begin my journey.

I expected AMICAns to welcome new members, and I was not disappointed. One of my first e-mail contacts was with Bryan. From the archived postings he had previously made to the member's bulletin board, I learned that he lived in Arlington, Texas, volunteered at the Fielder historical museum where he interprets old piano rolls, and that he was saving his pennies to refurbish "my English pumper." "I often find it interesting how other people became interested in our hobby," he wrote, which I took as a perfect opportunity to introduce myself.

Bryan was open about his passion for old automated instruments and eager to share his memories of discovering them.

> "When I was a very small child," he remembered, "the local Shakey's Pizza had an orchestrion that fascinated me. The fact that the restaurant was in a bad neighborhood, that I didn't LIKE pizza, and that it was bad pizza anyway had absolutely NO effect on me. I begged to go, and spent my time in front of the piano, plugging into it all the quarters I could find. Then when I was seven we bought the neighbor's old manual upright piano."
>
> "Were you a musician?" I asked.
>
> "No, but I looked at it and told my parents I would 'make it into one of those pianos that play by themselves.'"
>
> "Were you a mechanic?"
>
> "No, but I've rebuilt a few. I can't tell you how many times I had *Rebuilding the Player Piano* checked out of the library."

I had never imagined that an aficionado of pianos of any sort would be less interested in making music than in their restoration. This was shortsighted on my part.

When Bryan learned that I lived in San Francisco, he told me of his visits to the city, and how he visited the Musée Mécanique at the Cliff House in San Francisco. "Their collection had pianos, music boxes, fortuneteller machines, a dancing Tom Thumb," he told me, "but it has seen better days. The salt air and repeated playings take their toll and there's precious little left but love of the art to keep them maintained—certainly not money." Bryan sent me a picture of a bronze token, one of his prized possessions. On one side was a relief of the Cliff House shown in its Victorian glory. On the flip side was a statement of the coin's value: "Good for 10¢ Trade—Drop in Orchestrian."

He explained that this token was a fragment of the past that was lost when the Cliff House burned down in 1907. "The old Cliff

House is well known for what it looked like outside. But the orchestrion was one of the big attractions *inside*. This token is about all we have left of that."

The orchestrion, or what Bryan excitedly referred to as "the big guy," started as a late Victorian phenomenon. It, too, was a mechanical instrument, literally a piano with "all the bells and whistles" attached. It was an amusement park wonder featured in minstrel shows and on fairgrounds around the world. In 1890, a traveler visiting Glasgow in the United Kingdom wrote home about a festival that boasted twenty-five merry-go-rounds, all with band organs in the middle playing tunes embellished by blowing horns, swinging rattles, and crashing cymbals. Anyone within earshot would be made aware that this was "where the people were having their so-called fun."[1] Mechanized instruments like the band organ came to epitomize the fairground din. In France, a *piano mécanique* played music in *salon* settings with pins on a revolving cylinder tripping levers while someone cranked a handle as if it were a large music box. It was the birth of mechanical music. In San Francisco, the orchestrion was a featured attraction at the Cliff House at the dawn of the twentieth century. It was one of several mechanical instruments, a relative of the humble player piano, the instrument that over the next twenty years became the featured attraction in hundreds of thousands of homes from coast to coast.

I discovered that many people have some sort of memory or experience of a player piano, whether owned by themselves, a friend, or a family member. It often evokes memories of long-gone Christmas parties or of family rooms where the player was *the* center of entertainment before *entertainment centers* eventually replaced novelty pianos with TVs and stereos. Few of the vintage players are still in use. Many that exist are now silent, dusty pieces of furniture. They are garage sale feature items or heirlooms that do not work. Player pianos are to my parent's jukebox generation what cassette tape Walkmans are to the present MP3 generation.

Members of AMICA often collect everything they can afford pertaining to the heyday of mechanical musical instruments like the player piano, and other items that were part of life in the 1920s and '30s. Memorabilia are often smaller than pianos, such as lapel pins or posters.

"Would you call player pianos 'memorabilia'?" I asked one of the members. There appeared to be something unseemly about my question, as if my lack of appreciation for the importance of this object were morally akin to tossing it into the junk drawer of history. I should have known better.

"Are old books memorabilia?" was the thoughtful reply, drawing an analogy I appreciated as a historian.

True, I do feel differently about fragile manuscripts or rare books that exist in climate-controlled archives than I do about a digitally-scanned text posted on the web. I assign a certain value and importance to the original, un-pixilated, unenhanced text. However, the point was that the past must be preserved and treated respectfully no matter what kind of historical material we are talking about. "Memorabilia" implies a fragment or trace of memory, whereas the player piano was an archive unto itself. "Spirits live within the piano," remarked Bryan. "We have to learn to listen to understand what life was like when these players were at the height of their popularity."

To me, the past had always involved reading. The term *archive* suggested rummaging through boxes of manuscripts and learning to decode centuries-old handwritten script, or flipping through the pages of old newspapers and journal articles. I was now being introduced to a world I thought we had lost by being told to *listen*. I was anxious to hear what I would find at the Cliff House, my next research destination. My wife, Dorothy, and I knew the Cliff House was a restaurant perched above Ocean Beach overlooking Seal Rocks and the Pacific Ocean. The Cliff House as we knew it at the time was an undistinguished place for brunch with spectacular views, but I had never noticed any player pianos.

It was once a fashionable hotel, where, according to the *San Francisco Examiner* in 1907, "Princes, presidents, primadonnas and peasants, all had graced the hostelry during its long and busy life." The mining magnate and property tycoon Adolph Sutro had rebuilt it in the style of a grand French chateau after its first incarnation burned down on Christmas day in 1894. It burned down again after the 1906 earthquake, and despite repeated attempts to get the Cliff House back in business, it never returned to its former glory and ended up being a drain on Sutro's finances, requiring the family to sell off parcels of the vast property.

The first part of the Cliff House complex to sell was the amusement park known as Playland, just down the hill and across the street from Ocean Beach. It was purchased by San Francisco property developer George Whitney Sr. in 1928. Playland had roller coasters and theme rides, a fun house with games and wavy mirrors, a carousel, concession stands, and other features. Known as "the Barnum of the Golden Gate," Whitney described Playland as "a nickel and dime business, and we'll do well as long as people have nickels and dimes in their pockets."[2] Fortunately for Whitney, even the Great Depression that began at the end of the following year had left enough coins in people's pockets. They were eager for what Whitney described as "Good, clean, fun diversion." Even during those difficult times, Playland remained profitable. This was not so for the Cliff House restaurant, which Sutro also sold to Whitney in 1937.

Alert to the public fascination with games, and a man who enjoyed entertainment, Whitney stuck with what was a proven business plan and kept the fun machines in operating condition, ready to receive Playland's patrons' loose change. In the words of his son, Whitney was a "collector of collections," and Playland became a major tourist attraction, a mini–Coney Island of the West. It was the only amusement park to operate year round in America and boasted it had the "World's Largest Souvenir and Curio Shop." During World War II, according to Whitney Jr., "Playland did fantastic business. . . . Sailors had nickels and dimes."[3] So successful was Playland that it was one of the models that inspired Walt Disney's own amusement park, and George Whitney Jr. was hired as one of Disney's first "imagineers" in the 1950s.

Whitney Sr. died in 1958, and a decade later his son sold Playland and the Cliff House, which was closed for yet another refurbishment between 1969 and 1973. Since Playland was located on beachfront property, it did not take long before a millionaire developer named Jeremy Ets-Hokin acquired the park and began building condominiums in its place. Before the bulldozers razed the fun houses and roller coaster tracks in 1971, many of the coin-operated automata and mechanical musical instruments that were housed there were bought by a friend of George Whitney's, a fellow amusement enthusiast and collector of automated musical machines, Edward Zelinski.

Zelinski, who ran a painting and property management business, began his own collection when he was eleven years old with the purchase of a penny skill game that involved manipulating ball bearings into designated holes in a handheld box. Even this was a money maker. "I put pennies in it and taught my parents and friends to do the same," he recollected. "It acted like a bank."[4] He obtained his first player piano when he was doing a job for the Mills Novelty Company in Oakland and spotted a Seeburg player piano with a xylophone and mandolin attachment. The company manager was willing to part with the instrument since his employees were spending too much time playing with it instead of working. From there his collection grew to include more player pianos, orchestrions, an automated violin with a piano keyboard, antique slot machines, animations, and music boxes.

In the 1950s, Zelinski regularly had lunch with George Whitney Sr., sipping Scotch and agreeing to trade music boxes and pianos. When Zelinski subsequently acquired Whitney's machines, he found a new home for the collection in an annexed building on a terrace at the base of Cliff House and named it Musée Mécanique. Housed there for over thirty years was the historical collection of player pianos representative of the craze that had swept across America at the beginning of the century, revolutionizing the entertainment industry and introducing a new kind of musical experience for every stratum of society.

Prior to visiting the collection for the first time, I had been reading up on some of the social context of early twentieth-century San Francisco to familiarize myself with the local scene when these instruments first arrived on the west coast. "Get this," I said to Dorothy, citing a passage from an old book I had selected, *The Barbary Coast: An Informal History of the San Francisco Underworld.* "The 'parlor houses' in the late teens 'received a substantial amount of money from the sale of beer, hard liquor, and coins fed into electric pianos. A high percentage of the revenue then went to the police and politicians as graft.' So player pianos simultaneously entertained princes and presidents at the Cliff House and punters at brothels." Dorothy politely hummed. "It's probably the first time that music leveled society," I added. This was much more interesting than what happened at a pizza parlor.

As we descended cement steps to the back of Cliff House, I spotted a few people exiting the large camera obscura, the dark room which admits a beam of light which magically projects an upside-down image of the outside world onto a platform. "Why aren't there ever any signs," I complained, frustrated that this supposedly great tourist attraction was nowhere to be found. "There's one," said Dorothy. Tacked onto a piece of plywood that covered a door to an abandoned room was a sign that read "Musée Mécanique—Closed." "I think they mean permanently," I said, peering through a crack into a barren room with concrete floors.

Of all the research I have done as a historian—all the manuscripts I've consulted, the historical artifacts I have examined, and the delicate rare books I've read—I have been humbled by how much material is available for research. Though in an instant, while staring at the abandoned museum, on a historic site where this unique collection of Americana was once housed, I realized how fragile and impermanent historical research could be. I remembered the comment about how "love not money" preserved the past. How ironic it was that the machines—the "nickel-grabbing" pianos and music boxes which had funded themselves as a form of entertainment in a variety of ways—were now disappearing for a lack of money. These were the machines which, according to a common advertisement placed in *Billboard* magazine in the first decade of the twentieth century, were ideal for "Hotels, Cafes, Saloons, Restaurants, Dancing Pavilions, Skating Rinks, Summer Resorts, Ice Cream Parlors, Cigar and Drug Stores, etc."—but where were they now? How could they have just disappeared from view?

"What a sad coincidence," said Bryan, to whom I had immediately written with the bad news about Musée Mécanique. He had already discovered a few months earlier that the museum was closing, and he was one of the first signatories on a petition to keep the collection preserved.

Their efforts had in fact resulted in a publicity campaign that was covered in the pages of the *San Francisco Chronicle* throughout the previous year, which I had overlooked. The malefactors in this story were the "penny pinchers" at the National Park Service, a "confederacy of dunces," according to editorialists. "To federal bureaucrats, this is what is known as planning," declared *Chronicle* reporter Ken Garcia on March 12, 2002. "But in my corner of the world, this is what is known as war."[5] Yes! I cried. Those missionaries are on the right warpath; I was relieved to learn that I had caught a thread of contact with those who *do* care about history.

A week later, the *Los Angeles Times* announced that "Fans rally to save an offbeat museum of antique devices," which it dubbed "time machines." Quotes were offered by visitors from around the world decrying the decision to close the collection. Four months later, the *Chronicle* reported that the campaign had worked. Disney had made an offer to owner Ed Zelinski to house and maintain the collection in Anaheim, but at the last minute Port officials from San Francisco's Fisherman's Wharf had negotiated a lease with the San Francisco Museum and Historical Society to move the collection to Pier 45, my next destination.

Fisherman's Wharf on the northern tip of the San Francisco peninsula has a plethora of T-shirt shops, plastic models of the Golden Gate Bridge, and tourists. The Wharf receives twelve million visitors a year, many there to board the ferries to cross the bay for Sausalito or to tour Alcatraz. They also walk along the piers as they eat clam chowder poured into hollowed-out loaves of sourdough bread and marvel at the sea lions lounging on rafts. Many visitors arrive there via the famous Powell Street cable car that riders can catch just south of Union Square at Market Street. They hang on for dear life as it ascends and descends the steep city hills.

The Wharf has a small working harbor, notable for delivering Dungeness crab to the sidewalk stands and restaurants early in the morning, but most of the warehouses that line the long piers are either empty or are being converted into offices or bistros. Since its mid-nineteenth-century origins, the Wharf has been less bustling with longshoremen and stevedores than with curious visitors seeking entertainments that have existed throughout its colorful history, including appearances by card-playing pigs and skateboarding penguins. So it seemed a likely place to locate a museum of mechanical musical instruments.

Pier 45 is home to the museum and memorial of the *USS Pampanito*, a World War II Balao class fleet submarine. Immediately adjacent, at the base of the pier occupying the first warehouse space, is the new home of Musée Mécanique. As I walked through the large garage-door-type entrance, shortly after the museum opened on a foggy Monday morning, I spotted a small group of Japanese tourists in blue raincoats and yellow backpacks taking pictures of each other next to Laffing Sal, the bigger-than-life mechanical doll with bright rosy cheeks that gyrated while loudly heckling at the drop of a quarter. I had learned that this was the "twin sister" to another Laffing Sal that for years greeted visitors to Playland. That one ended up in the hands of a private collector, while this one emerged from George Whitney Sr.'s home collection. Laffing Sal is where I arranged to rendezvous with Dan Zelinski, Ed's son.

As I stood there looking around, unable to wipe the smirk off of my face from watching Sal, a forty-something year-old man with dark brown wavy hair wearing blue jeans and a denim shirt with a large name tag that read "I WORK HERE" approached me. After introductions, I confessed to Dan that through sheer ignorance I had trekked over to the Cliff House in search of the museum but then discovered the hullabaloo surrounding its closure.

"We love it here," said Dan. "It wasn't always certain that we'd be here, but luckily here we are." Dan had worked at the museum in the Cliff House since 1972, not long after it opened. He was young and in-between jobs when his father suggested he take up a job there. "Why?" Dan had asked. "What's there?" He was unaware that his father had opened what he called "an arcade" off of Ocean Beach. A typical disinterested teenage son, I thought, but that quickly changed when he began his new job. "Who would not enjoy working among such a collection of mechanical wonder?" I asked. We strolled down an aisle past wizards that rate one's sexual prowess, fortune-telling wax heads, and player pianos that churn out waltzes and raucous rags. Around us were over three hundred mechanical items with a history that reflected the evolution of an entertainment industry and continued to entertain up to the present moment. It is believed to be the largest privately-owned collection of mechanical musical instruments and automata freely open to the public.

We first reached a small wooden device which had a plastic placard that read "The Oldest Machine Here." The machine was called "Le Praxinoscope," a device to present animation by having a centrally placed stationary mirror reflect images of moving pictures circling around on a rotating drum. The first such device was developed by an engineer in Paris named Emile Raynaud in the 1870s, and the one in this collection, which showed a young girl skipping rope, dated from the late 1880s but had been modified to accept quarters to power the drum's movement. "I just think this is charming," said Dan. "It is also the quietest machine here," he added.

By the time we had strolled through a couple of aisles so I could survey the scope of the collection, about a dozen visitors had found their way to various machines, and I could hear laughter—both mechanical and very human—emanating from all quarters.

What I wanted to hear, however, were the pianos. So Dan reached in his pocket to fish out another quarter and we moved to the next aisle where the 1923 J. P. Seeburg KT special nickelodeon was placed. This was the first coin-operated piano that Ed Zelinski acquired for his collection. Known as the "Seeburg Eagle" because of the large stained glass bald eagle represented on the front panel (built by the Chicago firm of Drehobl Bros. Art Glass that produced stained glass panels for these Seeburg instruments in the 1920s and still exists today), the orchestrion contained a piano, mandolin effect, bass drum, snare drum, cymbal, castanets, triangle, tambourine, and Chinese wood blocks. The whole ensemble becomes animated at the drop of a coin, which starts a pneumatic system powered by an electric motor. I was treated to an automated rendition of Louis Armstrong's "When You're Smiling." The beat of the drum, the smashing of the cymbal, the ringing of the piano all suddenly echoed throughout the lofty warehouse, bouncing off the ceilings where pigeons flew among the steel rafters.

The KT special is known as a cabinet piano since it has no keyboard as one finds on conventional player pianos. Everything is hidden inside the large oak cabinet. Dan opened its front doors so I could observe all of the action inside. Seeing an orchestra inside a box was like peering into a Volkswagen Beetle with a hundred clowns stuffed inside. How in the world does everything fit? "The technology they came up with to produce this stuff is brilliant," said Dan. "There are some mechanisms inside these machines which are just amazing."

The design and performance of the KT special and the motion of the electric motor's wobbling back and forth suggested that it was not just the novel sounds that must have impressed early audiences but also the technological triumph it represented. In the early 1900s, when player pianos, orchestrions, nickelodeons, and the like first attained popularity, they did so in part because they symbolized American ingenuity. The J. P. Seeburg KT special in front of us was a pristine new cabinet design in the age of Thomas Edison, when people celebrated the modernity of light bulbs, the internal combustion engine, and the Kinetoscope, aka the peep-show machine. These were evidence that American "thinkers and tinkers" had become industrial innovators. This oak cabinet was a musical celebration of mechanical genius. As the KT special performed its music, I realized that one doesn't find music machines like this anymore. It had both ingenious construction and singular craftsmanship. "The machines are getting really old," said Dan, "but people are beginning to see what they are, which is just a beautiful work of art. The cabinet work on the machines is beautiful." Most amazingly, they were still performing some ninety years after being built.

We were soon surrounded by visitors with amused, and fascinated, expressions. They were easily entranced by the machine's performance. Another piano then began to play, then another from a different aisle. It was as if we had awoken a den of sleeping performers and had opened cages to let the spirits in the machines escape. We had alerted the first wave of morning tourists to the fact that it was OK to interact with the collection. "There are lots of people who come in here and they have never seen anything like this," said Dan. "They don't have a clue about what they are looking at. They don't know that you can drop a coin in and watch it go and listen to music or whatever. On the other end of the spectrum, there are people who grew up with these machines and who have not seen them in decades and they are just elated to be able to play them again."

So we were animating a musical history as the collection recreated musical memories and distant experiences. That is what gave this place meaning: that everything constructed from wood and pulleys, levers, gears, tubes, and leather belts—"miles of leather belts," stressed Dan—gave the immediate impression that this was no "arcade." But neither was it a museum. There were no red ropes keeping visitors at arm's length.

Dan told me about a trip he had made to the Deutsches Museum in Munich, which calls itself a "three dimensional encyclopedia" of the history of industry and technology. It has a large collection of musical instruments, including player pianos and orchestrions built by the German firm of M. Welte & Sons in the late nineteenth and early twentieth centuries. "It's a superb collection," said Dan, "but the instruments are kept silent and the docents don't play them for you. . . . My plan is to keep them open and working like they were originally intended to be used because that is fun."

I could hear that it was fun for the visitors, but maintaining a collection of three hundred automata and mechanical musical instruments for everyday use—how much fun could that be? Not long after Dan started working at Musée Mécanique when it was at the Cliff House, he enrolled in a machinery class at the local community college. That taught him the fundamental skills to use the shop equipment, especially the mill and lathe, to manufacture duplicate parts for those parts that broke.

> "So you started dissecting the machines to see what was inside?" I asked.
> "No," he replied, "they pretty much dissect themselves when they break. They just fall apart, so you just pick up the pieces and you try to duplicate them."

Maintaining the machines required ingenuity, patience, and dedication, and it was all driven by a youthful curiosity to venture back to an earlier world of engineers and mechanics to see how things were done then. Dan revealed his appreciation of and fascination with the skills that were disappearing as the instruments became older. His father, now deceased, faced the same challenges. When he acquired the Seeburg KT special in 1946, he asked an employee of the large San Francisco piano company Sherman Clay to come out and repair it. They visited his house, admired the piano, commented that they had not seen one like it in years, but could not provide an estimate for parts and labor since they had no idea if they could even fix it. So Ed decided to fix it himself. He started by removing one end of each pneumatic hose and blew cigar smoke through it to see where each led, and eventually figured out the system and got the machine working.

Now it was his son's turn to keep the machines alive, though living in modern California, he refrains from smoking. What intrigues Dan is that these machines are not only capable of handling long-term maintenance, but they also show evidence of hardy design. "Today," said Dan, "we have built-in obsolescence. Mass-produce it, use it, wear it out and get something new. The beauty with this stuff is that you can keep just about anything working—all you need is this." He pulled out his red handled 3/16-inch Philips head screwdriver from his breast pocket. "With this and an oilcan you can fix just about anything."

"Well, there are exceptions," he confessed. He took me to an area that was sectioned off by a high chain-link fence. Inside were hundreds of QRS music rolls stacked up against a brick wall. They had seen better days. "The reason there are not a lot of collections like this that are open to the public in this way is that you get this. . . ." He gestured toward the rolls, which looked damp, the boxes worn out. On an adjacent upright National Player Piano, Dan pointed out the scuffed legs and chipped corners of the cabinet. "If you look at the pieces in private collections, those things are mint. They are perfect. If you walk by them too quickly the owners get nervous. They come and look at a collection like this and grab their hair and cry 'How can you do this!'" At that moment he dropped a few coins in the player and "Walkin' My Baby Back Home," the 1930s tune later popularized by Nat King Cole, kicked in. It would seem unjust to quiet the instruments, I thought. "If this place is perceived to be or ever starts to turn into a museum, it will be inadvertent," Dan said. "I'll quit when this stops being fun."

When the Cliff House was going to close for refurbishment in 2002, Dan and his father's main concern was keeping the collection "alive"—intact and accessible. Other than the Disney offer, some people wanted to write a check and take the whole collection private, and many more wanted to buy individual pieces. "But luckily none of that came to be," he said, "and here we are." It is obvious that the location would not be a preservationist's first choice. Three dehumidifiers run all day and night, pulling up to 30 gallons of moisture a day from the air.

> "I try to keep the collection working and in good enough physical condition so people can put a coin in and realize that they actually do something," said Dan.
> "I guess what is good about the space is that there is plenty of room for you to work," I commented.
> "When we were at the Cliff House, it was really cramped. People could barely move around. Here at least we have space to grow, which is good, because I can't bear to part with anything, and history keeps stretching out."

That there was space at all for the effort to preserve a historic collection in this way was an incredible achievement, I thought. So much of what dies is simply thrown out. On a wall in Dan's workshop hangs a black and white picture of a heap of broken slabs of wood. It was a picture of a piano graveyard where sledgehammers were used to break them apart. "How can you have foresight that something is going to become a coveted item?" he asked. It reminded me of something his father wrote that I came across: "That's the way of a collector—you *should* have done this, and you *should* have done that." Dan errs on the side of collecting. "Quite literally, a lot of the machines were thrown away because something new would come out, like the jukebox, and the pianos would end up in the dump." He looked over to the picture. "You either pay storage for them, or get rid of them," he said.

It was a sign of just how common player pianos were in their heyday in the 1920s. More were discarded during the Great Depression than exist today. Some exist more as fragments of fading memories than as working artifacts. At least some collections such as this have survived and have not succumbed to modern money-making arcade games such as "Dance Dance Revolution" or "Redemption." "That's where all the money is now for this industry," said Dan. However, there was more involved with Musée Mécanique than money. It was love, I guess.

Soon the aisles of the Musee were streaming with people, and Dan needed to restock the change machine. I knew that since the beginning, these music machines had been money makers, but how could a business survive today on nickels and dimes? Even though a few of these musical machines were still called "nickelodeons" they no longer actually operated on a nickel. That would never cover the cost of the machine's maintenance. In fact, Ed Zelinski had discovered that the sheer novelty of the machines could sustain a regular price increase. For instance, he had a number of Mutoscope "motion picture" machines that originally cost a penny per play. "Then later," he wrote, "I changed them to a nickel and they received the same amount of play. Later on, I changed them to a dime and the number of plays increased. Several years ago, I changed them to a quarter and the number of plays tripled."[6] His son, Dan, encountered a similar pattern when he raised the price of one particular piano that was popular with the public in an effort to stave off overuse and excessive wear and tear. "Instead of a quarter, I raised the cost of a play to a dollar," he explained. "But people thought, ooohh, this must be *really* good, so they played the hell out of it. It drove me nuts."

Still, I thought, there is a delicate balance in allowing people to enjoy this collection and raising money to maintain it. Perhaps a corporate powerhouse such as Disney might have been willing to step in to rescue the collection because they could afford a relatively small nickel and dime collection as long as it helped to maintain a nostalgic theme. However, the Zelinskis were wise to have kept the collection under their control.

The background to the Whitney/Zelinski collection at Playland and the Cliff House suggested a connection between vintage mechanical musical instruments and a 1950s vision of recreating historic Americana in places such as Disneyland. When it opened in 1954, it had acquired a collection of some thirty machines, including a large Wurlitzer-style 32 Concert PianOrchestra that was built around 1912 (one of only three known to exist today), plus assorted player pianos, nickelodeons, and music boxes. These instruments had been purchased by Walt Disney himself in 1953 after he visited recently widowed Ruby Raney who lived on a ranch near Whittier, in southern California. Ruby and her husband, Albert Clifford Raney, had begun collecting coin-operated player pianos in the 1920s. Mr. Raney worked in sales, and he traveled extensively in the southwest. He took advantage of his travels and network of clients and friends to obtain a diverse collection of Navajo rugs and art, saloon memorabilia, and mechanical music machines.[7]

In the early 1940s, the Raneys built a large "music barn" to house their instrument collection, a barn that the state of California acquired through eminent domain and demolished to make way for the San Gabriel River Freeway (Interstate 605) a few years after Mr. Raney's death in 1949. Walt Disney's purchase of the Raney collection of mechanical musical instruments in 1953, therefore, came at a critical moment. (The collection of saloon and Navajo art was acquired at the same time by Knott's Berry Farm in Buena Park, California, which also had its own collection of Seeburg cabinet pianos and orchestrions). "The machines had found a good home, one where they will be cared for and appreciated," Mrs. Raney told a new friend, Terry Hathaway (a collector and later restorer of the machines who purchased his first player piano from her). "Otherwise," she said, "I would not have sold them to Disney."

Disney installed the machines in shops and alcoves along Main Street, U.S.A., in Disneyland to recreate the look and sound of a typical American town around 1920. The machines were available for the public to play, but there was also associated merchandise for sale that was related to the player pianos, such as QRS piano rolls that were sold by one of the shops on Main Street.[8] After the opening of the sister theme park, Disney World, in 1971, a number of the machines from the Raney collection, including the Wurlitzer Pian-Orchestra, were shipped to Florida for installation in the new Main Street Arcade. By this time, it seemed to automatic music aficionados that the Disney organization was less than familiar with their historical value. When rolls would tear, they would throw them away, much to the distress of collectors. At the time, Bill "Sully" Sullivan, who had worked his way up the ranks from having been a ticket collector in the 1950s at Disneyland to operations executive at Disney World, was a fan of the instruments and was determined to keep them on display for the public.

In 1990, Disney World had the good fortune to hire a technician named Bob Moore to maintain the collection. Moore grew up with a family life that revolved around the now defunct Roseland Park in Canandaigua, New York. He worked in the machine room of the carousel and learned to fix the band organs at a young age. He later came across a book by Larry Givens, *Rebuilding the Player Piano*—the same book that my AMICA acquaintance Bryan and many other aficionados had read. "One thing that impressed me from the very start was that [the Disney organization was] not running a museum," wrote Moore in a posting to the online *Mechanical Music Digest*. This meant two things: first, similar to Musée Mécanique, that the machines would be "hands on" to the public, and second, that they would not be maintained or restored to museum quality. "I had to balance the company's desire to have the instruments out where they could grab quarters against my desire to preserve valuable pieces of history," he wrote.[9]

However, there were inherent differences in the way that the principles of access *versus* preservation would be applied when comparing the maintenance of the instruments at Disney to that at the Musée Mécanique. Moore was an employee, and when Bill Sullivan retired in 1993, new management remapped space and awarded "profit points" to each square foot of property. The cost of maintaining an item such as the Wurlitzer PianOrchestra far exceeded the amount of quarters it could grab. So it, along with most of the rest of the Raney collection, was sold in the late 1990s, not long before Disneyland would make an offer to house the Musée Mécanique collection. (Rumor was that the corporate bosses at Disneyland were unaware of the sale occurring at Disney World.) In any event, the publicity generated by the acquisition of the Zelinski collection might have been considered worth the investment. Moore remembers the remorse he felt as the two large moving trucks pulled away with the collection en route to a dealer in Arkansas. Moore had spent the better part of a decade restoring some of the instruments, like a Seeburg nickelodeon, piece by piece from the inside out. Suddenly the order came to pack them up and prepare them for sale. "It was a great disappointment for me never to be able to hear the Seeburg H in person," he wrote.

Disney's sale of their mechanical instruments elicited critical opinions from collectors and dealers in this market. Tim Trager— "dealer, historian, lecturer, consultant, collector" of mechanical music in Illinois—decried the theme park's decision to sell their collection. Posting on the *Mechanical Music Digest*, Trager described his visits to Disney World, Disneyland, and Knotts Berry Farm around 1995 when he was shown storage rooms where the nickelodeons, orchestrions, band organs, and music boxes were stacked on twenty-five-foot-high shelves. The staff he talked to "had no memory of the instruments' time on public display," nor any "idea of the musical ability of the items." To Trager, this was evidence that the original aim of creating "a nostalgic mood of the place" had died and "a sycophantic corporate culture of professional management moved in."

"The coins taken in by the instrument cannot justify the maintenance expense," Trager commented. Consequently, the floor space once occupied by the instrument was allocated to gift racks "filled with high-profit trinkets made in China." "Every dime squeezed out is looked on as helping the profit margin and stockholder value."[10]

I wanted to follow up on Mr. Trager's comments about the fate of these historic collections and whether he thought private collectors could forestall the disappearance of a musical era. I assumed he was an instrument dealer, but during our first telephone conversation I learned that he was actually an attorney, accountant, and real estate investor who enjoyed "stirring the pot" by collecting items from the golden age of mechanical musical instruments. "I have a hobby that has gone way out of control," he said. "In fact, my real job is now collecting."

It is a hobby that has become family tradition. His collection was started by his grandfather in the 1930s with the purchase of a Werner player piano and a Tangley roll-operated Calliaphone from Chicago's famed Riverview Amusement Park. Then, when Trager was six, he went with his parents to visit family friends in Montana. "We went to Charles and Sue Bovey's restored ghost towns of Virginia City and Nevada City and I saw a vintage melodrama with a person playing a Cremona photoplayer. I also went to the Bale of Hay Saloon which was full of orchestrions, and the massive long hall in Nevada City which was full of band organs from Coney Island."

His family returned to Montana every year over the next decade, and later Trager visited other mechanical music venues and "roadside America" attractions across the country from Clark's Trading Post in New Hampshire to Knotts Berry Farm in California. He also discovered Musée Mécanique at the Cliff House. "That was quite an experience," he said. "Paint falling from the ceiling onto suspended plastic sheeting, waves crashing on the rocks below. . . ." These trips sealed what he calls the "electric thrill" of hearing the magical music.

Over the years Tim Trager's collection has grown to include twenty band organs and thirty nickelodeons and orchestrions, including a Hupfeld Phonoliszt Violina, Mills Violano Virtuosos, player banjo machines, a large Wurlitzer photoplayer, and a Wurlitzer PianOrchestra. He also acquired a French-made rococo-style 110-key Gavioli fairground organ that for fifty years was the center attraction at the skating pavilion at Euclid Beach Park in Cleveland, Ohio. Weighing over four tons, it was the largest fair organ in America. Its one thousand pipes, twenty-one-note bass trombone section, and brass trumpet and brass clarinet sections provide the full chromatic range of a one hundred–piece concert band. Trager remains enchanted by the quality of the marches, waltzes, and overtures it plays. After attending a concert of the Chicago Symphony Orchestra, he complained that they did not sound as good as his Gavioli fairground organ.

Trager's interests went beyond music to include a whole variety of machines and technological artifacts from the early twentieth century. He told me about his Wells Fargo stagecoaches, carriages, nautical antiques, automata, vintage cars, and a life-sized gasoline-powered elephant built by the cleverly-named English company "Mechanimals," which at one time strolled along Coney Island boardwalk. I asked him if he ever parted with anything or kept expanding his storage space to accommodate his collection. "Every collector is a little bit a dealer," said Trager, "because they sell off items and acquire others in order to enhance their collections."

I thought about Dan Zelinski's comment that some collectors have angst about the maintenance of their collections. I wondered about the extent to which these musical machines become pieces of antique furniture rather than items of entertainment. As "a bit of a dealer," Trager has suspicions that some items might be preserved, but above all he believes that one must keep these instruments in perspective. From the humble player piano to large classic orchestrions, these instruments are, he stressed, "a lot of fun!"—a unique diversion from the problems of the day. He mentioned the fact that what is fun can also be educational. He, too, appreciated that these instruments represent the fine artistic craftsmanship of their time. The high-quality cabinet designs range from Victorian to arts and crafts to Louis IV to art nouveau, Bauhaus, and art deco. "The music these instruments play captures another era like a time capsule," said Trager. "Turn on a roll and you hear exactly what they heard in 1905 or 1930. Through these instruments I discovered all types of music, from overtures such as the 'William Tell' and 'Tannhauser' to the concert waltzes of Emile Waldteufel to ragtime and 1920s jazz." Yet because of the maintenance and preservation efforts, even new music can be played on century-old instruments. While there were many reasons for owning these instruments and many places to display them from mansions to saloons, "one should never forget the enjoyable and entertaining side of these instruments," Trager observed.

Yet for all of the superlatives, mechanical musical instruments remain virtually unknown to current generations. They remain a well-kept secret. I asked Trager if this was because these instruments are for the most part rarely on public display and not part of our modern musical culture. If not for the public collections in the theme parks

that he saw in the 1950s and '60s, all his efforts to collect and preserve these instruments might never have come to pass.

> "Along the way I have met a lot of the pioneer collectors," said
> Trager. "We owe all these early collectors who rescued many
> of today's surviving instruments a debt of gratitude!"
> "Are there enough collectors to keep the history alive?" I asked.
> "I think so," he said. "Corporate executives might still celebrate
> when 'dead' assets become history—such as when they threw
> a party at Disney after the sale of the Raney collection. But
> things are not always about cost/benefit analyses. Popularity
> comes and goes. Right now, these instruments are so old they
> are new."

Trager's thoughts about the opportunities missed by theme parks
to display vintage mechanical musical instruments elicited a number
of sympathetic replies, though a general consensus seemed to be that
times had changed. The popularity of these instruments in the last
decade seemed to have been on the wane. Theme parks that still use
coin machines to generate revenue are seen as an anachronism. Musical tastes have changed as well. "Just listen to most Industrial,
Grunge, Hip Hop, or other nihilistic sub-cultural . . . 'music' today,"
wrote one contributor. "It's hardly suitable for the graceful instru-
mentation of a PianOrchestra or large band or fair organ."[11]

The technology and the nostalgia it evoked was appealing to a
decreasing proportion of the population. While reconstructing
America of the 1920s might have been nostalgic for theme park visitors of the 1950s, visitors today react that way to scenes of the 1950s,
'60s or even '70s. "When you are trying to attract literally millions
or tens of millions of people to a theme park," wrote Martin Roenigk,
another contributor to the discussion, "you have to go after the common denominator."[12]

People such as Tim Trager and Martin Roenigk might have had
slightly different perspectives on what benefits major theme parks
obtain by preserving vintage mechanical musical machines, but they
agreed that there still exists a market for such instruments. Roenigk
has a particular interest in the collection that was formerly at Disneyland since he and his wife acquired the Raney collection. It became

part of the stock of their business, Mechantiques, which operates out of their historic Crescent Hotel in Eureka Springs, Arkansas.

The town of Eureka Springs refers to itself as "The little Switzerland of the Ozarks." As a member of the National Register of Historic Places, it also refers to itself as being "So Unique It's Out of Time! Out of Place!" It was founded in the 1850s by Dr. Alva Jackson, who described himself as a graduate of Douglas Medical School in Kentucky and who proclaimed the springs to have medicinal properties. Throughout the nineteenth century and into the early twentieth century, Eureka grew into a fashionable resort, with wealthy invalids seeking constitutional restoration. The downtown area is adorned with Victorian architecture, steep winding streets, and a 240-foot-high, two-million-pound white concrete statue of Jesus that was carved by Emmet Sullivan, one of the Mount Rushmore artists. ("Jesus is big here!" quipped one tourist.)

Visitors to the Crescent Hotel and Spa are encouraged to absorb the historic ambience of its 120-year history: to enjoy carriage rides through the country, relish the half-century-old recipe for their huckleberry muffins, and listen to mechanical musical instruments. The hotel sits amidst a lavish landscaped garden. Heavy wooden pillars frame the lobby with a magnificent central white stone fireplace, while stained oak panels and rich red Victorian wallpaper decorate the walls.

A majestic Welte Philharmonic Salon Model 4 sits against one wall. Built in Freiburg, Germany, around 1912, this self-playing pipe organ stands over ten feet tall and eight feet wide with 250 pipes, two drums, and a cymbal, all of which operate from a library of over 150 music rolls. "It is one of three of this model still known to exist," explains Marty Roenigk. "The other two are in museums in Germany and Japan. One of the others was intended for the *Titanic*, and the builder, Mr. Welte, was to have accompanied it on the maiden voyage. However, the organ wasn't ready in time so both the organ and Mr. Welte luckily missed that fateful voyage."

Marty and his wife, Elise, have been collectors of mechanical musical instruments for over thirty years. They discovered Eureka Springs while scouting for a retirement venue in the region and took the opportunity to visit Floyd Miles, proprietor of Miles Musical Museum (a specialist in mechanical music), located just outside town on scenic Highway 62.[13] That museum was closed and its contents auctioned off in 1997, shortly after the Roenigks decided to buy and refurbish the Crescent Hotel and the nearby Basin Park Hotel.

Among the items they purchased at the Miles auction was a Mills Violano Virtuoso, a self-playing violin built inside a cabinet player piano. It is displayed in the lobby of the Basin Park Hotel. Along another wall of the lobby of the Crescent Hotel sits a Seeburg H coin-operated orchestrion purchased from Disneyland. These instruments add to the historic feel of the hotel and are a nice complement to the whole Victoriana ambience. "They fit in very, very well," he acknowledged.

"How do the visitors react to the instruments?" I asked.

"They enjoy them very much when they are playing," said Marty. "Unfortunately they are 'down' too often." He was referring to the wear and tear of the instruments on public display. "When working," he said, underscoring the efforts it takes to keep the instruments in good working condition, "they are played by the bellmen whenever requested, but not by the guests directly."

Luckily the Seeburg H orchestrion was 'up,' and I sauntered over to the bellman and asked to hear it. A moment later the machine began playing a lively ragtime tune. I could see the roll unwinding through the stained glass window as the keys bounced up and down. As we listened to the music, I glanced at some of the small framed pictures hanging on the wall. There seemed to be a warp in one of the pictures. "It's a ghost on the second floor," said the bellman. "You know this place is haunted, right?"

I then understood the little white squeezable ghosts for sale in the gift shop which I had previously spotted. Then there was the book. I saw an advertisement for a work of fiction "based on real facts" also sold at the hotel about a psychic who was drawn to the hotel by a restless spirit that lived in room 218. According to various sources, that was the very spot where a workman who was helping to build the hotel in the 1880s fell from the roof and died. "We have lots of pictures of ghosts," said the bellman. "The 'Ghost Hunters' team from the Sci-Fi Channel recently spent a week here filming them." I wondered whether the machine that plays by itself was also part of the "ghostly" legacy at the hotel—whether the spirit that sat at the machine and played its heart out might be in the photographs. "No connection has ever been made," said the bellman, with an austere look on his face. "We know this is a mechanical show. There is no explanation for the ghosts." It seemed as though a marketing opportunity was being lost.

I was there to visit Mechantiques, which bills itself as the country's largest dealer in mechanical musical instruments, advertising an inventory of over 125 items for sale, including music boxes, musical clocks, coin-operated pianos, band organs, and mechanical singing birds, "anything in antique mechanical music." Owners Marty and Elise are strict about the "antique" quality of their collection—accepting nothing made after 1930. Like many antiques, these fetch considerable sums. A carved oak Mermod Frères German cylinder music box that plays opera arias that "can make you cry" was for sale at the reduced price of $48,500. A charming brass birdcage automaton with two mechanical birds priced at a more down-to-earth $2,850. However, more in my budget was a folding "picnic style" portable phonograph with a faux red leather and metal case for $75. Long gone was the now well-traveled Wurlitzer Style 32 Concert PianOrchestra from the Raney collection that was at Disneyland. It was refurbished by the musician, historian, and automated musical instrument lover Arthur Reblitz in 2005 and moved to a private collection in Wisconsin.

Despite the Roenigks' decision to adopt what they call "the classical approach" to reducing their inventory by reducing prices, they were not overly eager to reduce their treasured collection. Even though (almost) everything was for sale, it was less a business than another example of a hobby out of control. As Tim Trager had said, in every collector there was a dealer. These instruments might not be "hands-on" to the public, but they have passed through the hands of many collectors and aficionados through their long histories. The world of circulating mechanical musical instruments was an international trade. I asked Marty why he thought there was such interest in mechanical musical instruments. "I expect it is all of us who can't play an instrument ourselves that are amazed that an 'ancient' machine can do it," he said. History is humbling.

People come to understand and preserve the past in different ways, and what constitutes an "archive" or a "record" depends entirely upon how one interacts with it. I discovered new ways by which people were rescuing fragments of the past that had been over-looked and taken for granted. As I had just learned, love and money worked both for and against these efforts. I would learn more about these as my travels progressed, but I wanted to start at the beginning. Who invented these automatic pianos? Who were the artists whose names appeared on the thousands of music rolls that were so popular at the beginning of the twentieth century? It was time to hit the history books. I was in search of those inventors and musicians who made the machines come alive.

Chapter 3
Chronic Mechanitis

"OHN McTAMMANY counts his patents by the hundred," boasted William Geppert, the editor of the *Musical Currier Extra* in 1915.[1] The fruits of his friend's labor over the previous thirty years had resulted, he declared, in the invention of the player piano, an accolade that McTammany had had etched into his gravestone in Canton, Ohio. Whether referred to generically as a "player piano" or "pianola," or specifically to the name of a company's own line of players (which Pianola was before it became a generic term), the instrument has assumed a variety of different forms and functions. Everyone knows the player piano plays "by itself." The power that enables the machine to come alive is derived either from a human operator, a taut spring mechanism, or electricity, depending on the age and design. While one might debate which method sounded best, the first impression of most spectators is one of surprise at the mechanical genius of a player piano.

Mechanical musical instruments had long been a curiosity, beginning with automata in the Age of Enlightenment. Eighteenth-century philosophers had accepted the view borne from the Scientific Revolution of the previous two centuries that nature, society, and the body alike operated according to mechanical principles. Thinking about the functions of machines became a way of understanding the secrets of nature. Music itself was thought to have derived from harmonies produced mathematically through the motion of celestial bodies, the "music of the spheres."

In 1814, the Viennese musical engineer Johann Maelzel pushed metaphysical philosophy by claiming that a chess-playing automaton bolted onto a cabinet worked by establishing a musical harmony with the mind of its opponent. For years the famous "Turkish chess player" mesmerized audiences around Europe by outplaying its competitors until the presence of a clever gamesman hidden under the automaton's gown was finally exposed. This discovery might have happened earlier had the public not preferred to have been entertained by the spectacle of the hidden powers of nature instead of the wizard hidden behind the drape. In fact, while Maelzel went on to immortalize himself by inventing "an universal standard measure for musical time," the metronome, he ended up in London pursuing his "metronomic dream" of devising a completely automated orchestra, hoping once and for all to transcend human intervention—a dream he failed to realize.[2]

In the 1770s, Pierre Jacquet-Droz and his son Henri-Louis constructed mechanical dolls designed to perform tasks while also appearing to breathe and glance around. On display in Neuchâtel, Switzerland, one boy doll draws pictures and challenges observers' philosophies by writing "I think therefore I am," while a girl doll plays a small pipe organ so that the tips of her fingers press the appropriate key.[3] From animated dolls to devices that animate pianos, innovations in the mechanization of music continued to flourish with contributions from all over Europe throughout the nineteenth century and in America prior to the dawn of the twentieth.

In 1900, the American lawyer and inventor Thaddeus Cahill patented a machine that had an alternating current generator connected to a piano keyboard that divided "an electrical current into a fixed and mathematically exact number of vibrations" per second to correspond to as many aerial vibrations per second in a note of the musical scale for which it stands.[4] The combination of technology and music promised to push the boundaries of the gradation of the octave, potentially revolutionizing music. In 1907, the Italian piano virtuoso Ferruccio Busoni wrote his *Sketch of a New Esthetic in Music*, in which he predicted that "in the new great music, machines will also be necessary and will be assigned a share in it."[5] This was a prescient statement since this was not an obvious direction for music to go in a period when music required live performances.

At the dawn of the twentieth century, the piano was found at all levels of American society. As the sociologist Max Weber pointed out, it proliferated outside the concert hall to become "a significant piece of middle-class furniture"—a necessary accoutrement to domesticity, as familiar as an armchair.[6] While it was "furniture" for the middling sorts, it was the "entertainment center" within poorer African American communities. In Harlem "rent parties," friends and family paid a modest fee to gather around a pianist for a night of revelry, often to help the host pay for that week's rent, but as often, noted the black sociologist Ira Reid in the early 1920s, "to pay the next installment on the Steinway piano."[7] One builder of Harlem apartment blocks even planned to put an upright piano in each unit, "just as other landlords build hat racks in the hall and china closets in the dining room."[8]

In this same period, previously marginalized forms of entertainment transformed American culture as commercial industry brought forth African American music, modern dance, and working-class mechanical marvels such as storefront nickelodeons to a diversified mass audience.[9] Entrepreneurs also created a mass entertainment market for player pianos that brought together isolated fragments of Americana from the fox-trot to ragtime, from amusement park automata to vaudeville theaters, from the futurism of avant-garde artists to mechanics hoping to revolutionize the "musical soul" of modernity.

Paradoxically, techniques for mechanical reproduction in the arts—in film, photography, and music—took place during a period when a Bolshevistic-style "smashing of the rules" celebrated new freedoms of artistic expression.[10] It was even more so that the public perception of a "live" performance was conveyed through machines. As the German literary critic Walter Benjamin said of the early motion picture, "what mattered was that a part was acted not for an audience but for a mechanical contrivance."[11] With the loss of corporeality, the entertainer became alienated from the stage as much as from himself. The performer expected to be observed, but mechanical interventions elide the entertainer. Benjamin's observation was relevant to the contemporary player piano. Many manufacturers also sold cameras and advertised them as improvements made on human eyes and fingers by means of lenses and keyboard levers.

As popular as pianos were during the first two decades of the twentieth century, player piano sales soared past those of the conventional manual piano. The automatic piano had arrived at a moment when American social life and industry were torn between the mechanization of labor and the aesthetics of freedom. They embodied the shift from experiencing machines as powerful, utilitarian muscles that worked to industrialize modern America to their being sources of entertainment, a sublime spectacle.

The possibilities of what could be done when "mechanics" were put to work on modernizing musical instruments quickly began to stimulate capitalist imaginations. In the 1910s, almost every piano manufacturer was rolling out its own specially patented player pianos. Already by 1904 there were more than forty different kinds of automatic piano on the market.[12] "The enormous growth and activity in the manufacture of self-playing instruments at the present time can be paralleled by only one other line of manufacture," stated the *Patent Review* in 1906, "namely, the automobile industry."[13]

For consumers of means, it was estimated that the player piano was the most expensive purchase Americans could make, after a house and car.[14] While they clearly caught the public's imagination and changed the way an entire generation would learn to listen to and understand music, it is unclear just what lay behind the public's intrigue. Was it that they were listening to the seemingly live performance of amazing pianists or were they more enchanted by the triumph of a machine, the success of an industrially ordered society? The ambiguity of this cultural enigma—an apparent clash between art and science, aesthetics and technology—was captured in the question posed by an attendee at the end of a player piano concert in Germany in 1926: "Should one applaud? For nobody is there. It is only a machine."[15] Regardless of whether John McTammany, an Ohio agricultural machinery repairman, had single-handedly "given birth to a new industry" (as his admirer Geppert asserted), it is not surprising to read Geppert's follow-up claim that "the player has been the subject of acrimonious controversy extending over a period of forty years, during which time it has raged in the Patent Office, disrupted the courts and clogged the pages of the press; has proved, in fact, an issue that has staggered the Supreme Court, convulsed Congress, engaged the attention of the President and demanded the amendment of the Federal laws."[16] American manufacturers allegedly suffered from "chronic mechanitis."[17] Millions of pianos which had been sold over the past century were, they envisioned, now sitting silently in middle-class homes. With a few alterations, a vast new market could emerge. A patent fetish ensued.

People enjoy discovery stories. Books retelling the history of science are full of examples of eureka moments and sole geniuses, though anyone who reads historical manuscripts or early published accounts usually soon finds that history is not so linear. People silently borrow ideas, gain inspiration from similar devices, infringe on patents, and improve on their own designs. Even though I was encountering a wide variety of mechanical musical devices—and once I was reprimanded for confusing a Pianista with a Pianola—I thought I'd try to set the record straight. A conveniently, if somewhat hastily, planned trip to Paris would help me to plot the evolution of the player piano, or at least what others believe was the order of developments.

An old professor friend of mine named Bob Hatch was teaching summer school in Paris and offered me his couch in a rented apartment in Montparnasse. Hanging out there, in the early twentieth-century hub of Parisian intellectual and artistic life, would provide a good setting in which I could perform some research.

One evening not long after I arrived we were visited by Dominique, a friend of Bob's who taught philosophy at the Sorbonne.

> "So, what do you plan to do in Paris?" asked Dominique, in broken English.
>
> "I'm doing some research on the history of music," I answered.
>
> "Ahhh, music, excellent! You know, zey say zat Paris is ze City of Lights, but I sink zat music is a real passion here. You write about French music?" he asked.
>
> "Well, a bit," I replied. I was unable to recall a famous French pianist nor could I think of any French piano rolls to make a connection. "Actually," I said, "I am trying to find out more about an instrument—the player piano."
>
> Dragging on his cigarette, Dominique stared at me.
>
> "*You* know," I said, looking at Bob, hoping his French might be able to clarify, but he puckered his lips and shrugged his shoulders to gesture (in the French way), *je ne sais pas.*
>
> "You like ze piano?" asked Dominique.
>
> "It's not a piano, really, it's a machine," I said uneasily.

I could not think of a way to gesture in explanation because tapping my fingers onto an invisible keyboard to emulate playing would be the inverse of what I was trying to convey—it is the absence of fingers, not the keyboard, which was important. "It is a piano that plays by itself," I added.

A brief moment of silence passed before Dominique shot his finger up into the air, "Ahh, oui, oui, piano mecanique!"

"Piano mecanique," I repeated, "yes, the mechanical piano, I want to learn more about its history."

I explained to Dominique that I planned to visit a few museums that specialized in mechanical musical instruments and perhaps visit with one or two members of the Association des Amis des Instruments et de la Musique Mécanique (AAIMM)—the French equivalent to AMICA. This association was started in 1975 by Claude Marchal, an electrical engineer who came from a family known for manufacturing automobile headlights and sparkplugs. He retired to the small village of Bullet, in Switzerland, which then became a pilgrimage for people interested in Claude's amazing collection of mechanical musical instruments (many of which, such as his music boxes and musical clocks, represented fine Swiss craftsmanship) and his collection of Boy Scout memorabilia, items he began to collect shortly after World War II when he became the international commissioner of the Scouts de France. He passed away in 1997, and this collection ended up in the International Scouting Museum in Las Vegas while his mechanical instrument collection was auctioned off in 2004 just months before my visit.

The AAIMM has around six hundred members, and its president, Philippe Rouillé, maintains a website providing information about trips the association organizes to villages throughout France and around Europe to visit historic automated music collections. One useful document he prepared was a walking tour of Paris for viewing the contemporary sites of places of historical interest, such as the Aeolian Company's French headquarters, where Gavioli's organ factory was, and the location of Jouets et Automates Francais, makers of automata and music boxes. I had plotted out a day trip and showed it to Bob and Dominique. "In my family house," said Dominique, "we have a Serinette—a small music box zat chirps like a bird. It has a little barrel with pins sticking out of it, which . . . uhh . . . open valves zat push ze air into pipes. It is quite old. I sink it is quite valuable." I said that music boxes were often found in collections I visit, which were not limited to player pianos but encompassed a wide range of mechanical musical devices. The Serinette was an eighteenth-century invention apparently used to teach canaries to sing, but its design is very similar to that of barrel organs played by organ grinders in streets across Europe.

Music boxes remain extremely popular among collectors all over the world, I noted, pointing out that they have their own dedicated fan base and collectors' clubs that enjoy a sort of rivalry to others interested in player pianos, orchestrions, and the like. As popular as they were, I speculated that organ grinders probably did more to popularize mechanical music (and alienate neighbors) in the nineteenth century than any other group, since they created the music of the street.

> "I remember ze tune zat ze box played so well," said Dominique. "*Savoir par coeur*, I know it by heart. I can hear it. I guess zat makes me a kind of machine, *non*? A kind of mechanical repetition, in my brain."
> A true philosopher, I thought. "Some critics argued that the mechanical reproduction of music takes the heart out of the music," I offered. "That is similar to what some German philosophers in the 1950s were saying about the mechanization of art, like the projection of images in movies," I added. "Machines eat away at humanity."
> "You know," replied Dominique, "zere are some philosophers who earn a living by arguing ze nonexistence of zeir own minds."
> "So we should be especially critical of what philosophers have to say?" I wondered.
> "You tell me if you feel ze spirit of music today, here, in ze streets of Paris." Dominique leaned on the railing and blew cigarette smoke over the railing. "We have ze new music of ze streets. All mechanical, *non*?"

Conversation stopped and I listened to what was going on outside. I realized that the evening rush-hour hustle was over—no more

endless moped horns and car engines revving—and music was emanating from all of the bars and cafes in the labyrinth of alleys and
streets below us. The area we were in is what the French call
"mixed"—multicultural, multiethnic. One could discern Irish, African, American, South American, and European music—music that
would beat on until five a.m., I would discover. But with my ears
newly tuned in to the musical world around me, I was looking forward to setting out on my journey to find the music of the past.

The ultimate destination on my day out was the Musée de la Musique Mécanique, a collection open to the public in the family home
of Henri Triquet in a cul-de-sac off of the Rue Beaubourg, around the
corner from the Pompidou Center. It was officially opened in 1983
by the then-mayor of Paris, Jacques Chirac. An old article in the travel
section of the *Los Angeles Times* described its "several organs that
grinders used to play in Parisian squares and parks," a Violin-
Virtuoso, an automaton "accordionist with a working accordion and
a drummer whose head moves back and forth with the beat," player
pianos that offer "the softest pianissimo to a drumming forte," and,
even more unusually, an automaton man dressed in a tuxedo who
slowly raises a lit cigarette to his lips, inhales, and blows out the
smoke with his eyes shut.[18] How very European, I thought, definitely
something that would not be appreciated at the Musée Mécanique in
San Francisco. It seemed a promising high point to the day where I
would finally wind up at a café near the Pompidou.

The first stop was across town to the Musée des Arts et Métiers a
few blocks from Réaumur-Sébastopol Metro. Founded in 1794, this
is France's, if not Europe's, oldest museum of "arts and trade," what
would be known in America as a museum of science and technology.
It had eighty thousand objects spanning over four hundred years of
technological innovation, from Blaise Pascal's 1642 calculating
machine to a 1986 Apple computer. The architecture of the museum
itself is enchanting, beginning with the entrance into the remains of
the medieval Priory of Saint-Martin des Champs, spreading over three
levels of modern halls housing exhibits and ending in an eleventh-
century chapel that is now a large gift shop.

Within the displays is the exhibit that most interested me: Le Théâtre des Automates, described in the catalogue as "a spectacle and
demonstration of living automata and mechanical music." I knew
from brief correspondence with a curator before my trip that they

had in their collection various musical automata and at least one player piano, an Aeolian Pianola built around 1900. However, my communications were sketchy, my French lousy.

I was hoping to find out whether they had any information on Jean Louis Fourneaux, who in 1863 took out a patent for a pneumatic apparatus rigged to a system designed to play piano keys. His invention, which he called the Pianista, was built into a case that was pushed up to the front of a piano so that its mechanical "fingers" were aligned with the keys of the keyboard. When a handle was cranked, the fingers depressed their respective keys, playing a tune it had been "programmed" to perform. The Pianista is what is commonly known as a "push-up player," which predated the design of the internal player that was contained within the piano itself. Where exactly in the chronology of invention the Pianista stood was a complex issue, but Fourneaux's invention certainly was an important early development in the evolution of the mechanical piano.

While it was a hot summer day, the air-conditioned museum seemed unusually quiet. Bob and I wandered past the history of scientific instruments, energy, and transport while I was studying the floor plan wondering where the music exhibitions would be. Eventually we found two large, closed wooden doors with a sign above them reading "Le Théâtre des Automates."

"This must be where we want to go," I said to Bob. The doors were locked.
"It's closed," confirmed Bob.
"Well that's just typical," I cried.

The room held what many people would regard as the most interesting collection of machines in the museum, which, in my cynicism, explained why it was closed. However, Bob had a plan. Despite its being the weekend, which almost certainly meant that no curator with any authority would be available, he disappeared and a short while later returned with a woman dangling a key. As she opened the door, Bob explained the situation, that I just wanted to take a quick look at a specific item about which I had had a lengthy correspondence with the curator. The woman did not speak, and flipped the minimal number of switches to illuminate the room. The few spotlights cast eerie shadows in the large dark space, shining on the porcelain faces of mechanical dolls, miniature circus sets, organs, and other objects. All sat frozen and silent.

"Ici," she said, standing next to a piano.

Bob oohed. "Merci, madame," always very courteous. I smiled and nodded, but she probably couldn't see my face. It was so dark in the room I could not decipher what kind of piano it was let alone read the label.

"Bob, do you think she'll play it for us?" I asked, incredulously, but Bob has that "why not" attitude.

"Madame, ce possible . . . ecoute . . .," is what I could decipher.

"Non . . . [something undecipherable]," was her reply.

But she did ask, in hesitant English, whether I wanted to take a picture. That was a good idea. The flash might help us to see something. Unfortunately, the camera's dead battery foreclosed that possibility.

While I had visions of being able to study a French player piano and quiz the curator about its social and cultural history, and this failed miserably, all was not lost. Serendipitously, as Bob and I were wending our ways through the textiles gallery, I spotted a machine designed to punch holes in paper rolls. It resembled a loom, and its plaque read "Mecanique Jacquard (type Verdol) 1883." "This looks like a player piano roll," I commented. "Look at those thousands of tiny little holes in the paper running through this machine."

What is generally referred to as the Jacquard loom, first invented around 1801, is a famous machine in the industrial revolution, but this mechanism caught my eye for its unintended consequences. Joseph Marie Jacquard had developed a way to use holes punched in cards to control the motion of hooks that wove threaded patterns into fabric, greatly simplifying and standardizing the manufacture of complex textile designs. It was also a technology that has been called the conceptual precursor to computer programming cards, but among mechanical music aficionados it has been argued that Jacquard's invention was linked to the production of piano rolls.

Even earlier than Jacquard, however, another Frenchman, Jacques de Vaucanson, was commissioned by the government to set up new silk mills in Lyon. Trained as a clockmaker and famous for building automata which he put on display in Paris, such as the well-known defecating duck and a mechanical flute player, he designed machines to automate the spinning and weaving of silk, which

Image by Brian Dolan

"Mecanique Jacquard (type Verdol) 1883." Jacquard's loom has been linked to the production of piano rolls.

included the use of pierced metal cylinders that functioned in ways similar to Jacquard's invention.[19]

There has been a long history of mechanical ingenuity applied to the worlds of both industry and entertainment, and the emergence of mechanical music, linked in various ways to the designs of automata, stems from these roots. In fact, the principle of perforated cardboard was adapted in England by the organ builder and noted "mechanical and musical genius" Justinian Morse, who adapted it to the operation of a mechanical piano as early as the 1730s.[20]

Then, in 1842, in France, a patent was given to Claude-Felix Seytre for the design of perforated cards for use in pianos. By the 1860s, Jean Louis Fourneaux was able to further adapt the principle of perforated cards and combine it with a pneumatic system for his crank-powered Pianista, which in France created a new category of musical instrument known as Pianista Automatique. Fourneaux, who was a maker of harmoniums (an earlier Paris invention) and organs, manufactured a number of Pianistas in the 1870s, at least one of which is said to have made an appearance at the Centennial Exhibition in Philadelphia in 1876.[21]

Soon after Fourneaux's "push-up" Pianista appeared, a number of manufacturers in France began producing similar *pianos pneumatiques*, with Nice in the south of France becoming one of the centers of manufacture of mechanical musical instruments.[22] However, these devices were limited in their operations. Initially, it was too difficult to design a mechanism that operated all eighty-eight keys, so only keys in the middle octaves played, usually between thirty-nine and sixty-five notes in all. Furthermore, before the perforated roll was developed, the size of the perforated cards imposed further limitations on the range and duration of music. They nevertheless provided enough entertainment for a new industry to develop.

I hoped I would get to see some of these historic instruments at the Musée de la Musique Mécanique. However, before that, I wanted to head over to Avenue de l'Opéra to take a look at the building where the Aeolian Company established its Paris offices in the early 1900s. This address was on M. Rouillé's guide. When I got there I discovered it was exactly as he had described it: a classic Hausmann-style six story building with balconies festooned with flowers.

Aeolian was one of the major early twentieth-century manufacturers of player pianos—a rival to Story & Clark, Baldwin, and others. The Paris office was one among many that Aeolian operated around the world when the organization was at its strongest. The company was established in 1888 by William Tremaine, who merged his Mechanical Orguinette Company with the Automatic Music Paper Company and bought all the patents of the Monroe Organ Reed Company. The name Aeolian, which derives from Aeolus, mythic god of the winds, had been used in literature to refer to winds that produce musical sounds, and had been used by others since at least the mid-nineteenth century. The Aeolian Company, manufacturer of automated pianos, was so named in 1898 when Henry Tremaine took over from his father and built the company into the giant of the industry that it would become.

During the 1890s, an ex-employee of the Mechanical Orguinette Company, John McTammany, began working on the design of his own push-up piano mechanism, a variation of the French Pianista earlier displayed in Philadelphia. Patented in 1895, the first Angelus produced did not appear until 1897. However, in the very year that McTammany was filing for his patent, an organ technician from Detroit, Edwin Votey, built his own push-up mechanical piano player. By the time McTammany was putting the finishing touches on the Angelus, Votey's company had already produced a number of his own version. The first model that Votey made is now in the Smithsonian. The Pianola, as he called it, was now being sold by the Aeolian Company. But the brand name would come to be used generically to refer broadly to any player piano.[23]

The turn of the nineteenth century marked the beginning of an aggressive marketing and production campaign by Aeolian to increase the popularity of the Pianola. They had factories in New York, New Jersey, and Connecticut, and sales offices outside America in England, Germany, Australia, and in the building that I was standing in front of in Paris.[24] An extant catalogue from 1902 states that they were sponsoring Pianola concerts in England. The cover of the gold-embossed program shows a woman sitting at the Pianola cabinet, which was attached to the front of a grand piano. At the base of the cabinet were pedals she would pump to activate the pneumatic system controlled by a perforated roll mechanism located inside the device, which controlled the mechanical fingers poised above the piano keyboard. Her hands manipulated small levers on the top of the cabinet that controlled the tempo and roll direction.[25] Standing next to her was a man in a tuxedo who would sing as she reproduced the music of Liszt, Blumenthal, Mattei, and others. In Paris, the Pianola was promoted by the Coupleux brothers, who imported the instruments and organized exhibitions and concerts. They later expanded into phonographs, cinema, and music recordings.[26]

My present trip to Paris was brief, time was running out, and my day was close to being over. I was ready to strike gold and check out the collection of mechanical instruments near the Pompidou Center that I had read about. After some inquiries, I learned that the Musée was no longer there. It had closed "long ago." I was ten years too late; the Triquet collection had been sold to a collector in Belgium.

After the Fourneaux invention, American engineers and instrument makers—among them McTammany and Votey, but also many others—began inventing and adapting new designs for pneumatic mechanical piano players. Companies large and small in Chicago,

Ohio, Michigan, and New York began filing patents for their own players. Paul Klugh, for instance, who had struggled to make a living selling organs to Michigan farmers from his horse-drawn wagon, accepted a job with the Cable Company of Chicago, which in 1904 decided to manufacture player pianos. Possessing mechanical skills and motivated by the possibilities that self-playing instruments offered, he soon began designing devices for the company's Carola Inner Player and Euphona pianos.[27] Large companies such as W.W. Kimball, which became the largest single producer of pianos in the world, entered the frenzy, as did Baldwin and Gulbransen-Dickinson. The "Gulbransen Baby" trademark—an infant in diapers kneeling on a player piano, promoting how "Easy to Play" it was—became as familiar as the Victor Talking Machine Company's "His Master's Voice" logo.

Image courtesy of QRS Music Inc.

The "Gulbransen Baby" Trademark. Gulbransen-Dickinson's famous trademark became as familiar as the Victor Talking Machine Company's "His Master's Voice" logo.

While New York had Tin Pan Alley and was a hub of showrooms and concert halls, the piano manufacturing industry was centered in the Midwest. Following the Great Fire of 1871, according to business historian Craig Roell, Chicago became "a national center in musical instrument manufacturing, especially organs and pianos."[28] In the first decade of the twentieth century, over forty companies were manufacturing pianos there, and Wabash Avenue became known as "Music Row," with a number of piano manufacturers and distributors having showrooms along the avenue.[29] Nearby was Orchestra Hall, the Fine Arts building, and the Auditorium Theater. With major retailers based there such as Sears, Roebuck, & Co. and Montgomery Ward, the market for the new mechanical instruments was given a timely boost.

One Chicago manufacturer, George Bent, eager to make a name for himself in the emerging market, claimed that he was the first person in America to sell a push-up piano player with the sale of a Wilcox & White Co. machine in 1897 (just as the Aeolian Company was promoting its Pianola). Bent, who went on to become the president of the National Association of Piano Manufacturers of America, later said that although he was enthusiastic about the device at the time, others thought that "such a thing as a 'machine' to produce piano playing was not only ridiculous, but the very *idea* was preposterous."[30] This view would not last long.

In 1904, a number of innovations marked the rapidity of progress in piano player design. The German firm of M. Welte & Son had opened up an American branch in 1866 and sold instruments that operated by means of perforated paper rolls. They obtained a number of U.S. patents in the 1880s and subsequently showed how elaborate automatic musical machines could be. At the St. Louis World's Fair ("Louisiana Purchase Exposition") in 1904, they displayed a colossal orchestrion over twenty feet high and thirty feet long—essentially three separate orchestrions put together and designed to play in synchronicity with one another. Further, another device they produced that year would make a definitive mark in the history of the more humble self-playing piano. They called it the Welte-Mignon—the first "reproducing piano."

The introduction of the reproducing piano revolutionized player piano design, and it encompassed two central mechanical features that would become the benchmark for the future of the industry.

First, it dispensed with the push-up cabinet with its mechanical fingers and built the player mechanisms into the piano itself (sometimes called the "inner" or "internal player"). This internalization of the mechanics fundamentally differentiates the mechanical "piano player," such as the Pianista and Pianola types, from the "player piano" that would subsequently become the ubiquitous and typical automated piano. The piano could be played manually or by pumping the pedals while the player mechanism did the work.

Engineers had been experimenting with this design innovation since the 1880s. The Aeolian Company had prototypes built by its experimental engineer, Robert Pain at that time, while a "pneumatic engineer" from Massachusetts, Theodore Brown—who later proclaimed *himself* to be the inventor of "the First Player Piano"—designed a similar mechanism called the Aeriol, which was sold by Aeolian in 1897.[31] In 1904, the design was improved upon and Aeolian began selling the "New Pianola," a foot-pedaled player piano with the music roll placed in its familiar location in the center of the upright cabinet above the keyboard. While this design was more convenient than having a separate push-up cabinet, the number of manual pianos already in people's houses was an impediment. Between 1870 and 1900, piano production increased at an average rate of three and one-half times faster than population growth, with manufacturers selling tens of thousands of instruments each year. This meant it would take some time for consumers to be willing to trade in their manual piano for a new automated model.[32]

The Welte-Mignon incorporated this internal player innovation but introduced still another feature that further distinguished this automatic instrument. Edwin Welte, son of the founder of M. Welte & Son manufacturers, collaborated with two other engineers, Karl Bockisch and Hugo Popper, to invent a system that would create specially perforated rolls that captured the dynamics or "expression" of a live pianist playing on a special recording piano. When played on the Mignon, their specially prepared rolls "reproduced" the performer's human expression. In their own marketing words, "not only does it play the musical notes, but it also brings forth every touch in technique, every subtlety of expression and tone color; in fact, you hear the *actual playing* of a master musician."[33] This claim remains a matter of contention. The idea that a mechanism could reproduce not only the notes, tempo, phrasing and attack of a composition, but something apparently as intangible as expression or emotional touch, was thought by critics to be counterintuitive to the essence of music.

In 1904, Welte-Mignon might have had some difficulty convincing its consumers of the accuracy of its claims, but by 1910 they had integrated their reproducing system into uprights and grands, a keyboardless cabinet piano, and a push-up version that could be attached to any piano, suggesting a commitment to the principle and enough public attention to pursue the idea.[34] It gradually became more and more popular, and an entire marketing campaign worked to persuade piano owners that they could have the "master's own hands" perform on their own instruments. One Welte-Mignon advertisement showed ghostly hands at the keyboard to illustrate that real hands created the original music.

Unlike "reproducing" or expression player pianos, such as the Welte-Mignon, mechanical piano players, or early player pianos, lacked the ability to perform with dynamic expression. A pneumatic system, sucking air through tiny holes in a paper roll, causing a mechanism to actuate a piano's keys, was *mechanical* sounding. It is ironic that the ingenuity of the design, which was celebrated as an example of the mechanical genius of industrializing America, was criticized for this trait. One answer might have been to change the way people learned to appreciate the sound of music—something that I would later discover begins to happen the more one explores the evolution of sounds through history. Another solution was to make machines out of people—to train them in some way to provide the missing expressive ingredient to the music they were reproducing.

This problem was addressed with the introduction of another technological innovation that made its way into the market by late 1903. A few years earlier, an engineer at Aeolian's London subsidiary company named Francis Young figured that if some sort of easy instructions could be given to "pianolists"—people who sat at the Pianola pumping the pedals and playing with the levers that regulated the tempo—then the limitations of what could be programmed into the perforated rolls has been overcome. His solution was simple yet ingenious. When one sits at a player piano and pumps the pedals, its pneumatic system kicks into gear and the paper roll passes over a metal "tracker bar." Those tracker bar holes uncovered by passing holes in the roll's perforations trigger associated small bellows to actuate individual piano keys. The speed of the pianolist's pedaling controls the force of the suction in the player's small bellows, which determines the force with which the keys are struck. How fast the roll moves over the tracker bar can be adjusted with the tempo lever. Young devised a way of helping pianolists control the intensity and the tempo of the resulting music. The technology also worked to control the actions of the pianolist.

The pianolist watches the music roll pass over the tracker bar. Young realized that if a wavy red line were to be printed on the roll alongside the holes corresponding to tempo changes, then following the red line with the movement of a lever would enable the pianolist to regulate the tempo. He attached an extension to the tempo lever at the front of the piano that moved a pointer placed alongside the piano roll as the lever was moved. All the pianolist needed to do was follow the red line with the pointer by manipulating the lever, and the tempo would be accurate. The pianolist then suddenly became part of the production of the music, an extension of the apparatus that regulated the reproduction of what the pianist had recorded. His device, which was equipped on Pianolas by the end of 1903, was called the Metrostyle.

In 1904, Aeolian announced that this innovation represented "an entirely new thought in musical instruments." For between $500 and $1,000, proud owners would be guaranteed that their piano would never stand idle again, and, above all, they would own a piece of cutting-edge technology. "Its advantages over the accepted type of pianoforte are so manifest," they declared, "that thousands of pianos heretofore satisfactory to their owners are destined to be disposed of to make room for this Twentieth Century production."[35]

The beginning of the new century that saw the beginning of a new love affair in the union between pianos and machines provided an opportune moment to pitch "Twentieth Century productions." However, there remained a design feature of the player piano, as well as push-up piano players, that seemed incongruous to bringing the new mechanical piano to its next evolutionary stage. Since about 1870, the standard piano keyboard had had eighty-eight keys. Yet, manufacturers and retailers of mechanical piano players from the turn of the century on had been working to convince the public that sixty-five notes alone were all that were required to play the classics. One manufacturer, Melville Clark, made a number of changes to the design of the player piano that would put the finishing touches on the revolution in mechanical musical instruments.

Census records suggest that Melville Clark was born in New York around 1848. A musician with an entrepreneurial spirit, he was trained at an early age to tune pianos and was employed by an organ manufacturer in Syracuse. When he was about twenty-seven years old, wanderlust struck and he moved to Oakland, California, where he started his own company, Clark & Co. He established himself as one of the first organ manufacturers on the west coast.

A year later, in 1876, he was on the road again and moved to Quincy, Illinois, finally settling in Chicago in 1879. In 1880 he bought out a manufacturer named Wright, who was contracted to make reed organs for the firm of Story & Camp, and Clark assumed those orders. Four years later, Hampton Story, one half of Story & Camp, sold his interest in that firm and joined forces with Clark, forming the partnership that in 1896 was incorporated as the Story & Clark Piano Co.

Hampton Story was slightly older than Clark and had built his first pianos in 1857 in a modest workshop overlooking Lake Champlain in Burlington, Vermont, before relocating to Chicago.[36] Quickly becoming a well-known firm in the bustling city, Story & Clark had two factories, one on Sixteenth and Jefferson Streets, the other on Canal and Sixteenth, which were dedicated to manufacturing pianos and reed organs, respectively. The first piano they manufactured was finished in the spring of 1896. As the business grew, so did Melville Clark's reputation within a notoriously difficult industry in which success was hard to achieve. In 1891, a trade journal ran a profile on him declaring that "there is probably not a single manufacturer in the country who has a superior personal knowledge of mechanism and principles of musical instrument manufacture than Mr. Clark, and certainly no man whose brain is more fertile in the originating of improvements."[37] Citing a number of patents he had been awarded for the improvement of organ manufacture, the article noted that many of his ideas were the results of his love of travel.

In 1890, Clark visited France and Germany, observing European methods of organ and piano building. "He returned," announced *Presto*, "with many new ideas." In a prescient statement, the article then went on to suggest that those in the organ and piano business "will have something new to think about." The allusion was to

Clark's interest in building new mechanized pianos. In 1900, Clark opened the Melville Clark Piano Co. as a factory on West Madison Street in Chicago dedicated to the development and manufacture of his new interest. The next year, he produced the Apollo Concert Grand Piano Player, a push-up player that was the first to cover all eighty-eight keys, playing every note on a 7 1/3–octave keyboard. This was the first piano player in the world to play all eighty-eight keys.

Alert to contemporary innovations that had begun to shift attention toward internalized playing mechanisms, in 1904 Clark introduced another revolutionary design: the first grand player piano, with an internal mechanized system that likewise played all eighty-eight notes. It created a sensation in 1906 when, at the St. Charles Hotel in New Orleans, it became the first "player-grand" to offer a performance in a public concert hall. This innovation created a new standard in the industry. Commenting on his own achievement in an interview with *The Musical Age* in 1909, Clark proclaimed that there "can be no question that the 88-note player has come to stay. . . . When you take into consideration the love for music and the ability to play, even by a mechanism, the best music, you will understand why it is that the player piano will hold a large place in popular favor."[38] In 1906, Melville Clark Piano Co. opened a new factory in De Kalb, Illinois, northwest of Chicago. Here he spent the next six years making a number of additional improvements to the player piano that would catapult him to a position whereby he became a major competitor of a mammoth company such as Aeolian.

The ability to play all eighty-eight notes overcame obvious limitations on reproducing music scores, and the Metrostyle tempo regulator that was increasingly adopted by different player piano manufacturers was a significant stride toward "humanizing" the machine. However, Clark—a foremost inventor by all counts—was not yet finished. Additional design innovations made the Apollo player piano unique. First, he altered the mechanism of the "pneumatic finger" which moved the keys from within the piano. His design allowed the keys to be struck in front of the key's fulcrum, which gave each attached key "the human stroke and a human touch and expression." Second, he invented the "transposing mouthpiece," which allowed the pianolist to change the music to any key to suit a singer's vocal range or an accompanying instrument. Third, he introduced a self-acting metronome and spring motor that was wound by pedaling—a system he called Dynaline—that compensated for any hard or clumsy pedaling by its operator and allowed the roll to be automatically rewound at its end.[39]

The multitude of adaptations and developments that went into the design of the player piano in the first decade of the twentieth century stimulated much discussion about ways that the machine, hidden within the piano, worked to produce less mechanical-sounding music. Media attention turned to reflect on ways that mechanization might actually embody human dynamic expression or "feeling." A pamphlet titled "Holding the Mirror to Nature," a marketing brochure published by Melville Clark Piano Company, emphasized the fact that their pianos were "modeled after a *human* musician."[40] While these mechanical contrivances were offered to aid the playback of the piano tunes, to allow them to sound less mechanical, there remained the reality that the music that was "recorded" in the piano rolls was not capturing the nuanced play of a human performer. Punching rolls for the player piano usually involved creating a master roll that served as a pattern for high-speed perforating machines. Those master rolls were often punched by hand, with hole placement guided by a keyboard-printed ruler for each note. This "drafting-board technique" is what caused the resulting player piano music to sound mechanical, rather flat, and lifeless.

The final development that Melville Clark made to the production of player pianos crowned his career. He invented the Apollo Marking Piano in 1912. The marking piano was designed so that each time a key was played, its associated stylus struck a roll of paper that rolled over a carbon cylinder, leaving a mark—note on, note off—on the reverse of the paper. Each of these marks would then be punched out, creating the music roll. As the pianist played, the trace marks left on the roll of paper recorded each note and sustained pedal action in real time with rhythmic subtleties. Some contemporaries likened this to a photographic image, but in the words of the 1950s music historian Alfred Dolge, Clark's marking piano "does more than the phonograph and photographic camera combined, because it reproduces the soul of the performer."[41] It was an accomplishment that marked a turning point in American music. Even John McTammany, ever anxious to lay claim to his own genius, acknowledged Clark's innovations as "an epoch in the history of the player."[42]

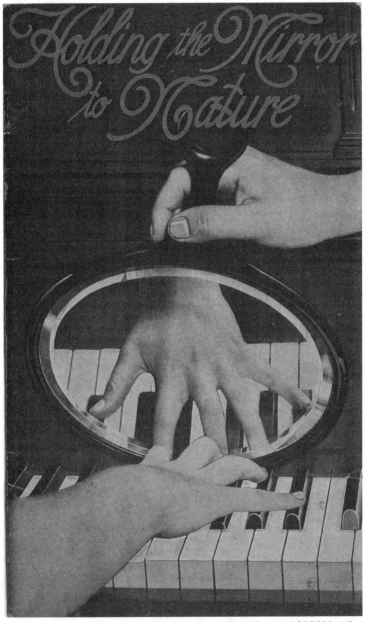

"*Holding the Mirror to Nature.*" This pamphlet was a marketing brochure published by the Melville Clark Piano Company.

Researching patents can provide a certain blueprint to reconstructing the past. While they represent a record of the development of musical technology, these patents also have their place in legal history, setting precedents that still impact the industry today. However, it was Dolge's remark about the "soul of the performer" that now held my attention. I had been preoccupied with mechanical ingenuity when I was suddenly reminded that music is an expression of much more. While the spirits appear to live on in the player pianos' performances, I wondered about the artists who interacted with the music roll recording machines. I was ready to set off to examine an original Apollo Marking Piano, which I hoped would bring me closer to understanding those who performed on it.

Chapter 4

Every Collector's Dream

$\mathcal{T}$HE FOUNDING of the Automatic Musical Instrument Collectors' Association (AMICA) in 1963 was spearheaded by San Francisco resident Richard Reutlinger. I visited Reutlinger at his magnificent 1886 Italianate Victorian home in historic Alamo Square, around the corner from the famous "Painted Ladies," the row of Victorian homes routinely photographed with the modern San Francisco skyline in the background. The juxtaposition of old and new captivates visitors to the city. Reutlinger's home was designed especially for entertaining—including a ballroom on the ground floor with a specially reinforced ceiling that eliminates the need for obtrusive pillars. This is the room that sold Reutlinger on the house, which he bought in the mid-1960s, and where he has since regularly hosted AMICA meetings, concerts, and public viewings during street fairs. It is a perfect venue to house his collection of automated musical instruments, the history of which he is eager to share.

Born in Nebraska in 1936 and now retired, Reutlinger was described by a local reporter as "a compact chap with a shaved head and amused blue eyes looking out through rimless specs." He first discovered a musical heritage during a family vacation to Virginia City in 1949.[1] Drama students from the University of Montana would come out to the theaters and perform vaudeville "and all of a sudden all this music came out of this place," he recalled, "and I thought, what is this thing?" What he was listening to was a photo-player built earlier in the century to accompany silent films in movie palaces. "I just thought, *Some day I am going to have one of those!*" And now he does.

Along the far wall in the ballroom is his 1911 Wurlitzer photo-player, which he picked up at a bargain price of eight hundred dollars but spent much more on its restoration. This was once located in the orchestra pit of a theater and used to provide music and sound effects for silent films. It has built-in percussion and brass and reed pipes. He has a dozen pianos and orchestrions in his collection, including a 1916 Seeburg G orchestrion that he recently acquired for seventy-five thousand dollars. It is the equivalent of a six-piece band, including pipes that imitate the sounds of violins and flutes, along with a man-dolin effect. On another wall he has a 1920 Mills Violano Virtuoso, an electrically operated instrument that plays a forty-four-note piano and a violin with celluloid wheels that excite the violin strings. When this automatic violin and piano duo was invented in 1909, the U.S. Patent Office declared it one of eight great inventions of the decade. When Teddy Roosevelt visited the Alaska-Yukon-Pacific Exposition in Seattle that year, he was so impressed with it that he ranked it among the finest American inventions along with color photography and the steam turbine.[2]

Next to the Violano is a 1917 Coinola coin-operated piano that entertained patrons at an Oakland bar until the mid-1940s, when it was replaced by a jukebox. He also has a number of other nickelode-ons and player pianos. One sports a framed sign that reads "Modern Dancing and Immodest Dress Stir Sex Desire: Leading to Lustful Flirt-ing, Fornication, Adultery, Divorce, Disease, Destruction and Judg-ment." I pointed to the sign and raised an eyebrow. "Much of the music produced here was considered 'evil' in its heyday," he com-mented, cryptically. Thus, I was anxious to learn more about the eve-nings of revelry he hosts.

In his hometown in Nebraska, Reutlinger played the accordion. "You know," he explained, "there was not a lot of talent in a small town, and you have to play for all the local lodges and stuff." One evening, after his western adventure, he was playing for a rotary ban-quet and was sitting across the table from one of the local furniture sellers, and he inquired whether the man happened to sell pianos. "It just so happened he had a player piano at the time," he remembered. "It was barely working and it was fifty dollars." Reutlinger, then thirteen, decided to sell his Lionel electric train to a friend and bought the piano.

"Of course, my parents did not know anything about this," he said. "I figured they would object, but I moved it into the house." This was the beginning of a few love affairs. The piano came with one roll: an old saloon tune called "Robin's Return." "The gal I was going with at the time had a younger sister, and we'd pay her a quarter an hour to pump the piano while we danced; and so I started looking for rolls because there was only one roll, and so I started asking around—all the friends of the family—and they would say, 'Oh yeah, I think we have some in the attic,' and eventually I managed to get a couple of hundred rolls."

In 1956, Reutlinger moved to San Francisco and discovered the Musée Mécanique at the Cliff House; he was floored by the collection, which served to whet his appetite for more. "There was a shop on O'Farrell Street I would pass on my way to work in the financial district, and one day in the front window appeared a player piano," he said. "There was no price or sign on it, but I used to make it a point to walk by the place during my lunch hour; but it was never open. . . . Finally, one night I had gone to the movies and I thought, 'Well, I'll just walk by there on my way home,' and it was open!" The two gentlemen working explained that they mainly repaired pianos in that workshop, and that this was ready to go. So, without considering the consequences of whether he would be permitted to have an upright player piano in the apartment he was renting, he purchased it.

Reutlinger admits that during the sixties in San Francisco he visited the Haight and grooved to the Grateful Dead, but his love and money were always dedicated to the sounds of piano rolls, citing QRS's Pete Wendling's version of "Darktown Strutter's Ball," the jazz tune from the 1930s, as a favorite. Before long, he discovered that others were equally interested in the music of these automatic mechanical instruments. Reutlinger began hanging out at a music shop that had been a speakeasy in the 1920s. There, he started making connections with others in the Bay Area who owned player pianos.

"It was fun to meet people like that," he said, "and because of people like that coming into the shop, I became interested in forming a local club of people who have these instruments, primarily reproducing pianos. That's how AMICA got started."[3]

"So, do the members of AMICA join because they like the history, the uniqueness of the instruments, or the sound of the music?" I asked.

"I think you have a couple of different schools of thought there," Reutlinger replied. "They get involved in the era. Some of them collect and rebuild antique cars. I don't know how it would break down by numbers, but AMICAns are into it because they like the era, the technology, but above all, they really dig the music."

"Do you work on refurbishing your own collection?" I asked.

"No! There are still skilled technicians out there who do this. I have spent thousands rebuilding this collection."

"Well, let's hear it," I said.

Reutlinger strolled over to his electrically powered photoplayer and placed a roll in the spoolframe. The piano in the middle of this three-cabinet assembly started to play. Advertised in the 1910s as "the Soul of the Film," it would accompany a movie such as *The Birth of a Nation* or *Ben-Hur*.

I had always thought of "silent movies" as, well, silent, but in fact these machines document the reality that the silent film era was usually the golden age of film music. Richard started tapping his toe to the piano music, and as the frantic music was building to a climax, he suddenly he reached up and pulled a cord. A train whistle blew. The music became dramatic. Then he pulled another cord that simulated gun shots. Even without the projected image, one could imagine an actress strapped to a railway track, with a train approaching or bandits on horseback firing their pistols in the air.

"That was great fun," I said, having never experienced "live entertainment" like that before.

"You should attend meetings of the AMICAns," he said. "I'm the treasurer. Join and you'll get the info about the next meeting."

I was there.

AMICA usually meets once a month in the home of one of its members. A newsletter announces what sort of instruments will be showcased and how long the festivities will last. Occasionally, I—now a proud member of this society of aficionados of Americana, the guardians of musical heritage—would read that local motels were available in case time slipped by unnoticed. I was anticipating quite an event. I RSVP'd to John, the host of the meeting who lived in the East Bay, north of Berkeley. It was the middle of summer, and Dorothy and I were looking forward to seeing some sun. San Francisco is a beautiful place, but I had no idea when we moved to the city just how thick, heavy, and cold the summer fog that rolls in from the ocean can be, nor how much a feature of everyday life it becomes during the hot months—hot in the valleys, anyway.

I remembered that the invitation called for people to bring some "libation," but I had forgotten to buy a bottle. I then remembered that we happened to have one or two spare bottles of champagne left over from a recent house party. I had imagined that we would be hearing gunshots, drunken yelps, and whisky bottles smashing while dudes dressed in cowboy outfits flew through swinging saloon doors. The background din of a player piano would fit in quite naturally, I thought. "You mean an early twentieth-century Western version of *Confederates in the Attic*?" I remarked, thinking about the Civil War reenactments that occur in the east. "You never know," said Dorothy.

We entered a large front room. The newsletter informed us that John had recently renovated his home to recreate a Victorian parlor for his antique instruments that had involved knocking down walls. In one-half of the room to our left were five or six people on benches and chairs lined around a grand 1926 Ampico player piano (manufactured by the American Piano Company). Eight other people sat on sofas or perched on a fireplace hearth to our right. We drifted over to the opposite wall to stand out of the way with the bottle of warm champagne in hand, when the door closed and John filled us in.

"Sally was just telling us about how she got involved with our group. It has to do with her parents. Go ahead Sally." Sally resumed her story. "So," she said, "if it was not for Mom and Dad's love of music and obsession for collecting those rolls, I would not be here. When they died, I was left with all this stuff—the pianos, the music rolls, the cabinets, the catalogs . . . I didn't know what to do with it."

Sally looked up at the ceiling. "Mom and Dad, if you can hear me from the great beyond, I just want you to know that I wish you had collected smaller things, like thimbles."

As I glanced around, I noticed different kinds of smiles on people's faces. Some indicated a kind of sympathy with her dilemma of what to do with someone else's collection of items.

"Well, that's very interesting," said John. "So, who are you?" he asked Dorothy and me.

"My name's Brian; I was in contact with the secretary of the society—Sandy."

"Oh!" shouted a woman who was sitting next to Sally on the couch. "Sandy mentioned him. She said he could be our reporter." This reminded me that I had previously revealed that I was interested in writing a history of the player piano.

I smiled and was about to elaborate on who I was, when John asked the gentleman at the door (whom I surmised was a senior officer of the society), whether "the meeting" was finished. Upon receiving a nod and a raise of the empty wine cup, John flipped a switch and the player piano at which he was sitting sprang to life. The room was filled with the music of "The Stars and Stripes Forever," an animated and patriotic tune that energized the group. One of the women who was sitting on the fireplace hearth came over and introduced herself. She took the bottle of champagne, and as she was leading Dorothy to the kitchen, I heard her ask whether we were interested in buying a player piano. I chuckled because there is no possibility of fitting a player into our condo.

I glanced around to admire the reconstruction that had been necessary to fit the Ampico piano into our host's home. The walls had red stenciled wallpaper and the windows were draped with heavy velvet. Framed pictures of player piano advertisements from the 1910s hung on the walls. Two antique wooden cabinets housed hundreds of rolls. On the other side of the room across from the fireplace was an orchestrion. Above the Ampico grand piano hung a Victorian-era converted library lamp with a brass base, decorated with muted greens and roses on its stained-glass hood. A couple of men walked over to inspect the mechanisms inside the piano rim. They resembled two guys peering under the hood of an automobile, but they were careful not to touch the piano, and their remarks of admiration for the cast iron plate that withstood forty thousand pounds of string compression seemed to be the musical equivalent of an appreciation of horsepower.

John was busy removing rolls from boxes and carefully lining them on top of the piano case, so I approached the gentleman who had let us into the house. He had just reentered the room with a fresh glass of wine and a handful of peanuts. Bing was from the Sacramento Valley but was an attendee of the monthly meetings. He was a computer software designer until his recent retirement, and he now spent his time traveling around in his white van with a piano keyboard painted on the side, repairing people's players. He began developing his technical skills in 1990 but had been a fan of mechanical music since childhood.

> "My mother was a beautician," he said. "After school I would walk to her shop. Next door there was an antiques place with a working nickelodeon. I spent all my time there."
> "And are you now a collector?" I asked.
> "Collector and repairer. I usually sell the old pianos I refurbish."
> "So how long have you been involved with AMICA?" I asked.
> "Since the beginning. I was recently the president of the chapter. I know everyone," he said. It dawned on me that this was one of the people Richard Reutlinger had mentioned regarding the restoration of his collection.
> "I hear you are writing a book," said Bing.

I had the feeling that I was being checked out to see if I was of appropriate character to be part of their club. I wondered if telling the secretary about my interest in writing a history of player pianos and the culture of collecting them would make anyone feel uneasy. However, Bing put my anxieties to rest.

> "Well, you've come to the right place. WE'RE ALL FANATICS," he cried. "I am a fanatic. Those guys are fanatics," he said, gesturing to everyone sitting by the couch, who glanced over at Bing.
> "Are you a fanatic about the music, the instruments, the collecting, the dealing . . . any particular aspect?" I inquired.

"The whole thing. Certainly about collecting."

"I once read a book on the psychology of collecting," I mentioned, referring to a book I had recently read following my visit with Richard Reutlinger.

New York psychoanalyst Werner Muensterberger wrote about the "unruly passion" of collecting, where he theorized that the "mania" people have for collecting things, whether stamps, baseball cards, or tulips, is actually caused by an anxiety stimulated by trauma such as "war, a parent's suicide, prolonged illness, physical handicaps, death of a sibling, or SIMPLY NOT-GOOD-ENOUGH early care."[4] Collectors might not appreciate this radical thesis, but when I asked my AMICA friends about their motives for collecting the sounds of history, I received a reply in good humor. "There's probably a lot of truth to that!" Bing exclaimed. "I've seen many private collections across the country—some are astounding. Have you had the chance to visit the Sanfilippo collection?" he asked.

I had not had the chance to visit this collection personally but was familiar with it since it was one of the collections featured in the elegant book *The Golden Age of Automated Musical Instruments* by Arthur Reblitz. The collection is owned by Jasper Sanfilippo, owner of one of the largest nut processing plants in the world, providing shelled pecans and peanuts to over seventy supermarket chains. His affinity for mechanical artifacts started in high school, when he built a small model steam engine. As his fortune grew, so did his collection, which moved into musical instruments after he purchased a seventy-eight-key Bruder Fairground Organ.

In 1976, he began turning his six thousand-square-foot Tudor-style home set in a fifty-seven acre estate in Barrington Hills northwest of Chicago into a shrine for his collection. Today the "Victorian Palace" has grown to over forty-four thousand square feet, including a multileveled music room with an array of orchestrions, Gaviolis, and fairground organs. A separate American Orchestrion Room houses numerous beautifully maintained orchestrions from Wurlitzer, Seeburg, and other manufacturers, some of which he acquired from the Musée Mécanique, all with elaborate stained-glass panels.

My old acquaintance, Tim Trager, believed that this was the largest and most comprehensive private collection of automatic musical instruments in the world. He had helped Sanfilippo acquire a number of the pieces, including a one hundred-foot-wide and forty-foot-tall steam-powered Salon Carousel. "Single-handedly," said Trager, in an interview for the *Chicago Tribune* reporting on this collection in 1992, "he is bringing back an era that should have been publicly preserved. He has been the first to put it together in its proper setting and restore them so magnificently."[5] It took a wealthy collector to put on display an important chapter in the history of Chicago, the hub of so many mechanical instrument manufacturers—something that even the Chicago Historical Society had not done.

Sanfilippo's interior designer, Marlene Lawton, who was hired to plan his music room, said that she faced a challenge that, when completed, not only cleared the clutter from doorways and windows but cured the angst of his family. "When the children were younger and living at home," commented Lawton, "they helped move these machines and often asked, 'Why can't Daddy just collect stamps or coins?'" Thus, collecting affects one's family, a dilemma that many collectors face: to buy or to stay married. As the British collector and piano roll producer John Farrell asks himself when contemplating a purchase, "Do I really need another instrument? If I get it, will the wife sue for divorce?"[6]

I asked Bing whether "fanaticism" and tearing down walls in a home to accommodate a collection of automatic instruments might add any strain to couples within AMICA, or whether it was a "family club." He seemed to know what I was saying. "Ahh, now there—he, *he* is a fanatic!" he said, pointing at our host. John nodded his head in agreement and finished putting the next roll in the piano, Gershwin's "Rialto Ripples"—the composer's only piano rag. It was a busy, lively piece of music, perfect for the player piano. Bing pulled two chairs over so we could talk to John.

> "This is a fine looking machine you have here," I said. John proudly nodded.
> "He's done a good job with this one," added Bing. "John here will go to no end for this past."
> "Sounds like you refurbished it yourself," I said.
> "You mean it sounds BAD?" yelled Bing, laughing and slapping me on the back.
> "I meant the other sort of 'sounds like,'" I demurred. "I *gather* that you did the work yourself."
> "I spent a year and all my spare money finding the parts to get this working," said John. "But it was a labor of love."

"John's the one for the job," said Bing. "He's got the patience and attention to detail. He's handy with tools. Have you seen the cars yet?"

I was informed that John was a restorer of classic cars. In his garage at that moment, he had two mint Packards: a 1934 Packard Victoria HT and a 1953 300 Convertible Coup. I noticed that John's hands were scratched and calloused. Oil stained his nails. They were not the hands of a pianist.

"Is that another hobby?" I asked.
"I've been rebuilding Packards for years. I repair cars for money but rebuild the classics for pleasure," he answered.
"For love, not money," I said.
"It's also admiration," said John. "In the '20s and '30s, Packard was the premier builder of automobiles in the world. They were built by hand and built to last. When someone bought one, they expected it to last forever."

This seemed to be another recurring theme: appreciation of the craft of manufacturing and of the era of its technological triumphs. John, among others I had met, enjoyed not only the mechanical but the historical dimension of the objects he rebuilt or collected.

"So is the connection between classic cars and old pianos the fact that they are old, or that they were built to last?" I asked.
"A classic car is anything over twenty-five years old. For real collectors and aficionados, 'classic' means having it restored to its original factory condition. I prefer to say they are vintage. I reproduce vintage cars. I was once delivering parts to a friend of mine, and in his garage he had a player piano that he had rebuilt to sell. I think it was a family piano. I had never seen one before. I ended up buying three of them within the next year."
"Did you do it for the mechanics or the music?" I asked.
"I did it 'cause I thought the mechanics of it were so cool. I had never heard a player piano before, but now I love classical music."

John explained that with each piano he bought, he received rolls. With one purchase he was promised seventy-eight rolls, but when he counted them there were nearly 180. "You got to get someone coming out of it," he said, referring to those no longer interested in the world of mechanical musical instruments. "That way, you know you are getting everything."

"One day you'll hit the mother lode," I said, with a tone of hope.

John nodded. I asked him if he had ever heard of Harvey Roehl's story "Every Collector's Dream." He let me indulge in a brief story.

Everyone in the world of mechanical musical instruments knows of the late Harvey Roehl. He was a World War II veteran, a major in the U.S. Air Force Reserves, a college dean and engineer by profession, and a private pilot. A member of the Piano Technicians' Guild, he and his wife, Marion, owned the Vestal Press, publishers of books on mechanical musical instruments, named after the town in New York where he and Marion lived. He died in 2000, his wife not long after. However, in 1964 he had written a short article for the *News Bulletin* of the Musical Box Society International about his first big find as a collector in 1957. He discovered that the best place to look for old player pianos and nickelodeons was to canvass "old-timers in the piano tuning profession, because most of them have been at the game throughout a lifetime, and can remember their younger days when these machines were plentiful and they had to service them."

During one trip to Providence, Rhode Island, he learned that there was a barnful of old coin-operated machines owned by a "junk shop" operator in his eighties, whom he arranged to meet. "When we got there I could hardly believe my eyes! It was a barn perhaps thirty feet wide and a hundred feet deep, literally jammed with old furniture—junk of all sorts; scores and scores of pianos, many of which were coin-operated, all in unbelievably dirty and decrepit condition." To Roehl, however, it was a gold mine. Among half-a-dozen or so player pianos that Roehl saw in the barn, he at first negotiated the purchase of one Pianolin, a player piano manufactured by the North Tonawanda Musical Instrument Works. When he was told that there were "about six machines" more like it upstairs, in a loft that was too cluttered even to enter, Roehl blindly negotiated to buy all the coin machines the owner had. He rented a thirty-three-foot tractor-trailer rig that arrived a few days later, and with the help that came with it, he managed to move aside all the clutter and saw for the first time his new collection. "I was flabbergasted," he recalled. "Where I thought I had purchased twenty machines, there were actually forty-five!" including a Wurlitzer Pianino and a variety of Peerless forty-four-note and eighty-eight-note player pianos, in addition to "a whole mess of music rolls, and about a ton of dirt!"

"One has to strike while the iron is hot," reasoned Roehl, "even at fifty cents a mile!" which he had to calculate for the added round trip from Providence to Vestal. Over the next many years, Roehl had all of the machines refurbished, sold most of them, which covered the cost of his original purchase, and kept four for his own personal collection. Above all, however, "I had in acquiring the lot of them and in disposing of them [made] a lot of new friends from among the collectors of this sort of memorabilia."[7] To be sure, the endeavor established him as an expert in the field and gave the Vestal Press much to publish.

There was a look of bemused interest on the faces of our host and the ex-president of the society. After we had exchanged some added details about the nuances of collecting, my attention was drawn to the remarks written by another guru of mechanical musical instrument restoration, Larry Givens. He authored the first text on rebuilding the player piano, as well as a history of the firm that produced the Ampico expression players, both published by Vestal Press. He also wrote an unpublished piece titled "Four Essays on Collecting," which I later tracked down in an archive at the University of Maryland.

In 1993, after forty years of collecting experience, Givens decided to write a mini–advice manual for those with a budding interest. It was a cautionary tale to help prevent a disease from getting the better of one. "It is easy for a newer collector to become so starry-eyed about the items that he collects," he wrote, "that he glorifies them unrealistically in one way or another. With regret, I must burst his bubble."[8] Collectors, he suggested, often think of the items they find as a manufacturer's gem—a glorious, unique product, designed to be a collector's item. In fact, one needed to remember that most products were made purely for commercial reasons, and that mechanical instruments were often only one more step in the evolution of musical production—a "step forward from earlier products they replaced." Instruments were of interest only until they were superceded by the new. The items that people had before then were discarded, much like black-and-white TVs after the introduction of color. "Heretical though it may sound today, the 1930s operator of a bar or restaurant would have been *crazy* to continue nursing his aging Seeburg H orchestrion along when he could replace it with a colorful chrome and plastic jukebox which took up only one-third the space."

Far from being preserved for posterity, or having been produced as a prize for future collectors, the things people played with were actually unremarkable at the time. I recalled the picture of the piano graveyard in Zelinski's office. Keeping this in mind, Givens suggested, would provide valuable perspective to modern eyes prone to overglorification and obsession.

Because times change, people tend to regret the fact that they have not learned enough about the remnants they come across, about the artifacts in relatives' homes. "Boys and their fathers discover that the old Chickering grand in Aunt Margaret's living room has a drawer to play a music roll and, miraculously, Aunt Margaret still has a closet filled with rolls for it. 'Say, do you suppose we might get it to play again?' The spark is struck; the timber ignites." The inquiring minds spend a few months searching for information, for parts, for more rolls. Months turn into years, they begin to see similar machines in other places, they meet people with shared interests, and suddenly fuel is added to the fire.

The toolbox comes out, garage space is sacrificed, and the machine is dissected. "Then somewhere in no-man's land" between what might be thought of as discovery and colonization, "a new life form appears on the horizon: the *dealer*." These people have grown up in an earlier cycle and have decided to turn their vocation to profit. They produce catalogs. New collectors' groups form, information begins flowing, discussions revolve around technical nuances of genres of machines. Ah, I thought—here is how "collectors become dealers." As societies and associations begin to mature, members eventually die. "*Time* has removed most of these original owners from the ranks of the living," wrote Givens, "and most acquisitions are now made from other collectors or from dealers. Occasionally an item can still be 'smoked out' from its original site, but only rarely."

So a new market emerges. The question "Are you interested in buying player pianos?" echoed in my thoughts. However, I had not yet experienced the more aggressive approach some collectors take to feed their habits. Early collectors find it increasingly difficult to find items to add to their collections since the market has pushed those objects into the hands of the wealthy. "As more 'men of means' join the game waving fat checkbooks, the 'little guy' who bought a rare item for $50 during Phase One days may find it quite impossible to turn down $15,000 or $20,000 for it. The long-postponed new room on the house, or a couple years of college tuition money, *break loose* the object, and the collector is left with only memories and a little bit of extra floor space to commemorate the instrument he once enjoyed." So, I thought, multimillion dollar mansions are squeezing out the collector who resorts to removing dining room walls to find a place to put the player piano. This, Givens argued, spelled the end to traditional collecting, that which was based on love but ends up being sacrificed for money.

Collecting mechanical musical instruments in the 1950s was a "dream world," said Givens. All one needed to do was ask around and one found dilapidated, dusty machines. He recalled asking the delivery driver of baked goods if, in the course of his numerous home visits, he had come across any, and he was told to visit a nearby roller rink which had recently closed. Through partially boarded-up windows he spotted a Wurlitzer 125 military band organ pushed against a wall front-first with music rolls stuffed into its brass trumpets and spilling out of the cabinet. He located the owner of the rink and asked how much he would ask to get rid of it. "Fifty bucks," was the answer, and Givens snapped it up. He installed a new electric motor and flipped the switch. "It began to play vigorously," he recalled. "I will never forget the *jets* of black dust which spurted out of each trumpet as it played for the first time in years!" This was not an isolated experience. "In those golden days of collecting," said Givens, "a person with a modest budget and a station wagon could easily acquire *one nice instrument per week*. Collectors of today, eat your heart out!"

For Givens, it was easy to collect with such high interest. The uncommonness of the machines was augmented by the fact that they possessed both audio and visual appeal. "To many people," he said, "these instruments seem almost *alive*." They become part of the family—they seemingly possess powers of attraction. "Do you own your collection, or does *it* own *you*?" asked Givens. Ultimately at some point, a collector's obsession may have consequences for his family. The point he wanted to make was: "*Just what should happen* to his prized possessions?" Few family members could maintain the musical machinery. Even fewer "would be as delighted by being bequeathed a large collection of instruments as they would be if they were the recipient of the same amount in *cash*."

John was fetching more boxes of rolls from his antique cabinet. Each one had a colored dot stuck onto it next to the title of the song. They were transparent and carefully placed over the "o" in Ampico. This was his roll preference system. A red dot on the box meant it was one of his favorites; green meant it was worth playing, and blue meant it was not worthwhile. I noticed that the red dots were mostly on the classical rolls. "I had never heard of these musicians before," he confessed, "but a world has opened up to me. Take Rachmanov for example," he said. He pulled out a roll with Rachmaninoff's Prelude in C-Sharp Minor on it. "This is one of my favorites," he said.

As John pushed back the piano bench the keys began to play. Dorothy had returned from visiting with others, and the small group of us watched the piano perform. The piece was so popular in Rachmaninoff's day—so often requested as an encore to his recitals—that the pianist took to referring simply to "It." *It*, therefore, was a natural choice for him to record for the player piano. Between 1919 and 1929, besides recording disks for RCA Victor, Rachmaninoff was commissioned to make paper rolls for Ampico. He performed thirty-four pieces, including the Barcarolle in G Minor, the Melodie in E Minor, his rendition of Rimsky-Korsakov's "Flight of the Bumblebee," and his arrangement of "The Star Spangled Banner." As the music in front of us rolled on, Rachmaninoff's soaring phrases, light touches, and overdone rubatos filled the room.

Rachmaninoff's broad hands easily spanned one and a half octaves. Witnessing the command he had over the keyboard was breathtaking. As the keys danced around, it was possible to visualize his hands hovering above, his body sitting at the bench, his famous stoic expression gazing out.

"Look at that," cried Dorothy. "He's sitting there. It's Rachmaninoff!!"

"When I go to hear the San Francisco orchestra, I wonder why I am listening to it when I can hear a better version of the performance in my own home," said Bing.

"That's why I never learned to play," John chimed in, "I could never play as well as the machine can."

"The machine is playing exactly how Rachmaninoff played," said Bing. He was emphatic on this point. "That *is* Rachmaninoff. That is how *he* played the music!"

It was easy to bestow such human attributes on the machine while arguing that Rachmaninoff was sitting in front of us. As I studied the movement of the keys on this automatic piano—itself from the era in which Rachmaninoff recorded—I began to feel as if there could have been another presence among us. It was the combination of the visual cues and the apparent authenticity of the music. It was said that at first Rachmaninoff himself was skeptical that the "recording piano" could capture the nuances of a pianist's performance. However, in 1919, after he recorded his first roll for Ampico, he was asked to listen to the master recording. "Gentlemen," he was quoted as saying, "I, Sergei Rachmaninoff, have just heard myself play!"

While I had explored and admired, as so many others had done, the technical ingenuity of the piano's design, I realized that I had overlooked the medium that gave the machine its expression. As John removed the roll and reached for the box, I asked if I could take a look at the paper. I unrolled the scroll a bit, gazing at the myriad tiny holes in it. The air that rushes through these holes breathes life into the machine. The pattern that presented itself was not just an unusual representation of a musical score, it had the signature of the performer. The invisible entertainer was paradoxically rendered visible through these holes. John and the others had moved over to the orchestrion on the other side of the room, and to the fanfare of cymbals, horns, and drums, we bid farewell. I was ready to set off to explore the mysteries of the rolls and the secrets that they might contain.

Chapter 5

A Musical
Morse Code

VINCENT MORGAN is a pastor of two Russian-speaking Baptist congregations in New York City and lives fifteen minutes away from JFK airport. He barely speaks Russian, but he has deep compassion for the people who attend his services, many of whom have suffered persecution for their faith. He finds any way he can to communicate with them. In the mid-1990s, his wife was given a piano roll. They pointed out to the donor that they had no way to play it, and so offered to pass it on to a friend of theirs. The friend responded by selling Vincent and his wife a 1920 Ampico player for one hundred dollars, and then referred them to the local AMICA chapter for help restoring it.

I had written to Vincent because I wanted to know if he had used the piano to play Russian music as a way of connecting with his congregation. He mentioned Rachmaninoff. They kept the piano at their home, but because they lived so close to the airport, they regularly received guests connected to the church and had entertained people from all over the world. He told me that a composer from the Ukraine was once visiting family who were members of their church. They had invited him to the house. The guest recalled having once seen a player piano at a theater but had never heard one play.

"As a composer and a musician who played many different kinds of instruments, he marveled at the piano that could play Rachmaninoff by itself," remembered Vincent. "He watched in awe as he saw the keys move as if in response to Rachmaninoff's fingers."[1]

"I know exactly what you mean," I said. "I recently saw a performance by Rachmaninoff myself. It takes a little getting used to."

"Young children are the most fascinated," said Vincent. "They call it the magic piano. One little girl who lives nearby says that we have a magic house and calls me the magic man."

I asked Vincent whether he had looked into finding rarer ethnic music in order to bring unique performances to his congregation that might have been left behind with their former lives.[2] He said that he had once learned of a producer of music rolls in Russia, but that they made rolls for Welte, and he had not come across anything beyond Rachmaninoff or Tchaikovsky.

Along those lines, said Vincent, "a Navajo pastor from Arizona wanted to know how he could get one of these for his church since no one there knew how to play a straight piano for the worship service. I told him that there weren't any Navajo songs available. He laughed and said that they sing regular hymns, but in the Navajo language."Even if Vincent had difficulty finding rare ethnic music, the piano nevertheless provides a spectacle that seems to unite those who hear it play. Like the sounds of much music itself, the experience transcends ethnic backgrounds—the way it seems to transcend historical background. "Look at how much fun it provides people from all over the world today," I commented.

I remembered comments made by various people at AMICA meetings who were amazed to hear music encoded by holes in rolls of paper. One writer to the *Mechanical Music Digest* who plays a calliope at public events noted, "It's been my observation that people are more fascinated in watching the music roll progress than anything else for a large part."[3] Such fascination with player pianos existed throughout the 1910s and 1920s. Roll manufacturers such as QRS realized they could add even more information to the roll to further enhance the musical experience. Just as player pianists were trained to follow the wavy lines of a metrostyle, why not print lyrics along the side of the roll to allow people to sing along?

The transformation of the player piano from a "toy and entertainer" into "a practical instrument of precision for musical education" was the topic of a promotional pamphlet published in 1922 titled "The De-Assification of Music." "This new form of musical transmission must, I believe, take up the work of doing for music what the printed book did for literature," wrote the author, Carroll Brent Chilton, whose address of Tompkin's Square in New York's Lower East Side was an area where Progressive Era reformers attempted to improve the education of immigrant children.[4] The author, who had written an earlier work on the appreciation of classical music, spelled out the technical details of a new invention, "The Universal Music Reader," which turned the roll on its side so that it scrolled from right to left, allowing printed words to be read in the familiar way of left to right. Not only did the author envision musical notes and lyrics printed on the roll, but the "audible music publication" would also include music criticism about the piece being played. While this system does not appear to have been manufactured, QRS did add more information to the roll.

QRS, which was originally organized by Melville Clark as a separate company to manufacture rolls for Story & Clark player pianos in 1900, began printing lyrics on them in 1916. The first lyric roll was the tune "Pretty Baby" played by ragtime pianist Charlie Straight. Later, they produced a set of six "educator rolls" intended to teach children how to play the piano the old-fashioned way, by hand. The rolls contained 132 lessons and sold for $11.50.[5] We don't know whether these rolls produced skilled pianists or not. However, it was not for want of attention to details. In the experimental phase, the best placement of the words on the roll was a consideration as was the size and type of the font. Finally, the color of the printed lyrics was tested with an eye to determine which one stood out best and was least fatiguing to read.

This trial was similar to what the British mathematician and famed inventor of the "calculating machine" Charles Babbage performed in the 1830s. Babbage's concern was that important scientific work—such as performing calculations and reading mathematical tables—might be compromised because of human fatigue. He wanted to lessen intellectual effort and mechanize acts of calculation—to transfer the labor of "human computers" to work that could be performed by machines. He built prototypes of his elaborate "difference engine," with which he entertained dinner party guests who were impressed with its ability to perform mathematical calculations. When he turned his attention to the printing of numerical tables, he tested a number of colors of ink printed on different colors of paper, including even the unlikely combination of black on black to see what was easiest to read. He determined that the contrast of a dark blue ink printed on off-white paper worked best. It was clearest and caused the least amount of fatigue on the eye. I was intrigued to learn that this was also the combination that the printers at QRS determined to be the best for producing legible lyrics on their piano rolls.

However, the association between Babbage and an early twentieth-century American manufacturer of player piano rolls does not stop there. Another connection lay in the very way that holes in paper were encoded to provide information that would be replayed through a machine. Throughout his life, Babbage struggled to improve on the basic idea of a calculating machine. Although he never built it before his death in 1871, he produced many plans for what he called the "analytical engine." What distinguished the analytical from the difference engine was that the former could be programmed using punch cards. He proposed that programs could be punched into paper cards so that the programmer only had to create the program once and then put the cards into the machine at any time to make it run. Babbage had envisioned the adaptation of Jacquard's punched cards to control the mechanical calculator, which—using the principle of looped action upon which the weaving machine was built—could produce results based on preceding computations.

When I thought about punched cards, encoded information, and experiments in printing, I wondered if player piano roll technology could be considered an evolution of Babbage's calculating machine. It was not necessarily a history rooted in music but rather an adaptation of early programming technology. I then discovered that twentieth-century science fiction writers had already picked up on this. "Have you ever seen a tape for an automatic piano—a player piano?" asked a character in Stanislaw Lem's novel *His Master's Voice*. The scene imagined a future world where no one understood digital computers, but some still possessed experience with preserved antique player pianos.

"By chance," explains the main character, Peter Hogarth, an eminent mathematician, "a program tape for a digital computer might also fit into a player piano, and although the program has nothing, absolutely nothing, to do with music—it might refer to some fifth-order equation—nevertheless, when it is put in the machine, it produces notes. And it might also happen that not all the notes thus produced will be in total chaos, but that here and there one will hear a musical phrase."[6] Inadvertently, people in the future might interpret digital computer tape as a kind of record of bad piano music.

In fact, as Robbie Rhodes, a mechanical music enthusiast and current editor of the online *Mechanical Music Digest* pointed out, there are records of surprising uses for player piano–like objects. In 1889, an astronomer in West Africa rigged together twenty-three telescopic cameras to photograph a total eclipse of the sun. An engraving of the setup showed a pneumatic contrivance designed to control the shutters, plate holders, and other moving devices to record the eclipse. The controls were operated by a perforated strip of paper, "similar to the music sheets now commonly used in automatic organs," reported a publication in 1899. "Each perforation in the eclipse sheet represented, not a musical note, but a mechanical movement of some particular device."[7] Apparently the system worked well, but unfortunately for the astronomer, the sun was obscured by clouds on the day of the eclipse.

An even more elaborate adaptation of perforated music rolls was devised through the improbable collaboration of Hollywood actress Hedy Lamarr and the avant-garde composer and concert pianist George Antheil. The two met in California in 1940 when Antheil diversified his interests and began writing articles about love and endocrinology for *Esquire* magazine. Their first meeting made an impression on Antheil. "My eyeballs sizzled," Antheil wrote in his 1945 memoir, "but I could not take them away. Here, undoubtedly, was the most beautiful woman on earth. . . . Her breasts were fine too, real postpituitary."[8]

It turns out that Lamarr's breasts were the very reason Antheil was invited around. She figured that with his knowledge of glands she could learn how to enlarge them. However, before long, attention to her breasts turned into a discussion of torpedoes and weapons of war. This was not entirely random. Lamarr's first husband, from whom she had separated three years previously, was a Viennese artillery

THE PNEUMATIC COMMUTATOR AND PHOTOGRAPHIC BATTERY OF
ECLIPSE INSTRUMENTS (TODD)

(As mounted at Cape Ledo, Africa, for the total eclipse of December 1889)

Illustration from David Todd, *Stars and Telescopes*
(Boston: Little, Brown & Co., 1899).

Telescopic Cameras. In 1889, an astronomer in West Africa put together twenty-three telescopic cameras in an attempt to photograph a total eclipse of the sun.

manufacturer specializing in shells and grenades. While she was occasionally responsible for entertaining foreign leaders, including Hitler and Mussolini, her husband was conducting research on launch control systems.

Following their divorce, Lamarr showed that she had absorbed much of her possessive husband's research and thought of herself as a good weapons designer, even planning to join the National Inventor's Council in Washington, D.C. Her idea, which she discussed with Antheil, was to devise a torpedo guidance system that employed frequency hopping so that a transmitter and receiver could coordinate the frequencies they were on while data was being transmitted. This would prevent the enemy from intercepting one frequency and redirecting the torpedo. Lamarr's concept was brilliant, but she had no means of synchronizing the transmitter and receiver. Antheil, however, suggested a solution: player pianos.

Antheil had composed music especially to be performed by player pianos, programming them to play in synchronicity in a piece called *Ballet Mécanique,* which will be discussed further along. Whatever his artistic motivations, the technical insight he offered Lamarr was based on the concept that two piano rolls punched with identical patterns could synchronize the transmitter and receiver. He even proposed that the system utilize eighty-eight different frequencies, the full range of keys that piano rolls controlled after Melville Clark and QRS rolls made that the industry standard in 1910 following an international music conference in Buffalo, New York.

The concept was sound, so to speak. In 1942, Lamarr and Antheil received a patent for their "secret communication system."[9] Although in the 1950s electronics capable of employing the principle of frequency hopping were finally developed, making the Lamarr-Antheil patent the basis of military communications, the military showed little interest in the proposed technology in the years immediately following their invention. Despite Antheil's canvassing, the Navy earlier dismissed the idea, apparently worrying about the size of the proposed system, mistakenly thinking that Antheil was proposing to put player pianos inside torpedoes.

Sending encoded messages reminds one of Samuel Morse. In the 1830s, he devised a plan for a telegraph built upon the principle of a binary code—that used by today's computers, languages with strings of 0's and 1's—which corresponded to a circuit's being either on or off. As a roll of paper was fed through a machine, a pen struck it as one's finger hit a key, leaving traces of dots or dashes on the paper. This technique was very similar to that subsequently used by Melville Clark's recording piano: lines drawn on moving rolls of paper that represent coded information. In the 1860s, when Morse code messages were to be sent more rapidly than a human could encode them, the rolls were converted to prepunched tape and communications were sent at rates of up to four hundred words per minute. Unsurprisingly, this device was sometimes referred to as the "electric Jacquard," but it also points to technological similarities to the principle embodied in piano rolls.[10]

Certainly there is some mystery surrounding the holes in paper music rolls and how their patterns are translated into a musical message. Edward, the Prince of Wales and future King of England, once even made a joke out of this marvel. "A sick man had his body covered with paper, on which his doctors pricked the locations of his various ailments. When they had gone, he threaded the paper into his pianola, and it played 'Nearer My God to Thee.' "[11] While probably unaware of this joke, the eminent mathematician Benoit Mandelbrot saw some value in the same concept. He thought that if one took the data from a patient's electrocardiogram and used it to perforate a paper roll of a player piano, it might systematically illustrate differences from one data series to another. "For instance, certain troublesome heart rhythms in the raw EKG data might produce a piano roll with a characteristic pattern of soft high notes, or an absence of notes around middle 'C'—each of them instantly recognizable."[12] Piano rolls would thus provide a kind of digital diagnosis.

To historians, the phrase "notes and records" sometimes refers to documentary archives of institutional history, as in the *Notes and Records of the Royal Society of London*. However, investigating piano rolls gave new meaning to the physical existence of notes and records. The punched holes corresponded to musical notes while the sum of their parts represented a record, not only in the early sense of an audio recording, but of a historical record. The notes and lyrics on rolls captured a moment of history. Like many books written throughout history, music rolls also captured expressions of a particular era. Sometimes the lyrics in songs revealed racist overtones, such as in some Klan marches of the 1920s. In other instances, what was *not* said in music revealed the contemporary social context. One example was the song "42nd Street" produced on a roll manufactured in Capone-controlled Chicago in the late 1920s. Its lyrics did not mention the terms *gangster* or *underworld* in the chorus, while the same song produced by Aeolian in New York did. (Incidentally, Dean O'Banion, Capone's chief rival of the underworld, enjoyed listening to his player piano every night, considering it his prized possession, according to his wife.)[13]

One contemporary mechanical music buff perforates rolls for his business, Artcraft Music Rolls, and has generated some controversy by re-releasing a few provocative titles. Douglas Henderson has been in the music roll business since the 1950s, including a stint cutting rolls for QRS Music. Besides them, he is one of the few who still service this niche market. "The perforated roll is an educator," he writes, "a fascinating performer (when 'guided' or 'monitored' by an *involved* human being) and above all, a PERMANENT arrangement for the future."[14] Just as many people dedicate their love and money to preserving the instruments, Henderson concentrates on what might be called the content side of things, the rolls, including the controversial ones.

In the late 1990s, Artcraft reproduced a roll from 1933 titled "Negro Heaven," which elicited condemnation in some postings on the *Mechanical Music Digest*. In response, Henderson allowed that he was going to discontinue selling certain divisive titles, but he defended his actions on the grounds that the music revealed a dimension of American history that should not be ignored lest it repeat itself. "I perforate all forms of social history," he wrote. Today, piano rolls are relatively hard to find. After all, they are made of paper and deteriorate over time. The vision of the stack of damp and mangled QRS rolls at the Musée Mécanique stays with me. However, Henderson made a point about what music rolls suggest about some aspects of the cultural history of music, of technology, and of social ideology. While they were one source of musical expression, paper music rolls preserved other secrets inside. To discover some of them, I set off to visit a location where more history of piano rolls is preserved than at anywhere else in America: the QRS Music factory.

I arrived in Buffalo, New York, eager to follow the spread of piano music on paths worn by early entrepreneurs, fortune seekers, and entertainers. Yes, Buffalo. An unlikely place, perhaps, but this is where the wealthy lawyer and manager of the Buffalo Philharmonic

Orchestra Ramsi Tick lived. In 1966, he bought QRS Music and moved the business from lower Manhattan to a modest building on the bank of the Niagara River where it still produces music rolls. The front entrance to what was once a streetcar maintenance barn opens to a showroom with oak panels, a wooden floor, some leather chairs, a variety of player pianos, and cabinets stocked with music rolls. A TV allows visitors to watch a video of a brief history of QRS. Down a hallway, one arrives at the top of a steel staircase overlooking the factory floor. Large prints of famous pianists hang on the walls above garage doors. In the center of the room sit three roll-perforating machines surrounded by wooden benches where machine parts, oil cans, boxes, and other manufacturing paraphernalia are placed. Two of the perforators have been out of service for years. The little demand that exists for newly punched piano rolls requires the use of only one machine, and even that is sporadic. The chief operating officer and my host—a thirty-year veteran of the company named Bob Berkman—saved up orders in advance of my arrival so that on the day I arrived I could see the perforator in operation.

Built in 1912, the perforator was made of cast iron and framed with wood, containing thousands of movable parts. Stacked behind it were fifteen two-foot diameter rolls of eighteen-inch wide coated paper that were unrolled and fed into the machine. The layers of paper then passed under a row of eighty-eight punchers, one for each key on a piano keyboard, which punched holes through the paper at nine holes per inch to create simultaneously fifteen copies of the piano roll music. The punches were connected to eighty-eight rubber tubes that led to a pneumatic device—the lungs of the machine—that controlled them. All of them were connected to the "nerve center," where the master roll fed the information to the tubes dictating which ones should perforate the layers of paper. In motion, the machine was loud and rhythmical with streams of paper inching out every second, shuffling through to the beat of air compressors, jolting metal, and sliding blades trimming the piano rolls to size as they folded, serpentinely, into a box ready to be carried off to the next stage of production, proofreading.

I studied the perforator and followed the paper as it wove through the system, beneath the bundles of hoses that supplied pressure to the parts, noticing the stigmata of nearly a hundred years of wear and tear. Underneath was a mound of paper chads that would

Image by Brian Dolan.

Spools. Multiple rolls are fed through an early twentieth-century perforating machine still in operation at QRS Music Inc. in Buffalo, NY.

eventually be shoveled out and used as packing material. A long musical history had passed through this machine. In its first fifteen years of operation alone, it—in combination with its two "sibling" machines—churned out some ten million piano rolls.

I followed the piano roll through the rest of the production line to the point where it was actually spooled and placed into the rectangular box with the familiar QRS label on its ends. This process was handled by two other employees, both of whom have been with the company for decades. They remembered when there had been someone working at every bench, with teams of employees managing each perforating machine. Roll production was a rapidly diminishing history. Along the brick wall at the opposite side of the factory floor were metal shelves with inventory awaiting shipping. This reminded me of the stack that was piled on top of my grandfather's ol' player, a comment I made to Bob Berkman, a youthful-looking fifty-year old.

Image by Brian Dolan.

The Perforator. Rolls exiting the perforator at QRS.

"If it was your grandfather's collection of old QRS rolls," he said, "then the boxes probably looked a bit different. We've restyled them a bit, but follow me." In between two rooms was a well-sealed, thick wooden door. Inside was a thin, long room lined from floor to ceiling with rows of old boxes containing some of the master rolls throughout the company's history. It was their music archive.

I now recognized the different style of script on the boxes and began reading through all the titles—"Burt Bacharach Medley," "Gershwin Medley," "Theme from the Godfather." Among all the various titles in one section something jumped out at me.

"Lots of these say 'Played by Liberace,'" I remarked.

"Those are from the 'Celebrity Series' that Ramsi Tick started in the early 80s," said Bob. "Liberace was flown in to record some rolls when we needed some fresh publicity. It was extraordinary. He went from a rhinestone-covered Las Vegas stage to a cramped room upstairs, packed to the ceiling with

Image by Brian Dolan.

The Archive of QRS Music Rolls. Over one hundred years of musical history is precariously preserved in a room adjacent to where CDs for digital "pianomation" are edited.

boxes of piano rolls, to play on the recording piano. I was sent to pick him up from the airport."

Liberace was not the only celebrity to arrive in Buffalo to record piano rolls, Bob added, naming a few others, including Vladimir Horowitz, Andres Segovia, and Beverly Sills. I pulled out a box titled "The Old Piano Roll Blues." "This one looks familiar," I said. Bob told me that it was part of the "Nostalgic Series," among the thousands produced in the heyday of the player piano. I noticed that many boxes in this section of the collection read "Played by J. Lawrence Cook." "They used to call him Cookie, but I think I'll stick to Lawrence," he said, with a slight grin. I was just becoming familiar with Bob's dry sense of humor.

"Lawrence was here for years," said Bob, "he was truly remarkable, both in terms of the quantity and quality of his work.

Owner Ramsi Tick used to say, 'J. Lawrence Cook is a great
arranger. Just ask him.'"
"What do you mean he was an 'arranger?'" I asked.
"He played 'the cow.'" I silently waited for elaboration. "Let's
go upstairs," said Bob.

"The cow" turned out to be the famous Apollo Marking Piano
invented by Melville Clark in 1912. It was where some of the rolls
that would be punched on the massive machine downstairs started
off. It too was rigged up with a rubber hose pneumatic system
(referred to as "the calf") so that each time a key was hit, air passed
through a tube that depressed that key's own stylus, which then
struck a roll of paper rolling over a carbon cylinder, leaving a mark.

"It records note and sustain pedal 'on' and 'off' information,"
explained Bob. "The innovation was that this was recorded in 'real
time,' with rhythmic subtleties." The lengths of the perforations are
determined by the periods of time for which each key is held down.
Thus, staccato notes produce little round holes about 1/32 of an inch
in diameter, a tribute to the agility of the fingers and to the rapidity
of the recording punches. The rhythm is determined by the spacing of
the perforation in the music roll as it passes through the recording
machine at a uniform speed—about eight feet per minute—and this
spacing is in exact accordance with the interval between the notes
played by the pianist.[15]

"So this is how one got an exact record of the artist's performance?" I asked.
"Well, almost an exact record," said Bob.

The carbon marks could not record the pressure with which a key
was depressed. Therefore, master roll editing was required to enable
the arrangement to sound more authentic. That is what "arranging"
for music rolls meant. Just as perforated music rolls enabled the
recording of piano music, so began the job of music editing. J. Lawrence Cook was the best in the business at making piano music sound
"authentic."

Roll editing was a difficult job. It took uncommon patience as
well as perseverance. Unlike modern audio editing studios, at that
time there was no such thing as instant playback. As Lawrence
worked at his editing bench, he used a ruler that was marked up to

resemble a miniature piano keyboard. He slid this up to the roll and, as each hole passed under it, he imagined the sound of music playing. Next to an errant note where the pianist's finger hit the wrong key, he marked an X. Where a note needed to be added, he put an O.

Since the very beginning of the use of the marking piano in 1912, the rolls so produced were sold on the proposition that they were as good as "live." However, when the public received their music rolls, the essence of the human artist who had created the music was lost in translation, rendered invisible by the artifice of arrangement. The room that Bob and I were in was the same one where J. Lawrence Cook spent the last few years of his long career arranging rolls, sitting at the very piano in front of me, where Liberace, Horowitz, and many other entertainers recorded their performances.

On the wall next to the piano was a framed, faded color picture of Lawrence, taken from the position I was standing in. He was in his 60s, the same decade the picture was taken. He was a thin African

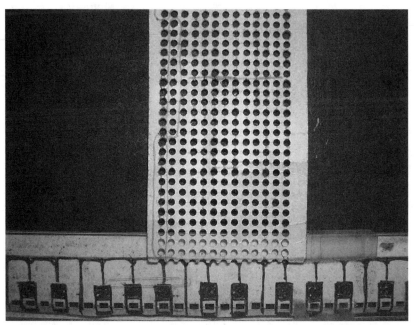

Image by Brian Dolan.

Cook's Ruler. J. Lawrence Cook, a wizard at editing piano rolls to make their playback sound "natural," slid his handmade keyboard ruler over the roll's perforations while recreating the piano tunes in his head.

American wearing classic '60s horn-rimmed eye glasses. He was wearing a short-sleeve collarless shirt; his suit jacket hung over the back of his chair. A swirl of cigarette smoke rose from the long-stem ashtray next to him. His hands were on the recording piano, but he was glancing over to flash a grin for the camera. He appeared to have been coaxed into the shot. He looked modest, almost embarrassed.

The photo was taken after a career that had spanned five decades. He was twenty when he was hired by QRS in 1919 to make some roll recordings of the new "race" music, the stride and ragtime that was gaining popularity in the clubs of Hell's Kitchen. He proved to have had a much more diversified career, much of which is only slowly coming to light now. He intentionally hid himself.

As I studied his picture, I wondered what life was like for him in 1919, working for an all-white company that was beginning to take Tin Pan Alley by storm, poised to revolutionize the music industry with their new inventions. I decided to begin a search for the origins of this entertainment. I wanted to learn more about the man who was hidden behind the music.

Chapter 6

A Search for Identity

ROUND 1905, the first motion picture to be shown in Columbia, Tennessee, was *The Crucifix*. A large white sheet was hung in the middle of a room, which had the dual function of being a projection screen and a divider to segregate the white from the African American audience. The African Americans sat behind the screen, forced to watch the movie and read the titles in reverse. Local ministers were given free tickets to attend the show. Since he lived in a small parsonage with his Presbyterian minister grandfather and his grandmother, this allowed six-year-old J. Lawrence Cook to attend. One of the things that Lawrence remembered about such events was that next to the ad-hoc theater was a shop showcasing player pianos. They were unlike other self-playing pianos that he had seen since they did not require a separate cabinet to be pushed up to the piano with its felt-covered "fingers" aligned to strike the piano's keys. With these new pianos, the player mechanism was hidden inside.

The association between early motion pictures and player pianos was something that many moviegoers would make because silent movies were often accompanied by pianists. Photoplayers provided orchestral effects as well as whistles, bells, and other sound effects. Piano rolls with generic movie theme music were also cut to loosely accompany the movies in theaters that did not have a live pianist to create the appropriate background music. For young Lawrence, the player pianos he saw in the store were a spectacle. Besides the amazing phenomenon that they played automatically, they also allowed a virtuoso performance to be heard by an audience which might not have otherwise had an opportunity to hear one.

J. Lawrence Cook mostly listened to his grandmother at the reed organ, which she played for Sunday School services. Occasionally the canvas straps on one of the pedals would break, and Lawrence would crawl underneath "and pump the pedal like mad by hand."[1] At the same time, he recalled in his brief autobiography, he began playing the keys on a children's toy musical instrument, and "I began to get the urge to want to be a pianist." Such a sentiment increased when he heard the music of virtuosi. "I always felt very much emotionally moved by performances of some of the most capable pianists who played mostly ragtime and jazz," Lawrence said. He was one of many.

About the time that the young J. Lawrence Cook saw the early motion pictures in Tennessee and discovered the attraction of playing pianos, he also began to wonder what the "J." in his name stood for. That was how his mother Zella signed his name on the back of a baby picture before she died when he was one year old. He was born in McMinn County, Tennessee, on July 14, 1899, in a small neighborhood of about twenty families, according to a 1900 census. It was a respectable community with most heads of household employed in the service industry as teachers and merchants.[2]

Lawrence's father, Jacob Lincoln Cook, was a preacher. Their immediate neighbor was a music teacher, the other a cook. However, life changed at age three when his father died and he was sent to live with his grandparents. Years later, no one had settled upon what the J. in his name represented. When people would ask, he would shrug them off. "I didn't feel obliged to give a detailed explanation," he said. To resolve the issue, he considered naming himself "Jay," and there the matter remained. He continued to sign the letter J. and use the name Lawrence.

What he was called mattered less to Lawrence than the music and prayer that figured so prominently throughout his life. Both provided some spiritual relief from increasingly difficult circumstances. His grandmother was buried on his eighth birthday. He was sent away again to Chattanooga to live with his aunt Nora, her daughter

Image courtesy of QRS Music Inc.

J. Lawrence Cook (1899–1976). Cook was a musician and piano roll editor/ arranger who pioneered the manufacture of player piano "race rolls" at QRS. He promoted African American talent including James P. Johnson, Fats Waller, Eubie Blake, and thousands of other pianists throughout his long career.

Lavetta, and her husband Hugh, "the meanest man in the world." There was no name for the place they lived—no street name at least— just a shack at the end of a dirt trail. In this wilderness, Lawrence watched on numerous occasions as Hugh would beat Aunt Nora unmercifully, then draw his gun and threaten to shoot her. "I have seen her beg that he not shoot her," Lawrence said. Then he would turn to beat Lawrence and Lavetta with a cedar limb, "and seemed to enjoy the thrill of our flinching at the sting an' on seeing the welts that he raised." Here, Lawrence spent a lot of time crying and praying. "The crying was a childish reaction," he said, "but the praying remained with me for the rest of my life."[3]

When Aunt Nora wrote to his grandfather reporting on what was happening, Lawrence received some money to return to Columbia. Through the intervention of an uncle, a Tuskegee graduate and an instructor in tailoring at the Snowhill Institute in Alabama, Lawrence was able to attend school. That uncle was also the bandmaster. When Lawrence learned that he would need to support his way through school by working in a carpentry shop by day and attending school at night, he said "I didn't mind at all. I was fascinated by the fact that I would have the chance of learning an instrument and playing in the band."[4] The uncle gave his twelve-year-old nephew a self-instruction booklet on how to play the clarinet, a vacant position in the band. During the weekends, Lawrence borrowed the keys to the instrument room and practiced on everything: trumpet, baritone, bass, alto, trombone, and drums.

One of his old friends from Columbia, with whom Lawrence kept a correspondence, had become envious of Lawrence's stories of playing the clarinet and persuaded his family to let him take piano lessons. Upon learning that his friend was before long performing hymns as the church organist, playing the old reed organ at which his grandmother once sat, Lawrence himself became jealous, and turned his attention to the piano. "I worked hard at it," he said, "with pleasing success."[5]

Despite his grandfather's desire that Lawrence pursue a career in carpentry, all Lawrence could think about was "the possibility of taking a piano course" at a technical institute nearby, and attempted to "lure" his grandfather by his jazz performances at the piano. When he was fifteen his wish was granted. At Haines Normal and Industrial Institute in Augusta, Georgia, "I spent every free moment practicing on one of the pianos" and studying those new wonders of musical reproduction, player piano rolls. Much to his pleasure, during his first summer there, someone had donated a player piano to the school's music department. "Wow!" said Lawrence, "I could touch this any time I wanted."[6] The Haines Institute was founded in the 1880s by

Lucy Craft Laney, a pioneer of African American education who had been one of the first graduates of Atlanta University in 1873. Following a passionate appeal at a Presbyterian Church convention, Laney received a donation of ten thousand dollars from Francine Haines, president of the Women's Department of the Presbyterian Church, which led to the institute's foundation.

While researching J. Lawrence Cook's upbringing, I came across another researcher interested in the same area: the British composer and Ferdinand "Jelly Roll" Morton biographer, Mike "Doctor Jazz" Medding. Medding maintains an extensive website dedicated to the history of ragtime, player piano music, and biographical information on early jazz pioneers, including J. Lawrence Cook. He mentioned to me that he was making a tour of the American South in search of an elusive World War I draft registration card for Jelly Roll Morton, and took the opportunity to check in on places Lawrence was involved with. It turns out that the old Haines Institute was knocked down in 1951 and a new school built, the Lucy Craft Laney High School. "The current headmaster and staff are unimpressed by Cook's activities," Medding told me, "and despite more than one attempt at making an appointment to meet the staff, I gave up."

I told Medding of my saga of trying to locate museum collections of mechanical musical instruments only to find that they were long gone, and shared his frustration of the ephemeral nature of institutional history and personal legacies. However, Medding did find a gem in the Atlanta archives. While he was unable to locate Jelly Roll Morton's registration card, he and another researcher, his friend Millie Gaddini, came across J. Lawrence Cook's draft card. It seems it took a world war to settle part of a question of identity.

In September 1918, Lawrence was required to register for the draft and told that he needed to spell out his first name. He decided on Gene, a name he was told that his mother had originally contemplated. Having studied some French at the Institute, he decided to spell it following the French custom, "Jean," even though "it might be mistaken for the name of a female."[7] Having at long last settled the issue of his name, it was ironic that he was renamed "Cookie" by friends in the music industry. He was about to embark on a new career. The war had ended and Lawrence had graduated from the Haines Institute. In 1919, he moved to Pittsburgh and took up a number of odd jobs with a desire to break into the music business. The player piano industry gave Jean Lawrence Cook just that chance.

In the first decade of the twentieth century, Tin Pan Alley in New York represented a multimillion dollar industry. In the second decade, the sale of player pianos was surpassing that of manual pianos, while piano rolls were taking the lead over the sale of sheet music.[8] In 1918, the *New York Times* reported on an "unprecedented rush of orders for player-pianos. . . . The result is that manufacturers, while they have a large stock of the plain type of pianos on hand for which there is little demand, are finding it increasingly difficult to meet the swollen call for player-pianos."[9] During the same period, American attitudes toward music began to change. Ragtime tunes and dances such as the Turkey Trot and the Texas Tommy began to transform social life outside the walls of home and business. After 1910, according to the "tune detective" Sigmund Spaeth, even "the publishers of popular music became more and more insistent that a song must be danceable in order to achieve real success."[10]

The "Dance Mania," as it was called by the periodical *Public Opinion* in 1913, was spreading the wealth around all aspects of the music industry, including technologies that were beginning to rival player pianos, such as the phonograph. In 1914, the trade magazine *Talking Machine World* reported that "dance music records have proven a great business builder" with assets booming, notably in the sixty-percent jump in Victor's sales between 1913 and 1915.[11] So serious was the competition becoming that player piano companies such as Aeolian diversified their product portfolio and introduced their Vocalion phonographs in 1914.

Yet despite the sales, the quality of sound on the discs left much to be desired—an acknowledgement made in Aeolian's own marketing pitch, which claimed that a "Graduola" lever, which muffled the sound emanating from the horn, "can reduce harshness of tone or other faults in a record to a minimum."[12] A competition began to establish scientifically that player pianos provided superior sound quality. The Standard Music Roll Company secured the expert testimony of Alexander Graham Bell, who wrote that "the superior music rolls made" by them means that "the instrument cannot be said, in any sense, to produce 'machine music,' as all means of expression are so completely and instantaneously under the control of the performer."[13] Blasius & Sons, another manufacturer of player pianos in the 1910s, listed Thomas A. Edison, who wrote that "I have been using your piano for the last two years for experiments on the phonograph

at the laboratory. Of all the instruments tried, my experimenters prefer the Blasius." This prompted the company to declare themselves to
have the "Tone Standard of the World."[14] However, it was the artists
themselves who made the most powerful case for player pianos' possessing more fidelity than acoustically recorded phonographs.

In the 1890-1920 period, as the University of Delaware historian
David Suisman points out, phonograph companies had a difficult
time recording piano music, and a number of pianists were reluctant
to make phonograph records.[15] Paderewski, for instance, did his first
recording for the Welte Mignon reproducing piano in 1906 and was
afterwards critical of disc recordings. Igor Stravinsky was another
composer who preferred the player piano. He discovered its potential
in 1914 and wrote compositions specifically for it, saying that he
hoped to make rolls of all his works as "a means of imposing some
restriction on the notorious liberty, especially wide-spread today
which prevents the public from obtaining a correct idea of the
author's intentions."[16] He eventually switched allegiance to the phonograph in 1928 with the advent of electrical recording that vastly
improved sound quality.

Manufacturers were eager to convince the public that when they
heard their player piano play, they should think not of a machine but
of the pianist. "In the case of [Moritz] Moszkowski, those compositions are his own. He marked them himself," announced the Aeolian
Company in 1903, drawing attention to its new Metrostyle rolls that
allowed player pianists to identify themselves with the maestro by
being guided through the interpretation of the piece. "Any one desir-
ous of playing these compositions of Moszkowski [can do so] just as
Moszkowski desires them played, to the very lightest and most subtle
shading and nuance." This was also true of the rolls recorded by Paderewski and Mlle. Chaminade and many others, they added.[17]

The sales and the musical preferences promoted by music roll
recordings should have translated into big business for musicians, but
this was not necessarily so. First, roll artists were not paid royalties.
Early on, music rolls were not even protected by copyright, and roll
companies did not pay music publishers for the rights to reproduce
their tunes in this form of medium. A lawsuit was filed by the music
publishers, but it was quashed by the U.S. Supreme Court's ruling
that copyrights protected only information that was read by humans,

not by machines.[18] In 1909, the roll companies began paying the publishers tune rights, but royalties were not paid to the recording artists until later.

Pianists were usually paid a set fee for producing a specific number of rolls. George Gershwin, for instance, then a mere sixteen years old, went from song plugger for Remick & Co. to recording piano rolls in 1915 for Standard Music Roll Company (and later, Aeolian) and was paid thirty-five dollars for six master rolls.[19] However, the main interest that many well-known artists, such as Paderewski and Stravinsky, had in recording piano rolls was the quality of sound preservation and the ability to exercise a degree of control in the reproduction and interpretation of the music. The act of recording rolls was not then a highlight of these artists' careers. Gershwin seems never to have discussed his experiences as a roll artist. Music journalists at the time gave little notice. Rather, these articles were most attuned to concert performances and employment in high-paying public establishments in the city.

On the other hand, ragtime, an emerging form of popular music, was catching on largely through the sales of piano roll music, where the performers were invisible to the public eye. There were two benefits for those who made piano roll recordings in the 1910s. First, because of the rules regulating performances set by the American Federation of Musicians, a union that African Americans were excluded from joining, and because of the lack of support groups for black musicians (notwithstanding the creation of James Reese Europe's Clef Club in 1910), musicians who played ragtime music had few opportunities for public recognition and thus more income through public performance.[20] Recording piano rolls gave them an opportunity to earn money, and the distribution of the rolls helped to spread their musical reputations. Second, because of the complexity of the style and the skill required to play ragtime arrangements, player piano rolls, which could be distributed across the country more quickly than a pianist could travel, created a niche employment market for talented ragtime musicians. Not every ragtime recording was performed by a black musician—Gershwin's "Rialto Ripples Rag" (1916) is one example, but Gershwin was an exception to the rule.

Historians of ragtime and jazz have pointed out that such music translated very well to the medium of the player piano. For a combination of the various reasons just cited, many of the leading African

American ragtime pioneers recorded player piano rolls. The first piano roll recordings made by African American musicians—in fact, the earliest recordings of African American music—were made in 1912 by QRS. In that year, John "Blind" Boone recorded ten rolls of light classical pieces such as "Woodland Murmurs" and "Sparkling Spring," as well as piano rags including "Rag Medley No. 1" and "Blind Boone's Southern Rag Medley No. 1."[21] The sobriquet "Blind Boone" resulted from a childhood illness which took his eyesight early enough in life that he never had any recollection of seeing at all, but he had an incredible ear for music. He also had a special feel for the keyboard, a talent he acquired through studying the key motions of a player piano.

According to his first biographer, who published in 1915, a year before Boone's death, "It is by this player that Boone learns most of his music . . . by the method of the player he learns his selections perfectly."[22] A hazy illustration in the book shows Boone at his piano, with a player piano covered in boxes of rolls in the background. It was, perhaps, in appreciation of the profound impact that the player piano had on his own ability to play that Boone was especially attracted to the idea of recording for it. In any case, it is a historic and fitting mark of achievement. Another early ragtime player, Eubie Blake, started recording rags, blues, and popular songs in 1917 and made his last rolls for QRS in 1973 when he was ninety years old.[23]

During his early years of making rolls from 1917 to 1921, Blake was also touring northeast America, with singer Noble Sissle performing vaudeville. During this time he met J. Lawrence Cook, forging a friendship that would last throughout their lives. Cook was still working at menial jobs in Pittsburgh but was spending his free time composing some songs and teaching himself how to cut piano rolls. Back when he was a student at the Haines Institute, he came across an issue of *The Etude*, a magazine dedicated to music and pedagogy that was published until 1957. Thumbing through its pages, he read an advertisement for a machine used to perforate rolls by hand, inviting the reader to "make your own piano rolls." "I tore out the page and saved it for so long that it began to turn yellow," said Lawrence. "My ambition was to purchase one of these hand-perforators one day and use it to make rolls of my compositions."[24] Eventually he found the machine.

For fifty dollars, making ten-dollar installment payments, Lawrence purchased a Leabarjan perforator. Invented by John Lease, a business partner of Carl Bartels and Franz Janzen (the first three letters of each name forming the name of the machine), it was designed to punch holes in small-run rolls, up to four at a time. The manual described how to read sheet music and how to transcribe that information onto paper via punched holes. The company thought that the market for this perforator would be school music classes where students would learn the basic principles of music.

While Lawrence did not record any details of his early meetings with Eubie Blake, he makes it clear that they talked about piano roll production and related opportunities for employment. In fact, Lawrence does attribute his decision to move to New York to Blake's advice that that was the place where one could make it big-time in the music business. So, in 1920, Lawrence moved to New York, weighted down with his Leabarjan perforator, bundles of sample rolls, and manuscript compositions. While encouraged by Eubie Blake, Lawrence was also inspired to be following in the tracks of "his first idol," James P. Johnson.

James P. "Jimmy" Johnson was born in New Brunswick, New Jersey, on February 1, 1894. His father, William, was a mechanic and his mother, Josephine, was a maid. He was the youngest of five children, with three older brothers and a sister. His mother saved enough money to buy an upright piano from one of her employers so she could teach herself to play hymns for the choir at the Methodist church. James, already tall and slim by age seven, sat beside her and worked the pedals. This was not an unusual introduction to music. Like many families, they found hours of entertainment around the piano.

"The piano makers had a slogan," James later commented, reflecting on these days, "What is a Home Without a Piano?"[25] However, the sounds of music were soon silenced in the Johnson home.

When James was eight years old, the family headed for New York but ended up going no farther than the last stop on the railroad before the Hudson, Jersey City. To help pay for the moving expenses, the family sold their prized piano. They settled in the tenderloin area between the wharves and the warehouses, an area filled with hustlers and "ticklers"—pianists who fondled the keyboard and the women who worked the bordellos in which the ticklers played. James's older brother befriended a few young lads hoping to find work in the cabarets. Between them they shared all they knew about how to play "ragtime," so called because it was characterized by its "ragged" rhythm—the rhythm of black dance that spread north from New Orleans' Congo Square.[26]

James followed his brother and his friends around, imitating them at any keyboard he could get his hands on. He later recalled with a laugh how that same year a woman who heard him at a piano enticed the eight-year-old with twenty-five cents to play in her parlor so long as he did not turn around.[27] He didn't know it at the time, but many of the ticklers he listened to with admiration through closed doors were big-time pimps playing songs "that would touch the ladies' hearts," a spiritual haven in an otherwise downtrodden life for those whom he referred to as "sporting women."[28]

Life became even more intriguing for James when six years later his family once again relocated to the northern tip of Hell's Kitchen, a section of New York City that ran from about 34th street to 69th, west of 9th Avenue. It was "probably the lowest and filthiest" part of the city, according to a shocked *New York Times* reporter some years earlier, writing about its tenements and factories.[29] It was here that fourteen-year old James was exposed to what he called "real ragtime."

Slipping out of "the Jungle" (the northernmost streets of Hell's Kitchen) in the evening, James passed the rowdy cabarets and clubs and visited McFarland's Irish Society Hall in a cellar at 100th and 3rd Avenue. Dropping his school bag in an empty coal bin, he headed down to the basement dance hall to listen to four- and five-piece orchestras until they finished late in the night. As the band retired to the bar, the proprietor rolled an upright piano onto the floor that James was allowed to play until the early hours of the morning while everyone else became drunk. "After a little sleep," he said, he would head off to school, but it was not long before he abandoned all attempts to keep this routine. His talent was rapidly developing at the piano. Stints of summer work entertaining at Coney Island over the next couple of years were earning him up to eighteen dollars a week. "That was so much money," he said, "I didn't want to go back to school."[30]

When he turned sixteen, James decided to return to Jersey City. He did not mind living next to pimps and drug pushers as long as he could play the piano. After all, entertainers were "real celebrities" in his words. "They had lots of girl friends, led a sporting life and were invited everywhere there was a piano. I thought it was a fine way to live."[31] Despite gaining enough admiration as a pianist to earn some money and keep him playing, his talent was based on a remarkable natural ability but no formal training in music. Unable to read or write music, he attributed his skill to hours at the piano imitating what he had heard played in local saloons. "I was born with absolute pitch and could catch a key that a player was using, and copy it," he said.[32] The preeminence of the piano indoctrinated a whole generation of musicians through imitation in much the same way that playing the banjo had caught on a few decades earlier. In fact, one music critic writing in 1881 believed that there was an effect that the banjo had on the way the piano was learned without the aid of formal training. "Did you ever hear negroes play the piano by ear?" the critic remarked. "They use the piano exactly like a banjo."[33]

When James was nineteen in 1913, a fellow tickler introduced him to "old professor" Bruto Giannini, an Italian music teacher. He charged a dollar a lesson using the works of Bach, Beethoven, Puccini, and other classical artists as a way of learning harmony and counterpoint—arranging "note against note" so lines of music would form a harmonious whole. James was shown where each finger belonged on the keyboard. "I had to throw away my fingering and learn to put the right finger on the right note," he said.[34]

By the time of James's classical music lessons, the better-known ragtime musicians such as Jelly Roll Morton and James Reese Europe were performing with such ability that the music had come into its own. Because of teachers such as Giannini, a number of New York black pianists were being introduced to "the European method," the system and styles that audiences in concerts and cafes in the city were familiar with. If there was more money and opportunity to be had, the musicians knew it was through embodying the techniques of the European concert pianists. "The ragtime player," observed James, "had to live up to that standard."[35]

To that end, James worked to develop full, round chords with a heavy bass supporting the right hand. According to the jazz scholar Gunther Schuller, James never missed a Hofmann or Rachmaninoff recital at Carnegie Hall.[36] Before long, his keyboard technique improved exponentially. He practiced in the dark and would play difficult pieces through a bed sheet draped over the keyboard to develop a clearer touch. He traveled around "listening to every good player I could. I'd steal their breaks and style and practice them until I had them perfect."[37] Substituting different chords and harmonies, he took what he heard, learned from his training, and concentrated on his own favorite music, such as the "Jelly Roll Blues." "I played rags very accurately and brilliantly," he said, "running chromatic octaves and glissandos up and down the keyboard with both hands." His music played off the sound of the feet shuffling across the dance floor. "It made a terrific effect."[38]

Before long, James's identity as a musician was beginning to crystallize. His own rag tunes were adapted—"stole," he said—from a variety of styles that were developed by others following the early introduction of ragtime at the World's Columbian Exposition in Chicago in 1893. Ben Harney, who called himself "the inventor of ragtime," was the first to dazzle audiences in New York by playing two pianos at the same time in vaudeville theaters. There was the ragtime of Scott Joplin, whom James credited with teaching him all he knew about "classic rags." There was Luckey Roberts and Eubie Blake, who have been said to "lay somewhere between classic ragtime and popular semi-classics." There was the distinctive style of the concert pianist Blind Boone. Jelly Roll Morton's New Orleans "western" ragtime was now beginning to be imitated. As did everyone else, James borrowed bits and pieces of them all. A virtuoso could detect the variations, but to much of the audience in the clubs, it was all the rage.

Slim and "dapper," as he described himself in his early twenties during these times, James donned a dark suit with long black tie and played at Drake's Dancing Class on 62nd Street, also known as "The Jungles Casino." The "class" appellation was a ruse for getting a dance license. ("It was very hard for Negroes to get a dance-hall license"). A coal bin was handy to receive a stash of liquor "in case the cops dropped in." When he started playing, the "pupils" started dancing. "Instead of playing straight, I'd break into the rag at certain places," putting the "James P." signature on the music, and the youth "would scream when I got good to them with a bit of rag in the dance music."[39]

Only a few years earlier, when he had started to play the clubs and cabarets in Jersey City, James had been approached by the African American music publishers Gotham & Attucks—who produced the music of Scott Joplin, George Walker, and others—wanting to represent him. However, James could not write any tunes down and, at the time, did not know anyone who could help him. Friends of his would attribute this to his shyness offstage. By 1917, however, he found a new opportunity to spread his music and to add a distinct "player piano" ragtime to the different styles of rag on the market.

The Aeolian Company's Aeolian Hall, an imposing eighteen-story building on 42nd Street, featured performances that rivaled the symphonies, choral concerts, and piano recitals of Carnegie Hall. Besides having studios for musicians and showrooms for their pianos, including Steinways equipped with their Duo-Art reproducing system, the company offered free public lectures on the proper use of the player piano.[40] This was, they believed, the future of music. They were at that time the largest player piano manufacturer in the world, and in 1916, the pianist they hired to demonstrate their instruments was James P. Johnson.

Since taking lessons in classical music under the tutelage of professor Giannini, James's reputation as one of the best pianists on the East Coast had soared. Over the previous few years, he had done a lot of "visiting around," playing in cabarets in Jersey City, dance halls in Harlem, and clubs in "the Jungles."[41] Having now learned to read and write music, James also began composing his own songs rather than only "stealing" and adapting others' tunes. He arranged what he called "homemade blues" such as "All Night Long" (later made into a popular song by Shelton Brooks), a tribute to all the nightclub owners who never needed to lock their front doors. It was music of pure emotion. "The Blues are the feelings of the people," James said, "their protests, hopes, loves, hates; a mingling of feeling all rolled together."[42] Such fusion was expressed at the keyboard where he also composed rags that would become famous, such as "Steeplechase Rag" and the popular "Carolina Shout." James pushed the limits by combining styles, and his unique mix of blues and rag solos was given a new name: stride. The term described the walking motion of the pianist's hands up and down the keyboard, creating counter-rhythms.[43]

The songs from Tin Pan Alley, which were previously marketed as sheet music, now began drawing attention to music rolls, driven by the same innovating energy used to improve the performances of player pianos. While remarkable talents such as James P. Johnson played at clubs and private parties in elite homes such as the Vander-bilts and Wanamakers, the music industry began to take his music to the masses. However, sheet music could not bring the pianos in middle-class parlor rooms to life. Who could possibly play like "James P."? Anyone who owned a player piano could, according to the Aeolian Company.

Twice a month Johnson visited the 42nd Street studio and played ragtime and his own brand of stride on Aeolian's recording piano. Over the next twenty months, Aeolian built a catalog of twenty rolls of his music, seventeen of which were original Johnson compositions. At the time, he prided himself in believing that he was the only black musician to record his own piano rolls. In fact, he was following the lead of Blind Boone and Scott Joplin, the latter having recorded a few rolls before he died in 1917. However, James's reputation spread even more widely through Aeolian's rolls. Other companies were quick to sign the rising star to record for them. The New Jersey firm of Ben-nett & White, who manufactured rolls under the "Artempo" label, recorded James's most well-known roll, "Carolina Shout," which helped make his reputation.

"The greatest gift of the Negro people," wrote W.E.B. Du Bois in his book *The Souls of Black Folk* (1913), was their music. The music that traveled from Hell's Kitchen to Carnegie Hall was increasingly imitated but never matched. "Even the ragtime music of white com-posers falls short of the genuine dance compositions of negro musi-cians," said James Reese Europe, a prominent ragtime exponent of the 1910s and founder of the Clef Club. It failed to "breathe the spirit of a race."[44] Such facility seemed to transcend raw technical skill, such as reading sheet music. "White musicians can play exactly what is put down on paper," observed J. Rosamond Johnson in 1915, who recorded his own rags for Ampico, "but Negro musicians are able to put into the music something that can't be put on the paper; a certain abandon which seems to enter in the blood of their dancers."[45] This spirit kept the people dancing like crazy and drove music publishers to attempt to figure out ways to capture this on paper for resale. What couldn't American innovation commercialize? Now the white folk (some of whom had once possessed blacks) owned machines whose music, allegedly, possessed what they could not otherwise create: black soul.

As if this new music (and the resulting dance craze that so offended puritan sensibility) was not threatening enough, the self-playing piano enabled a person who owned one to become the entertainer who was otherwise invisible in all but mechanical manifestations. Those white dilettantes who learned to pump pedals in the right way—no more difficult than learning the steps to the foxtrot—could overcome their lack of skill. They could become virtuosi and could, as the poet Langston Hughes said in reference to the humorous innuendo that permeated the lyrics of postbellum blues, keep "laughing to keep from crying."[46]

Chapter 7

Possession

FTER HEARING the lyrics to a popular hymn, "Nearer my God to Thee," sung as "Nero, My Dog, has Fleas," a New York music teacher complained that ragtime was destroying every musical tradition and ideal. The *New York Tribune*'s music critic concurred. Ragtime dances "are threatening to force grace, decorum, and decency out of the ballrooms of America," he wrote.[1] It was no longer just cabarets—basement dance halls, amusement parks and, increasingly, New York hotels were installing dance floors for nonballroom events. Homes across the country abandoned the genteel standards that used to establish the values of Victorian home-making.

Worse, however, was the threat that "Negro music" posed to the moral probity and spiritual welfare of Christian America. Ragtime and blues had a parallel with the fervor of religious expression in Baptist and Methodist churches. Romping down on piano keys was, in the words of James P. Johnson's youngest daughter, Lillie Mae, "just like the Baptist people sing." Church itself was a form of musical performance: "There's ragtime in the preaching," she alleged.[2]

To be sure, the Christian sentiment evoked the ennobling harmony of classical music—Beethoven, Wagner, and Bach—as the summit of spirituality. "The masterworks of instrumental music are the language of the soul and express more than those of any other art," declared Theodore Thomas, conductor of the New York Philharmonic (whose granddaughter became a "musical missionary" to spread the classics in the U.S. provinces). "Light music, popular music, so called, is the sensual side of the art and has more or less devil in it."[3] Not only the music but the machines that played the music were similarly associated with divine providence.

"Music is something we think of when we think of heaven," wrote Thomas Pletcher, general manager of QRS, in a 1916 leather-bound booklet titled *Confidential Selling Information*. Advising his sales team about why Melville Clark's Apollo Player Piano was better than anything the competition had, he drew an analogy between the production of the machine and God's handiwork where beauty is in the detail. "The theologist gets up and talks to his congregation and convinces them that they should live rightly and according to the laws of the Creator. If they do, they will be rewarded; and if they do not, they will be punished. The hope of reward is the talking point for a godly life."[4]

The connection Pletcher saw between the theologian and the salesman was the commonality of offering rewards. Music, he said, "is decidedly not a luxury, but a necessity—something without which human life is incomplete." However, the proof of the proclamation was in the detail. A well-built player piano, where "for every penny's difference in price there is a dollar in extra musical results and standing-up qualities," brought one a more fulfilled life. What better way to make the public understand the importance of technological innovation than to appeal to the core of American appreciation for the middle classes: the automobile.

Already by 1916, Americans were becoming motor crazy. It was the beginning of the U.S. addiction to gasoline. Salesmen of player pianos were therefore instructed to think about their customers' prized possessions. Pletcher here again provided some recommendations as to how to engage the customer's interest. "Without knowing anything about it," they were instructed to comment, "I venture to say that your car contains a gasoline engine, water cooled. All right, Mr. _____, why did you want that type of engine? Simply because you knew that it was the standard principle of motor construction." So what about player pianos? The standard of construction became the talking point. "Now you are buying a player piano," says the salesman. "It also contains a motor and in proportion the motor of the player piano is called upon to do just as much work and do it just as faithfully as the motor in an automobile."[5] God and automobiles. How Republican. How very unlike a sales pitch for an instrument that was also known to be perfect for playing ragtime music.

However, a problem developed in the sales strategies. The sale of popular music, particularly ragtime, was on the rise. While in the first two decades of the twentieth century classical and orchestral music made up a majority of roll sales, ragtime was reaching ten percent of all sales.[6] Yet the majority of the trade press, in whose pages of musical reporting player piano and roll companies needed to advertise, still claimed that popular music smote religious ears. "In Christian homes," argued a critic in the pages of the *Musical Observer* in 1914, "where purity and morals are stressed, ragtime should find no resting place."[7] These debates went beyond musical criticism and religious fundamentalism to include testimony from missionaries and even academics such as post-Darwinian anthropologists about the deleterious physiological effects unleashed by such "sensual" (i.e., "primitive") music performed by African Americans. "As I understand it," volunteered Dr. Henry van Dyke, a Presbyterian minister and Princeton professor, "it is not music at all. It is merely an irritation of the nerves of hearing, a sensual teasing of the strings of physical passion." As such, he said, "jazz put the sin in syncopation."[8] For the musician, "ragtime will ruin your touch, disable your technic, misuse your knowledge of pedaling, and pervert whatever sense of poetry and feeling you have into superficial, improper channels. Shun it as you would the 'Black Death.'"[9]

Darwinian and Freudian theories provoked more alarm. Contemporary Christian and medical conceptions of demonic possession in an age preoccupied with spiritualism linked anthropological accounts of diabolical "primitive rituals" of music and dance with the subconscious. The language of "degeneration theory" threatened the imminent collapse of (white) civilization through the pernicious spread of promiscuous and diseased musical mores that sowed the seeds of physiological, as well as spiritual, destruction. Missionaries told stories of their encounters with possessed, "demon-haunted" natives of China, India, and Africa. These claims by liberal and orthodox Christians alleged a relationship between the soul and unconscious "animal instincts." The newly discovered unconscious or subconscious mind provided a fertile medium for demonic possession.[10] In America, a watchful eye and attentive ear were kept on the behavior of those exposed to the new music.

Yet the spirit was meant to be liberated. In the run-up to the roaring '20s, the songs that once had modulated the work rhythms of black laborers were reinvented by mechanization and urbanization. "Black music," commented the historian Lawrence Levine, "found a new home in leisure time rather than work time."[11] According to Houston Baker, a professor at the University of Pennsylvania who wrote *Modernism and the Harlem Renaissance*, the "hard won song" of Afro-American modernist expression was "designed to move the spirit of freedom."[12] However, for white audiences, embracing black modernist expressions was seen as an expression of their enlightened values, which did not involve a move away from the ethos of slavery but a transformation in Victorian and Puritan values. The "exoticism" of ragtime and stride, which created a new social order in which black pianists reigned supreme, is said to have been transfigured by the bourgeoisie to become an aesthetic to be colonized and possessed by the privileged for their own social ends. "Most white Americans know by now," said the historian Paul Carter in 1971, "that the only reason the period [of the 1920s] qualifies as *the Jazz Age* is that it was the time when middle-class whites first discovered this musical idiom."[13]

However "liberating" the music of African Americans symbolically became to a once enslaved population, it also became a way for whites to create a context to engage with the "new Negro," to invent the fantasy of Harlem as Happytown.[14] Some roll-production companies took the bold step of defending ragtime by explaining "to the Musician with a Head of His Own" that it was merely the rhythm that differentiated it from all other music, and that this was not to be feared. "What is rhythm?" began a brief educational catechism produced by Melville Clark.

A.—The best definition obtainable is: "A symmetrical fluctuation of the intensities."

Q.—Then what is ragtime?

A.—It is any piece of music, light or heavy, good or bad, intensified by syncopations.

Q.—Why does this rhythmical treatment make the piece dispreputable?

A.—Of course, it doesn't. This idea is the flim-flam of the fossilized "ancient" who has kicked it with both feet since he first came up against it—and couldn't play it.

There were two points: first that lack of talent, or "technic," created a pretense against the music, an objection based on resentment. Second, they want to turn the wheels of progress backwards. In the veins of those who embraced ragtime ran "the red blood of the 20th century. . . . Common sense will override all 16th century prejudices. To turn up the nose at ragtime without discrimination reveals a 'loft to let.' "[15]

The limited fidelity and poor quality of the early phonograph records meant that player pianos were essential to the spread of ragtime, whether considered a "contagion" or modern liberation.[16] The player piano, and the new styles of music popularized by it in the 1910s, thus became a machine that mediated old and modern values—a transformation from nineteenth-century suppression to twentieth-century expression. To entertain in the age of abandon meant bringing "live" music into one's home and assuming the role of an entertainer. Sitting at a player piano and taking control over a tune's crescendos and diminuendos was regulating the rhythm of the party while gaining moral, social, and aesthetic authority in the transition that turned passive audiences into active participants in the expression of new principles of liberty.

The player piano allowed complicated and avant-garde music to enter new contexts, which challenged the superiority of classical music. Previously there was no way of experiencing such music outside clubs or parlor houses, and it made its new audience uncertain as to how to react to it. As one musicologist put it in a historical article on jazz and modernism in 1983, "Unlike some 'classical music' audiences who understand that 'their' music is difficult and demanding intellectually, many jazz listeners 'dig' jazz in an atmosphere, a context, that encourages an emotional rather than an intellectual response."[17] It was precisely that different genres of music were moving into different contexts and provoking emotional responses—behavior that might have deleterious physical effects on the population—that worried commentators and subjected the instrument of musical transmission to scrutiny. "Can it be said," asked a writer to the *Musical Courier* in 1913, "that America is falling prey to the collective soul of the Negro through the influence of what is popularly known as 'rag time' music?" "All psychiatrists" thought so, he claimed. Could this be embodied in piano rolls and the "possessed" player piano? It was a concern that the industry needed to address, and it was quick to do so.

"MUSIC WILL HELP YOU," assured a magazine advertisement from 1919, "To Harmonize Yourself with your condition, Your work with your pleasure, Your family with your home."[18] The medicinal and spiritual qualities of music were augmented by other health-giving properties embedded within the music of the player piano. "The Player Piano is the Heart of a Happy Home," announced an advertisement for the Standard Pneumatic Action Company in the 1920s. "It's the kind of 'active' relaxation I love," offers a cartoon face of grandpa in an advertisement for the Pianola.[19] "Music has peculiar curative powers," stated the *Standard Player Monthly*. "It works on the body through the mind, the soul, the delicate, responsive membranes of the mind. It affects the nerves. It will not cure all human complaints, but it most assuredly will relieve a great many popular conditions which often baffle physicians. According to the facts of the case, every home should have a player piano, just as one would have a family physician."[20]

In the 1940s, the Music Research Foundation produced a series of booklets titled "Music for Your Moods" that registered compositions arranged by mood classifications of "Gay," "Lilting," "Meditative," "Soothing," and "Stimulating." The foundation "has encouraged psychologists, physicists, and musicians to perfect the use of those great sources of human stimulation—sounds and rhythms scientifically controlled, blended and administered." A natural development to their program of research was to enroll the scientifically controlled expression of music in player pianos as instruments of curative administration. To gain support for this, the foundation contacted Melville Clark, nephew of Melville Clark of Apollo Player Piano fame, and president of what was Clark Music Company in the 1940s—a Syracuse-based player piano and Irish harp firm (whose ill-fated mechanical "player harp" nearly put him out of business). The foundation invited him to attend an all-Chopin concert to appreciate how his music "communicates feelings of joy or sorrow or triumph far more rapidly and far more intensely than any spoken or written description," but no collaboration between the parties seems to have resulted.[21]

Up to the present day, the therapeutic benefits of the exercise one gains from pumping away at a player are discussed among aficionados. "Someday I hope to find in the *New England Journal of Medicine* a double-blind study comparing longevity of nursing-home residents with access to a player piano to those of age-matched inhabitants without access to a foot-pumped player," wrote Bob Baker, a contributor to the *Mechanical Music Digest*.[22] "I know from first hand evidence and experience that cardiovascular surgeons highly recommend pumping a player piano as a means of exercise," replied John Tuttle, another contributor.[23] "In one instance I was asked *not* to improve the air-tightness of a unit because it would be too easy to pump. The owner weighed over 300 pounds and she could not ride a bicycle, which at that time was the preferred method of exercise." It was later revealed that the patient lost seventy pounds in one year by "pumping off" at least five rolls a day.

The power of the player piano to harmonize life was demonstrable when placed in the most unsettling situations, such as in the midst of war. According to a press release issued just after the end of World War I, the *USS Delaware*, which patrolled the North Sea with the British Grand Fleet, was one of a number of warships equipped with player pianos that were in daily use to improve the morale of the troops. This and at least nine other battleships had them in the officers' mess hall. A photograph from 1911 taken onboard the battleship *USS Connecticut* shows five junior officers sitting around a player piano with the caption "A Good Cigar—and the Autopiano." For the Autopiano Company of New York, which supplied the Navy with the pianos, it was proof not only of their utility but their durability.

The Autopiano Company was following a marketing strategy that had already worked for another company. In 1907, the Aeolian Company provided twenty-six Pianolas for the U.S. Battle Fleet under the command of Admiral Evans, which sailed from Hampton Roads in Virginia on a voyage around the world as part of a demonstration of U.S. naval power organized by President Theodore Roosevelt. The player pianos traveled forty-five thousand miles on the high seas through arctic cold and tropical heat, were jolted with each battle gun practice, and were "used constantly by scores of individuals." When they returned to New York in February 1909, Aeolian proudly proclaimed that they were "in excellent playing condition." "Today more Pianolas are in use on ships of the navies of the world than any other instruments of the player-piano type," they announced. In 1919, a representative from the Navy Department, Bureau of Navigation, in Washington, D.C., wrote to Aeolian asking them to prepare an article on how to care for player pianos for the "preservation of their recreational material."[24]

During World War I, another company designed a poster showing a forlorn woman at a player piano pedaling out the music to "Over There" with a superimposed cloudlike image depicting troops in trenches. The player thus had some ostensible effect on the civilizing process by evoking memories of home for troops fighting abroad while fostering empathy among those waiting for the soldiers to return. If it was good for the Navy, reason suggested that automatic piano music would be a means of boosting morale for other organizations, too. James West, Chief Scout Executive of the Boy Scouts of America, wrote to Weber Piano Company in 1920 explaining that Palisades Interstate Park in Tuxedo, New York, had the largest camp—2,200 boys. "It would be of splendid assistance to this large number of boys," he wrote, "to be able to have one of your [player] pianos located in some of the mess halls." The same year, Mr. Fletcher, the advertising manager of the Aeolian Company, received a letter from Miss B. M. Gage from Harlem House, a community house that was anxious to obtain a player piano for their dancing and gymnasium classes and hoped the firm would be willing to donate an "out of style" piano. "Our people are a music-loving race and we would deeply appreciate a donation of this sort. . . . I feel that when you realize the great need for music in our work and the fact that we have been established for over twenty years, that you will cooperate with us."[25] There is no record as to whether or not the companies agreed to these requests.

Overwhelmingly the marketing of player pianos relied on the proposition that one wanted to play rather than just possess a piano. The player piano was sold on the premise of the attainment of a different kind of engagement with modernity: achievement through a "de-skilled" performance that would otherwise have taken years to achieve.[26] Laborious studying and training were not necessary. William Geppert, editor of the trade journal *The Musical Courier* in the 1910s, explained that John McTammany "could see no good reason why the masses should subject themselves to years of drudgery and expenditure of money in the development of the technic by the human fingers when the same result could be produced by the technic of the piano itself."[27]

The "masses" referred to belonged to the swelling middle class. A player piano was no small investment by the late 'teens: a standard upright would cost between $300 and $500, while top-of-the-line Steinways—which produced player pianos in agreement with Aeolian and Melville Clark Piano Co.—could cost between $4,000 and $5,000.[28] Even each roll was somewhat costly, between $1 and $3 each. However, to own one was to be associated with the ranks of the elite. The trade journal *The Purchaser's Guide to the Music Industries* showed pictures of player pianos "in the finest homes," including Sandringham, the Queen of England's summer estate.

Individual companies regularly published the names of their prominent patrons: the Roosevelts, Carnegies, Rockefellers, Vanderbilts, Mark Twain, George V, King of England, and an array of Dukes, Duchesses, Earls, Countesses, Lords, and Barons were all mentioned in numerous advertisements. The Aeolian Company was notable for drawing attention to its patrons, producing an illustration of Pope Leo XIII giving a private audience to the Pianola in the Throne Room at the Vatican, and declaring in *Everybody's Magazine* in 1911 that "The *Rulers* of nearly *every substantial power* are owners of Pianolas."[29] Story & Clark player pianos were installed in educational institutions including Harvard, Columbia, Amherst, the University of Wisconsin, Tufts—right down to the Public Library of Evanston, Illinois, and Public School Number 12 in Indianapolis, Indiana.[30] Whatever their wealth, the customers whom player piano manufacturers had in mind were refashioning themselves along lines where such purchases identified them as participants in the modern world of entertainment. Player pianos were marketed not only as machines for a certain class but as particularly suitable for a specific gender.

"What connection is there between a piano, or organ, and a sewing machine?" asked the musicologist Arthur Loesser in 1954. Both, he answered, "were moderately bulky objects that women liked to play with around the house," at least at the end of the nineteenth century, he said.[31] That was when both items became symbols of America's triumph of engineering and industrial organization, making each affordable and the object of ladies' proper domestic pursuits. By the first decades of the twentieth century, piano manufacturers could not rely on the Victorian sensibility of the "angel in the house." Irene Castle, the ballroom dancer who has been called "the first representative of the 'New Woman' of the twentieth century," declared that women should no longer be domestic matrons but active and free. Dance and music had an important role to play as did the player piano.

"How many thousands of American parlors contain that shining monument to past girlhood—a silent piano?" wondered player piano manufacturer J.T. Wamelink & Son of Cleveland, Ohio, in 1905.[32] Why were they dormant? Since at least the eighteenth century, particularly in Europe, young women were given lessons on the pianoforte to encourage them to become well suited to provide evening entertainment as well as agreeable companions to their husbands in their arranged marriages. It was a duty rather than a passion to play.

A story in *The Musical Times* in 1924 pointed out why the new technology of a player piano might change women's appreciation of music. A young lady was brought up in a Scottish provincial home in the 1880s, "where the sense of duty was inculcated by precept and punishment," and the sense of art received little recognition. She had pianoforte lessons, "but teachers in those days seemed to regard it as a duty to instill only difficult and dull music," she said. She studied for years, attended concerts and operas, but left to herself, she admitted, "I should never again willingly have read of music or listened to it." The piano on which she was once forced to demonstrate her polite talents was promptly abandoned.

However, she underwent a "conversion" that resulted from three significant events. First, she got married to a man who, "although preoccupied with scientific research, yet realized the joy of music, and consequent recognition of the fact that 'there was something lacking in me, that some unknown sense required development.'" Second, she took an interest in the dancing of Maud Allan, who choreographed and performed dances to the music of Bach, Schubert, and Mendelssohn. Third was the "purchase of a player-piano upon which the Maud Allan music could be played." It was reported that this woman now returned home every evening and practiced reproducing classical music on her player piano, which allowed for her "personal musical growth."[33] The player piano allegedly saved her marriage.

In America, an advertising blitz of the late 1910s and 1920s featured women as players. "The American Player Piano in the Home is the Delight of the American Girl," said an Ampico advertisement. "How Your Daughter will Love a Reproducing Piano!" assured Welte-Mignon, whose advertisements featured a ghostly illustration of the "phantom hands of a thousand immortal pianists" hovering over the keyboard. With ease, the pianos that sat silent could now come alive again and provide a means of stimulating one's artistic passions. "The Pianola action affords the individual a means of playing the piano and giving artistic expression to [one's] own ideas of music," explained an Aeolian Company advertisement.[34]

Aware of the conservative critiques of the "New Woman" image and the condemnations of moral guardians who attacked the "perversions of play," companies needed to promote a range of music, including ragtime rolls, while pitching the benefits of a player piano for the conventional study of music. The Melville Clark Piano Company produced a pamphlet for the Apollo Player titled "A Word to the Cultured Woman" and asked, "Do you want the HIGHEST type of music in your home? If you are not an accomplished pianist yourself . . . you will want a player in your home, one that will render the greatest musical compositions in an artistic manner."[35] Above all, the once contemplative and "intellectual" music of the European masters—what was laborious or "dull" to learn—was now accessible.

"I *like* my lessons," said the young girl in the *Saturday Evening Post* advertisement for the Standard Pneumatic Action Company, which pointed out that their self-playing mechanism made the job of a music teacher easier. With the disembodied heads of classical musicians gazing over a woman in a dinner gown sitting at a player piano, a 1914 advertisement by the Starr Piano Company asked, "What Stands Between You and the Music of the Masters?" Nothing! Their upright piano "removed every barrier of technical inability and gives you access to all the music of all time. With one of these players at your command the most classical selection is no more difficult than the latest popular song and [with their piano] you can produce the grandeur of one or the ragtime swing of the other with equal success."[36]

The enjoyment of "player pianism," the technique of properly controlling the player, was quick to catch on. As early as 1912, Gustav Kobbé, a music critic and prolific author, wrote a tract called *The Pianolist*—a guide for pianola players—after experiencing its effects first-hand. "One night I was at my desk in my study, when, suddenly, I heard the strains of this impromptu"—Schubert's "Rosamunde." Enchanted by the "sweet and tender, graceful and expressive" character of the performance, he hurried to his drawing room to see what virtuoso was at his piano. "Entering it, I found my fourteen-year-old daughter seated at a Pianola."[37] It was less remarkable that his daughter was performing Schubert with such expression than that Kobbé was ostensibly deceived into thinking a "live" pianist was in his home. Indeed, he later invited two friends around, one a "great virtuoso" and the other a druggist from Detroit and was bemused by the fact that a schoolgirl could play like the virtuoso while the druggist was offering playing tips to the music critic. "What a leveler of distinctions, what a universal musical provider the Pianola is!" he declared. The musical elect and those who would have formerly remained "outside the pale" were now on "common footing." "This may not always appeal to the musical elect," he thought, "but think [of] what it means to the great mass."[38]

While women's tastes and musical talents were an important point of appeal in the commercial culture of early twentieth-century America, men were also included, but to a much subtler degree, in the sales hype of player pianos that underscored the masculine element of mechanization: men should be particularly interested in player pianos because of their interest in machines.[39] By inviting middle-class consumers to participate effortlessly in, rather than passively listen to, musical performance, piano manufactures forged a new way to pursue "a revolutionary musical democracy in America."[40]

The "masses" did not disappoint. In 1909, 45,000 player pianos were sold. In 1919, sales jumped to a staggering 208,000, generating almost one hundred million dollars in revenue.[41] In 1918, the *New York Times* reported on the "Rush for Player Pianos," stating that people were arriving at dealers in hoards to see what kind of arrangement they could make for exchanging their old piano for the player type. "The result," it said, "is that manufacturers . . . are finding it increasingly difficult to meet the swollen call for player pianos."[42] The potential for producing a new order of virtuosi on a mass scale, converting suburbia into "Tin Pan America," startled the *American Architect*, a magazine that began reporting on practical methods for noise abatement. The American comic writer J. P. McEvoy immortalized his feelings about living in the player piano age in his 1919 poem "The Player Piano Upstairs":

> My soul once was cluttered with gladness and joy,
>   My heart was a haven of glee;
> Each syllable uttered was larded and buttered
>   With gayfulness airy and free.
> My garret cephalic with japeries Gallic
>   Was crammed to exclusion of cares,
> But all this has passed on the winds of the blast—
>   There's a player piano upstairs.
>
> And now ev'ry morning when faint for repose
>   I hear its matutinal fuss,
> Which when I no longer may slumber grows stronger
>   And stronger till madly I cuss,
> Yea, bitterly cuss the sarcophagus ghoul
>   Who chauffeurs with murderous fin
> Insane permutations of sad syncopations
>   Accented, I'd say, on the 'sin.'
>
> It tortures the Poet and Peasant all day,
>   And Rubenstein's Melody F,
> And C. Rusticana that ghoulish pian-a
>   Abuses in every clef.
> The Rosary, too, from its wallops is blue,
>   And Killarney it tatters and tears—
> O, words are inutile and puerile and futile
>   To limn that piano upstairs.
>
> And that's why my soul, once a clutter of joy,
>   And my heart once a haven of glee,
> Are sadly senescent, with sorry liquescent,
>   A dunnage of dreary debris.
> My onion cephalic once gayfully Gallic
>   Is now an asylum of cares,
> My loony medulla, alas! Is the fool-a
>   That player-piano upstairs.[43]

An article in the *New York Times* titled "Commercialized Pianissimo" suggested that in the future a prospective property hunter will begin with the question: "Is it soundproof?"[44]

For all the claims about "Perfection without Practice," however, performing at the player was not as easy as it was set out to be.[45] Some novices who sat down at the piano and began pedaling away, unfamiliar with the role that the levers in front of the keyboard had in regulating the tempo or the sensitivity required by the feet for controlling pneumatic suction, were aghast by what they heard themselves produce. One woman said she found herself "horribly at the mercy of the demon," the phantom that was contained within.[46] While amateurs did not want the trouble of learning to play an instrument, dealers did not want potential buyers to learn that this particular instrument required study. On the other hand, for all the emphasis that was placed on the player piano's ability to avoid practice and resurrect the life of dead masters through mechanical wizardry, it is ironic that it did prove effective as a means of teaching individuals how to become highly skilled musicians. Player pianos did in fact make pianists out of people who had no other inducement to study music.

Chapter 8

Expression

"There will be no 'boos' tonight," a man at the front of the room announced. "No booze!" cried those around me. "Champagne is included in the price of the ticket!" "*Boos*, my friends, we will not boo the pianist!"

TYPICALLY good-spirited banter at these events, I thought. I was once again at the magnificent Victorian home of Richard Reutlinger, who was hosting an evening ragtime and jazz concert by the trio Ivory & Gold, with Connecticut-based ragtime pianist Jeff Barnhart; his wife, flutist Anne; and drummer Danny Coots from Nashville. Barnhart, who has been playing ragtime since he was fourteen, is a self-described "pianist, vocalist, arranger, bandleader, recording artist, composer, pedagogue and entertainer."[1] He has toured the world, performing at festivals, at concerts, and on cruises; is the manager of the jazz band Titan Hot 7; and has his own record label, Jazz Alive Records. He met Reutlinger about a dozen years ago at a jazz festival, and after seven years of prodding, the group finally included this intimate setting during a West Coast tour.

About forty guests showed up for the event, which took place in Reutlinger's drawing room. Eighteen-foot high ceilings and expansive bay windows kept the air circulating. The velvet chaise lounges and high-back chairs had been pushed into the adjacent dining room to make space for five rows of folding chairs facing the 1928 Steinway grand fitted with Aeolian's Duo-Art player system. As we filed into the house, we could hear ragtime emanating from the piano.

"I wonder if that is the pianist or the player piano," I commented to another guest.

"You have seen Richard's collection, then," said another guest. "It is remarkable, isn't it?"

"Are you a fan of automated mechanical music?" I asked, not assuming that there would be an overlap between the membership of the West Coast Ragtime Society, where this concert was advertised, and the AMICAns, even though ragtime music is so characteristic of the music in the heyday of player pianism—the music all AMICAns "dig," according to Reutlinger.

"Oh, yes," the guest replied. "I have well-developed legs from all the pumping I did as a child. I loved 'The Maple Leaf Rag.'"

As we entered the drawing room, the music stopped. Jeff Barnhart was standing next to the Steinway. I didn't ask if what I'd heard was live or a piano roll. As we settled down, Barnhart announced that given that he was trained in jazz, while his wife was trained as a classical flutist, there was only one obvious genre of music they could play together: ragtime. "Often in ragtime you can hear undertones of European classical music come through," said Barnhart. "Most ragtime players were trained in the classical style." When asked what they were going to be performing that night, Barnhart replied that they would be *creating*. "Performing," it seemed, was too much like repeating another artist's composition. "It's improvisation. New patterns and rhythms emerge in the context of performance. We've put together versions that you've never heard so you can't compare us to anyone else."

It seemed an unusual trio: a drummer who alternated with the bongos, a flutist who touched on the whole register of notes on her twenty-four-carat gold-plated flute, and a pianist who commented on the uniqueness of playing piano keys covered with real ivory. However, the combination worked wonders. They started off with Charles Hunter's "Back to Life"—"He didn't get to play in the Reutlinger mansion," said Barnhart, "he played in much less healthy places"— and after an hour that incorporated the works of Eubie Blake, Gershwin, and others, they were ready to break. "Richard's magnificent pianolas downstairs are itching to be played," said Barnhart, "and I'm eager to hear them."

As I made my way through the ballroom downstairs where the bulk of Reutlinger's collection is housed, I spotted Coots, the drummer, admiring the Mills Violano. "An amazing technology," said Coots, "the music of magic." I told Coots that I was quite interested to know what musicians think of automated mechanical musical instruments, given the experience and familiarity with their own.

"I think they are great," said Coots.

"How do you feel about automated drums?" I asked.

As if overheard by the spirit within a nearby orchestrion, suddenly the sound of smashing cymbals and beating drums flooded the ballroom. "There you go!" said Coots, with a childlike grin on his face, "It can keep the beat, and it's about a hundred years old!"

"What do you think when you listen to this?" I asked. "Can you sense people playing—entertainers hidden within the technology?"

"I don't think of people," said Coots. "It just captures the context for me. It captures the edge of the music. The sounds are not like they are today in mass-produced music. We're listening to the way it was heard when the technology and the music was new. This is the era of the birth of American music, ragtime, and this technology was born at the same time. That is what is captured here."

"We're listening to the sounds of history," I said.

"Yeah, music as it was heard *at the time*. It provides a sort of connection to that place in history when everything was new."

"Does this connection allow you to learn something about ragtime?" I asked, "something that reading sheet music wouldn't allow you to do?"

"It is within the quality of the machines themselves. The way these sound is not like our modern instruments. Listening to these and how the music is put together, how the music was arranged for it to be recorded on these instruments, is getting into the mindset of what it was like to record a hundred years ago. It is about different recording styles. Not only is it the sound of history, it is the history of different recording styles. We've gone through our own changes with this recently—we used to record each instrument separately then put it together on a track. Today we all play in the same room at the same time when we record. We want that edge."

"I want that Steinway," said Barnhart, who had joined the conversation, tapping his toe and sipping a large flout of sparkling wine. "The quality of it is incredible. I put the sustaining pedal down and Anne plays the flute over the strings and the harmony reverberates throughout the room. You don't get that on cheap pianos."

"It is amazing it was built in 1928," I said, "around the same time as most of these machines. What do you think—do these capture the essence of the entertainer who originally recorded for them?"

"No," said Barnhart, definitively. "That's like asking does a circus capture the essence of . . . you know, I can't think of a metaphor of what a circus can capture."

"You!" said Coots. "The circus is the essence of *you*."

"No, really," continued Barnhart, "they are ingenious machines, but they don't capture the dynamics or the rubato of the music. They don't take the place of the human. We're not out of jobs yet!"

"You know, there were musicians who allegedly believed that the player pianos *did* capture the way they themselves played," I offered. "When they heard their recording on the player, some, like Stravinsky, claimed that it was the only true interpretation of his music, and he was glad that history would preserve that."

"If creation occurs during performance, then what does that say about recording it and replaying it?" wondered Barnhart. "How could it be said that what we are listening to was *the way* the artist wanted his music interpreted, when if the artist were to play it again new patterns might emerge?"

"Yeah, and who gives a——what the artist wants?" said a guest from the crowd gathered around us. "Ragtime and jazz—it is not about control or imprisoning a particular expression. It is *freedom* of expression."

Thus, a small debate ensued about whether the player piano—or any recording for that matter—only captures a memento of what the music is all about: the performance as it was at that time, freezing the music in a moment, rather than perpetuating its life. The musicians themselves, especially ragtime and jazz performers, did not repeat their performances exactly. As the jazz musician and conductor Gunther Schuller wrote,

> The musician played what those who hired him wanted to hear and in the manner in which they wanted to hear it. It was the *milieu*, ranging from rough honky-tonks to the sedate salons of the rich gentry, that determined how and what he played. He might indeed play "The Maple Leaf Rag" in any and all of these establishments, but he'd play it one way here and another there. He'd clean it up there and dirty it up here. He'd play it straight here to impress his host, and he'd "fool around with it" there to arouse his clients to greater heights of spending.[2]

"Perhaps it would be truer to form if the player piano was programmed to improvise some notes," I suggested to the others. "But then there is always the way that a person who pedals an old player piano can change the tempo and so on to reinterpret the piece." I recalled the story of Scott Joplin's 1902 rag "The Entertainer." Thanks to the movie *The Sting*, people have become familiar with it as a fast-paced tune. But Joplin's version was meant to be played at a deliberate tempo. When people hear a rag played at the original speed on a player piano, they ask for it to be played at a faster tempo. "Maybe it is not the intention of the composer or the limitations of the technology but popular opinion that decides how something is played," I remarked. It was a sentiment borrowed from the music critic (later CIA spy) Henry Pleasants from his 1955 book *The Agony of Modern Music*; he said that jazz "has taken music away from the composers and given it back to musicians and their public. The simplicity sought by serious composers through intellectual and technical experimentation has been achieved by practicing musicians guided by popular taste."[3]

Since Reutlinger also has in his collection an Aeolian player with the Metrostyle feature which allowed people to perform the piece according to the composer's intentions, I took the opportunity to mention the comments offered by the *Musical Courier* in 1903 just weeks after the Aeolian Company first advertised the Metrostyle:

> What is going to be the result of this thing? Here we have an invention which is going to be the first to perpetuate interpretations. For instance, a Chopin nocturne can be indicated by Paderewski, by Rosenthal, by Bauer, by Busoni, by d'Albert. These five pianists all play a composition differently and their interpretations of Chopin differ, and yet by means of the Metrostyle and the Pianola we can obtain records of Chopin nocturnes interpreted by these five masters, and in five, twenty-five, fifty-five, or a hundred years from now people will be able to play them on the piano exactly as these pianists play them now! . . . They are on record now. At any time hereafter any performer can learn exactly how Moszkowski interprets his own compositions.[4]

While I was able to offer only the gist of this opinion in the *Musical Courier* to the discussion, the point was that player pianos were seen in the industry as devices that could capture and preserve artists' intentions—his or her own interpretation of their music. In a sense, contrary to the spirit of ragtime and jazz, the player piano—which nevertheless worked so efficiently in spreading the music that ultimately put improvisation and freedom of expression on the musical map—was ironically seen as a device that worked against freedom of interpretation. It seemed that classical composers appreciated the ability to capture, or freeze, their performance in time. African American music, however, which stressed the emotion and soul of the performer, fostered expression that could not be reduced to mechanical principles. Given this reality, I began to wonder how African American artists became so involved with the player piano industry. However, this thought was preempted by one last mechanical music performance before the second half of the ragtime concert.

Reutlinger had most of the crowd gathered around him and the photoplayer as he started to perform the music that would accompany a film, just as he had demonstrated it to me months earlier. He pulled one cord and the train whistle blew, while tugging at another cord produced the sound of gun shots. As his show came to an end, a guest yelled out, "You play very well, Richard." "Don't I?" he replied.

I left the concert at Reutlinger's thinking about the musicians' attitudes toward the capabilities and limitations of automated musical instruments. Clearly, spectators were captivated by musical instruments that play by themselves, often remarking about the feeling that the spirit of the musician resides within the machine. However, musicians, I figured, would be more weary of the allegation that musical expression could be captured. I wondered about the degree to which Stravinsky's comments might have been commercial spin-doctoring, a mere advertising ploy by the manufacturers following an old and established strategy of using celebrity endorsements. However, the more I explored press accounts from the early twentieth century, the more I discovered that such claims about the humanlike interpretations of the machine were widespread. Perhaps this was due to the sheer novelty of this kind of recorded music. With the exception of the poor-quality phonograph records and pin-barrel music boxes, in the early 1900s there was no listening to instruments that were not played "live." Therefore, getting the entertainer *out* of one's mind was no easy task.

An advertisement from Chickering & Sons pianos, which were built with its parent company's (the American Piano Company) Ampico player system, featured "The Hands of Liszt," a title that was printed in bold face at the top of a cardboard poster. An engraving in the upper left corner showed a detail of long, bony fingers playing a Chickering piano, with the caption "Drawn from life in 1876" printed below it. A Chickering is what Liszt owned during his career at the Royal Conservatory at Budapest. In his own words, "I must declare them perfect, and perfectissimes [sic] (superlatively perfect)," by which one presumes he refers both to his hands and to the Chickering piano. The text was brief and to the point: Buy a Chickering and you buy Liszt's hands. "Hands that caressed the keys of the piano, drawing from the instrument the sobbing beauty of a nocturne or awakening Jovian thunders of tonal splendor."[5] With the Ampico system built into Liszt's preferred piano, customers were told they could possess those famous fingers forever.

Another elaborate advertisement by Welte Mignon that appeared in *Harper's*, *Atlantic Monthly*, and other fashionable magazines reproduced a typed, signed letter from Vladimir de Pachmann. In it, he stated that "I have always looked for a mechanism which would serve to perpetuate my playing for future generations so that I, as an interpretive artist, might end my career with the assurance that my art would live forever." He found it, he said, with the Welte Mignon, though he had tried to immortalize himself by recording for the Gramophone and Typewriter Company in London as early as 1907.[6] It was the piano rolls, however, that he felt best preserved his pianism. "In them I found my 'alter ego,' the sound of my own playing coming out of a piano without a pianist, invisible hands rendering the spell of my Chopin, my Liszt."[7]

Music critics were also seduced by the humanness of the machine. "I have never heard a machine produce music like that," wrote the noted German conductor Augustus Manns in Britain's *Daily Mail* in 1903. He had just attended the Musical Instrument Exhibition at the Crystal Palace and listened to a Cecilian push-up player manufactured by the Farrand Organ Company in London. "It expressed all the delicate nuances of the skilled musician, and the quality of its tone was beautiful. There is no reason why any man with the 'heavenly spark of music in his heart' should not produce music from it as fine as that of a Paderewski. A dozen Paderewskis in one could not play finer scales. No pianist could produce a greater effect upon my feelings than that machine did."[8]

At about the same time that Manns was singing the praises of the Cecilian player, a pianist trained at the Royal College of Music in London named Reginald Reynolds first came across the same model. He was manager of the piano department at Maple & Co., a department store in Tottenham Court Road, which had a Cecilian on display. So enthusiastic was Reynolds about the artistic possibilities of the push-up piano player that he arranged to give a public recital with it at London's Steinway Hall. While some people expressed skepticism that he could play an accompaniment with the machine, Reynolds insisted on testing the limits of the piano player. In front of a "good-sized and appreciative" audience, he accompanied a talented soprano named Maggie Purvis, who sang Francesco Tosti's "Goodbye" and Schubert's "Who is Sylvia?" "There being perfect control of the tempo," reported Reynolds, "I was able to follow all the effects of rubato these artists chose to introduce into their performances."[9]

Following this successful performance, which was among the very first public player piano concerts ever, Reynolds was hired by Farrand, who manufactured the Cecilian, and continued to offer recitals at a hall in Great Marlborough Street in the West End. While Reynolds noted the occasional dismissive remarks by "pompous" professors of music in his memoir, he also noted the rising interest in and admiration for this presentation of music. Aston Johnson, a well-known music critic, even sent Reynolds a note after he attended a recital, "saying that he had heard the great pianist Busoni play the same work the previous day and that he preferred my performance!"[10] Reynolds, who was dubbed "the Paderewski of the Player Piano," was next offered a job at the Aeolian Company's London offices, and throughout the 1910s he managed the recordings of various artists for the Duo-Art system. Referred to by the British press in 1934 shortly after his retirement as "probably the world's best player-pianist," Reynolds was convinced of the benefits of player piano roll recordings. Comparing all the pianists who performed at Aeolian Hall in London who left "no trace of those delightful sounds with which they have charmed their audience" to those who made their way to the top floor of the Aeolian building, where the recording room was, he proclaimed that the latter "there discovered a means of perpetuating their interpretation for all time."[11]

These and other accounts suggest that a number of artists, recorders, and an increasing number of consumers were claiming that a player piano roll *did* manage to preserve and reproduce a composition according to the interpretation of the original artist. Moreover, not only was it valued because the interpretation was preserved—safeguarded against *misinterpretation* by future pianists—but because it preserved a moment in history for future generations to appreciate. In ways similar to the way in which the daguerreotype or early photograph gave people the opportunity to envision a time when others would look at aspects of the lives of their forebears, paper music rolls offered the prospect of artistic immortality. There was a supposition that some spirit was preserved in the magical roll. Given this element of artistic preservation, I wondered whether something more personal about the entertainer could be revealed by studying this medium that would not have been preserved in phonograph recordings. I discovered that music historians had already begun this novel form of research.

Sheet music may be regarded as an instruction booklet: it is a representation of what one should do to achieve a certain result. However, a lot of improvisation, interpretation, or fiddling around emerges in the space between the printed symbol and a human performance. What is particularly useful about automated musical instruments is that their operations can be reviewed and approved by the artist to confirm that the end result is that which was intended. Therefore, a study of the way a machine was programmed can sometimes reveal the "thumb-print" of the master. Some musicologists have turned into sleuths by looking for original pieces of mechanical music that might give them further insight into the idiosyncrasies of a particular artist. In other ways, mechanical music can be investigated as a means of recovering musical history that is on the brink of obliteration. One remarkable find was the result of examining an instrument from an early era of automated mechanical musical instruments—a barrel organ built at the beginning of the nineteenth century. Such barrel organs were constructed with a rotating wooden cylinder studded with brass pins and elongated staples that actuated levers as the barrel rotated. The levers opened valves that allowed pressurized air to flow into organ pipes.

In 1819, an organ was built by a Dutch instrument maker who supplied a repertoire of barrel music. A century later, this organ was housed at the Nationaal Museum van Speelklok tot Pierement, in Utrecht, Netherlands. An examination of the barrels revealed an arrangement that was determined to have been written by Wolfgang Amadeus Mozart, for which no written score was known to exist. That the barrel preserved a "lost" Mozart piece is itself a curious find, as well as the fact that it was heard for the first time based on a performance "arranged" by an early nineteenth-century instrument maker. However, when scholars began investigating other barrels in their quest for lost music, they discovered something else of interest.

In the 1920s a piece identified as having been composed by Haydn was discovered on another barrel, and its notes were transcribed into staff notation by a musician. Subsequently, an original score of the piece with subtle notational differences was discovered in Haydn's hand. The music played on the organ was exactly what Haydn had written, but the differences between the composer's and the music as transcribed from the barrel lay in the style of notational interpretation, suggesting that conventions of notation have changed.

The implications of this find were stated by the author and mechanical music enthusiast, Arthur W.J.G. Ord-Hume: "Without documents such as these to demonstrate to us what was intended, styles of musical interpretation remain blurred and, with the passing of time, whole new meanings are read into music while other, authentic ones are obliterated."[12] Without the "recorded" piece on the mechanical musical instrument, there would have been no opportunity to transcribe the music, and then later to compare that against Haydn's own staff notation. This offered a reverse demonstration of differences in interpretation—the piece was heard first then interpreted into notation.

Music rolls have their own ways of documenting differences between them and live performances as well. In 1950, a University of Minnesota professor and professional musician, Russell Roth, was investigating the history of ragtime in light of the recent "ragtime revival" that followed the appearance of a popular biography, *Mister Jelly Roll*, by Alan Lomax. Roth became interested in Scott Joplin and listened to a live performance of his work by the white ragtime pianist S. Brun Campbell, known as "Joplin's disciple" since he studied with Joplin at the Maple Leaf Club in Sedalia, Missouri, in 1899. After the performance, Professor Roth tracked down a number of Joplin's piano rolls and compared them to the performance he had heard. He determined that Campbell's playing was "stiff" and "European" sounding, "rather than Negroid in style, uncertain in tempo." It was somewhat of a revelation to Roth, who appreciated the fact that the piano rolls permitted him to listen to a style of playing—"performing their own music as they [the artists] intended that it should be played"—that had otherwise disappeared.[13]

Roth's remarks convey the implicit assumption that ragtime performance sounded different when played by whites as opposed to blacks—an insight he gained by comparing the Joplin recorded roll of "The Maple Leaf Rag" and other tunes to a performer who allegedly trained under Joplin. Some piano rolls might therefore be said to possess a certain element of ethnicity, derived from the cultural background of the recording artist who produced the roll.

Additionally, music rolls might also figure in a historical debate that stems back to the period when ragtime and African American music generally were first becoming popular: Could white musicians (re)create it? Playing ragtime is difficult—handled best by talented performers on well-maintained instruments. One white musician with exceptional keyboard ability was George Gershwin.

Of Gershwin's ability, Eubie Blake remarked that "James P. Johnson and Lucky Roberts told me of this very talented ofay [white] piano player at Remick's. They said he was good enough to learn some of those terribly difficult tricks that only a few of us could master."[14] Beginning in 1915, Gershwin recorded piano rolls for the Standard Music Roll Company, continuing later with the Aeolian Company and Welte-Mignon. Studying his rolls offers insight not only into his capabilities but into his flashes of inspiration. Pianist and music historian Artis Wodehouse, who in 1993 organized the release of his piano rolls re-recorded onto a CD titled *Gershwin Plays Gershwin*, found that "Gershwin interjects original ideas in the introductions, breaks, and riffs; enriches or alters harmonizations; and fleshes out bass lines beyond the published sheets."[15] Listening to Gershwin play his own compositions recorded on rolls that he produced over a number of years, Wodehouse detected moments when he employed popular piano tricks such as using parallel fourths and fifths for the basis of his compositions. His rolls revealed traits of his evolving style of play. Not only was a particular performance preserved but characteristics of the individual performer as well.

Since the *Gershwin Plays Gershwin* CD, which *Time* magazine called "A remarkable example of technology put to the service of art," a number of other piano roll performances have become available on CD.[16] These seem to appeal to customers who want the authenticity inherent in music rolls. One can now buy a compact disc titled *Classic Movie & Broadway Show Tunes from Rare Piano Rolls*, and the New York Public Library has a collection of 33 1/3 rpm LPs from the 1970s with parlor piano solos recorded from "rare piano rolls," an ironic expropriation of one means of recording by another that was once (if not still) considered inferior. This suggests that the artist's intention can be preserved within the technology of the piano roll, and a player piano can bring it back to life.

Through modern forms of audio reproduction, millions can hear precisely the same song. Nothing sounds "live" about it. Indeed, the difference between listening to a live performance and a recorded song is striking. It can be doctored so much in the studio that even the original artist might not be able to duplicate it. Yet in the early twentieth century, despite the praise of those who marveled at the ability of the player piano to reproduce the nuances and expression of the original artist, some music critics held that the imperfections were precisely what made music beautiful. For them, any mechanical reproduction of music was monotonous. Art should move "from soul to soul," reported a 1929 article titled "The Esthetics of Contemporary Music" in the *Musical Quarterly*.[17] Differing from the opinion that player pianos and other mechanical musical instruments were marvels of technological wizardry, the Dutch composer Willem Pijper thought that the association with speed and power that lies within mechanically produced music was the antithesis of "the mystery that was the living center of all art."[18] As the historians of technology Trevor Pinch and Karin Bijsterveld have alleged in their study of the introduction of new musical technologies in the twentieth century (particularly the Moog synthesizer), the mechanical style of this music, despite its novelty and its own mysterious effects, was distinct and characteristic. Player piano music produced a "clearness, exactness and preciseness" that distinguished it from a live performance.[19] Hence, the elimination of error from a roll recording made it seem less plausible that one was hearing live music.

Not only music critics but the manufacturers of piano rolls recognized that the recording of a pianist's performance would not sound natural to the ear. Surprisingly however, this had less to do with the presence or elimination of errors in play than with manipulating the arrangement to add unplayed notes to the roll. While the advertising hype remained centered on the assertion that this was *how the artist wanted a tune to be heard*, what was not well-known was that an editor, or arranger, of the roll had a hand in its final form. In order to make the roll sound "natural," to render the desired expression, it often had to be doctored in a way that is impossible for an artist to perform. The subtle and nuanced art of arranging piano rolls became a major element in the successful sale of player piano rolls. To these invisible technicians fell much of the work of making saleable music. This career fell into the lap of J. Lawrence Cook.

The first stop on Lawrence's job-hunting list after he arrived in New York in 1920 was unsurprisingly the Aeolian Company, the producers of James P. Johnson's rolls. However, when the president of the roll division heard the arrangement they asked him to create, he said, "Well, Lawrence, it ain't brilliant enough."[20] Lawrence's talent as a pianist was not being judged. While he did play for them, the job he was attempting to obtain was that of arranger, the person who converted the marked ("recorded") roll to a properly checked and edited arrangement of punched holes. Thus, Alfred Dolge's opinion that the metaphor of a photograph was not an accurate one to describe the recording piano is appropriate, but not because of his assertion that a piano roll captured the "soul" of the performer. If anything, the process captured the interventions of a skilled technician who adapted the live performance to suit the capabilities of the player piano.[21]

Disappointed but not dejected (Lawrence described himself as "cocky" and was sure his abilities would be recognized), he kept his job as a busboy and practiced his technique of arranging rolls with his Lebarjean perforator. The arranger whose rolls he studied as a model was Victor Arden, dubbed "King of the Piano Roll." Throughout the 1920s, he and Phil Ohman recorded hundreds of songs and piano rolls featuring the duo's "pyrotechnical" keyboard style. "He's the one person that I thought had done the most to develop this as a separate art in the music field," said Lawrence, who was one of the first to appreciate the skill of editing music rolls as a new musical craft. After some further study, Lawrence decided that he "had the art of arranging down pretty good, mechanical arranging," and he was off once again to see about a job, this time where Arden was employed.

Victor Arden was an accomplished musician, a graduate with a music degree from the University of Chicago and the American Conservatory of Music. In the late 1910s he moved to New York and played piano to accompany short movies and to provide popular music for "talking machine records." In 1919, he was hired by the QRS Music Company as a "player roll artist" and in their words brought "individuality and charm" to their business.[22] And what a business it was! QRS was one of the three businesses overseen by Melville Clark, who, in the words of a reporter in 1918, "has a superior personal knowledge of mechanism and principles of musical instrument manufacture than anyone else."[23] Besides the roll business, he owned the Melville Clark Piano Company and half of Story & Clark Pianos, both of which had rapidly grown over the past two decades.

In 1901, Melville Clark had opened a new factory in Grand Haven, Michigan, for the production of Story & Clark player pianos, keeping their general offices on South Wabash Avenue in Chicago. Everything was crafted in-house. White spruce was used for the sounding board, rock maple for the bridges, with a mahogany finish. "The cases are the creations of artists," the company stated in a booklet explaining their production, "not merely draftsmen or copyists— hence the appealing originality of the design of all Story & Clark pianos." It took six months to produce a piano, and over three hundred thousand of them had been manufactured since the company was founded in 1896. Teams of workers concentrated on specialized tasks. Pictures showed a room with a dozen women working with the ivory used to cover each natural key, while other rooms were full of craftsmen carving the cabinets and assembling the pieces. They were producing, they said, "an instrument not only for a single lifetime, but for many lifetimes—*an instrument worthy to become a family heirloom.*"

Roll production, the other side of Melville Clark's business, was also flourishing. Such were the sales that by 1911 QRS was created as a separate company in De Kalb, Illinois (where the Melville Clark Piano Company, which produced the Apollo) was built. One legend suggests that the origin of the company name stemmed from the overflow of roll orders (filed under "R") being stuffed into the empty adjacent "Q" and "S" slots in the office's mail filing system. Whatever the precise etiology of its name, the rolls they produced later printed a slogan that captured the company's mission: to provide "Quality Real Service."[24] Over the next decade, the company grew to become the largest manufacturer of player piano rolls in the world.

In 1918, Melville Clark passed away. The Melville Clark Piano Company was purchased by Wurlitzer, while Story & Clark continued to be controlled by the descendants of Hampton Story. It was eventually sold to CMI, Chicago Musical Instrument Company, which was bought by Lowrey Organ Company in 1962.[25] In late 1918, QRS was bought by a veteran employee of the company, Thomas Pletcher, who oversaw the opening of factories in San Francisco, Toronto, and Sydney, Australia. The New York offices on East 135th Street were opened in 1919, the year Victor Arden was hired. Two years later, Lawrence was interviewing for a job with the same company.

Everything was going well for QRS at this moment. One of their Chicago employees, the general manager of the recording department named Max Kortlander, had just shot to fame after turning his attention from classical music—which, like Arden, he had studied at the American Conservatory in Chicago—to composing "popular works," ballads, and music for the fox-trot. He had just moved to the New York branch when Arden joined the team, and that same year one of Kortlander's compositions, "Tell Me," was sold to the Remick publishing firm for one hundred thousand dollars, providing the basis of a family fortune.[26] With lyrics by J. Will Callahan and a recording by Al Jolson, among others, it became a huge hit.

The efforts of Kortlander, Arden, and another QRS artist who joined the "fellowship" in 1919, Phil Ohman, resulted in the soaring popularity of songs from Jolson, Gershwin, and others whose music they arranged on player piano rolls. In total, QRS employed five hundred people and was turning out fifty thousand rolls a day.[27] One thing they lacked, however, was a specialist in ragtime and blues. In December 1920, things were about to change.

Since his rejection at the Aeolian Company, Cook had been cutting rolls freelance on his home perforator for a company that paid eleven dollars for each master roll they liked. During this time his skills developed and his reputation began to spread. It was Kortlander's keen eye that spotted his talent, and Lawrence was summoned to the offices of QRS.

Kortlander was by now not only a famous musician but a skilled businessman as well. As concerned about the success of QRS as its owner, Pletcher, Kortlander kept a close eye on everything the competition was doing and had collected a number of their rivals' rolls. A stack of these were on his desk when Lawrence walked in. "Lawrence, these rolls here," said Kortlander, "I don't know, this is kind of bothering us. It's getting that U.S. [the United States Music Company that bought Lawrence's homemade rolls] is beginning to outsell us. They've got some guy. We hear it's you."[28]

This must have inflated Lawrence's ego to no end and immediately put him at ease. When Kortlander slid one across the table, Lawrence knew it well.

"I did it."
"What about this one?" asked Kortlander.
"Yes, that's me."
"Did you do all this counter stuff?"

Image courtesy of QRS Music Inc.

Max Kortlander (1890–1961). Kortlander was a musician-businessman who earned a fortune from royalties on his hit 1919 fox-trot "Tell Me." Having seen the amazing success of QRS as an employee when it sold 10 million rolls in 1927, Kortlander purchased the company in 1932 and saw the piano roll business through the trying times of the Great Depression; he witnessed its early revival beginning in the 1950s.

This made Lawrence proud. QRS, the largest manufacturer of piano rolls in the world, with a huge new plant across town filled with machinery punching thousands of rolls to mass-produce the music, was impressed with Lawrence's home-punched work. "Well, how'd you like to work for us steady?" said Kortlander. "You mean full-time?" asked Lawrence.

He did not know what to say, but one thing was clear: Kortlander "was not going to let me get out of there without a signature."

The significance of that moment cannot be overstated. The teaming of black and white musicians to work in such a business context was unprecedented. Lawrence—"Cookie"—joined the fellowship and published his first roll for QRS, "Dying with the Blues," a few months later. This was quickly followed by an arrangement of a song by his first idol, James P. Johnson: "Carolina Shout."

Chapter 9

A Race for
the Rolls

J. LAWRENCE COOK was the first full-time African American creator of piano rolls. His arrival at QRS Music Rolls marked the beginning of the piano roll industry's answer to phonograph companies' early stake in the jazz and blues market and their interest in creating so-called "race labels," similar to the Black Swan record label.[1] The black musician to whom Lawrence turned his attention as a source for piano rolls was his idol, James P. Johnson. "I did everything that Johnson did," he said, referring to the corpus of James's music.[2] While James still continued to publish his own rolls for Aeolian, he was by now New York's top African American pianist, if not the best in all categories. So, from Lawrence's first 1921 "Johnson" rolls, a number of renditions of his songs became available through QRS.

The version of "Carolina Shout" that Lawrence arranged was different from the one that Artempo produced in 1918. It had slightly different bass patterns and rhythmic phrasing. Being an interpreter as well as an arranger meant more than "getting holes in paper in the right place," as Lawrence once wryly described the process.[3] Each roll combined the notes of a composition, the traces of a live performance, and, finally, the personalized touch of the editor. Each roll—within the arrangement of thousands of holes—carried the "signature" of the person who created it. Therefore, anyone who studied the performance of a composition by sitting at the player piano (in the manner in which the companies suggested one could use it to learn to play) was experiencing a presentation by a secondary invisible entertainer, a hidden technician. It is thus arguable, then, that one of Lawrence's first "pupils" was Thomas "Fats" Waller.

In 1921, seventeen-year-old Waller had reached his final height of 5'7" but had not yet grown into the 285-pound man with stubby fingers that earned him the "Fats" sobriquet. He was also still learning to play the piano. Waller was born and raised in the heart of Harlem. As a delivery boy for a local delicatessen in his teens, he made many rounds to the clubs and rent parties where, as Willie "the Lion" Smith said, pianists "would wake up on the piano and then we went to bed on the piano." Fats's friend Wilson Brooks, a fellow student at Public School 89, had a player piano in his home, where Fats spent hours following the keyboard strokes with his fingers, imitating the motions that a live pianist would have made.[4]

One day Wilson's older brother, Russell Brooks—himself a talented stride pianist—walked in the room when Fats was at the player. "He was kind of embarrassed," said Russell. "Fats was practicing James P. Johnson's 'Carolina Shout'" using the newly released QRS roll. Russell thought it was good. A few months later, Waller performed the song with a conventional piano at a talent contest at the Roosevelt Theater and won.[5] At about the same time that Fats was enjoying newfound success as a stride pianist, he was frequenting the Lincoln Theater, one of two Harlem movie houses that catered to African American audiences. There he watched Mazie Mullins perform an elaborate accompaniment to the silent movies, and during intermission he was allowed to perform at the pipe organ. The Lincoln was a popular spot where many musicians attended shows, including Russell Brooks and J. Lawrence Cook. On one evening James P. Johnson was in the audience. Later that night he mentioned Fats to his wife, Lillie Mae, who had previously heard Fats play at Leroy's cabaret where she was a singer. "I know I can teach that boy," James said to Lillie. Fats had no idea that his idol had been in the audience.

A few weeks later, Russell Brooks happened to run into James on the street. "I asked him if he knew Fats Waller, the kid who played

the organ at the Lincoln."[6] James knew exactly whom he was referring to. Russell told him how much Fats wanted to meet him and
suggested that maybe James could "help him a little." He agreed. The
first time they met, James pulled up a stool and sat next to Fats. For
the first time Fats could see the entertainer's fingers at work, playing
trills and strong bass configurations. "He taught me more in an afternoon than I had learned in ten years," he said.[7]

With James P. Johnson as a mentor, all sorts of doors were
opened to Fats Waller. He was playing in clubs regularly, had rented
his own apartment, and soon had a wife and son. Despite his increasing popularity, though, money was as tight as his schedule. Only seventeen years old, he was more interested in playing the party circuit
than spending much time with the family. By his baby's third birthday, Fats was looking for a new place to live, extra money for ali-
mony, and—whenever he played the piano—another Mickey, a half-
pint of liquor. Knowing Fats needed a regular income, James had a
suggestion that would help. He was earning fifty dollars for each
player piano roll he recorded. He thought this would be a good line of
work for his "understudy" (as people called him) to get into. Having
admired the results of J. Lawrence Cook's interpretation of "Carolina
Shout" on the player piano roll, and appreciating the fact that Kortlander, Arden, and the others were musicians rather than just businessmen, James and Fats headed over to QRS Music Rolls.

This was another magical moment for the piano roll business,
enabling Lawrence to develop the "special department" that catered
to "race" music. In 1923, just after Cook had selected tunes for Fats
to record, QRS made the announcement that Waller and James P.
Johnson had been added to their list of recording artists, "through
which the characteristic music of the Negro Race would be made
available for the player piano and recorded by artists of their own
people, thus insuring accurate interpretations."[8] The trio made up of
the famous musician whose first commercial hit was a player piano
roll he recorded, the skilled technician devoted to producing rolls of
great entertainers, and the young student who learned to play the
piano by studying such piano rolls, made for a remarkable collaboration.

I had met quite a few people who appreciated having a player
piano because they were unable to play the instrument any other way.

I was also familiar with the advertising of the 1910s and 1920s proclaiming that possessing a player piano was the easy way to become an entertainer. The sales pitch of being able to play to "perfection without practice" made the point that the technology did all the work for the otherwise untalented customer. However, Fats Waller's experience with the player piano was a new twist to the tale. Instead of using the device to sidestep the acquisition of a pianist's skills, it became a surrogate instructor. For many Harlem youth surrounded by the buzz of excitement over the new sounds of African American music, with black musicians' reputations spreading across America and even to Europe, and desiring to be the centers of attraction as respected pianists, the only way to study music was with a player piano. It was a form of self-instruction technology with no need to pay a professor for tutelage. All the talk about having the master's fingers in one's home took on a new meaning. The player piano was not merely a spectacle of entertainment but also a form of education.

Associations were made between a collection of piano rolls and a library of books. One patron of QRS rolls explained that his library had two bookcases. "The one on the left contains the undying names of literature written in great books—my old, good friends. Here are Thackeray, Hawthorne, Eliot, Dickens, Scott, Hugo, and a score of the Titans who have journeyed on . . . .The other bookcase is filled with the names of masters also, the world's masters of music. Here is Beethoven's name, Chopin's, Wagner's. Here are the names of Liszt and Mendelssohn and Brahms, and many others besides. Here, too are the 'best sellers' in the music of our time."[9] Like a collection of books, the collection of music rolls provided instruction in the classics.

The educational value of mechanical music was also stressed by one defender of such instruments in the face of charges that machine-made music would spell the death of professional music. "This fear is groundless," wrote the poet and musician Robert Haven Schauffler in *The Century* magazine in 1914.

> Mechanical instruments will no more drive the good pianist or violinist or cellist out of his profession than the public library, as many once feared, will drive the bookseller and the author out of business. . . . The supreme value of mechanical music is its direct educational value. By this I mean something more than its educational value to the many thousands of grown men and women

whose latent interest in music it is suddenly awakening. I have in mind the girls and boys of the rising generation. . . . The reason why America is not more musical is that we men and women of today did not yesterday, as children, hear enough good music. Our parents probably could not afford it. It was then a luxury, implying expensive concert tickets or an elaborate musical training for some one in the family. The invention of mechanical instruments ended this state of things forever by suddenly making the best music as inexpensive as the worst.[10]

Also in 1914, an elaborate, quarto-sized, gold-leafed volume titled *The Weight of Evidence* was published by the Aeolian Company. Pitched to a wealthy audience, the book, itself a showpiece to be displayed near the Pianola, explained the many ways that the player piano makes music accessible, and therefore provided an educational function. "Our treasured heritage from those masters who spoke in music has been hidden in printed notes, and locked in instruments that called for gifted fingers and long and laborious training to search it out and give it back to us all to whom it belongs. But music is the inaccessible art no longer."[11]

Owing to the wonders of mechanical music, musical expression would become possible for "all of mankind." They considered the invention of automatic instruments to be equal in importance to the development of printing. "Just as the printing press opened the world of knowledge and literature and thought to all men instead of to the few, so the Pianola opens the world of music, of emotion, and of self-expression to all instead of merely to the few with talented fingers." The development of libraries and textbooks eventually helped to standardize the way children learn. Likewise, the player piano provided a new means for students to study music. As Aeolian said, "It provides the musical technique which throws open the doorway to the vast library of the world's musical literature . . . [to] all who would enter. . . . It imparts to the children a knowledge of and a taste for music of the highest type. It enables them actually to study music, not merely dull, monotonous technique, and brings to their daily practice hour the enthusiasm of appreciation and understanding."[12] It did this by "mental association," enabling the student to "watch" the expert play right in front of them.

All of this "evidence" was meant to echo music critic Gustav Kobbé's observation in 1912 that the player piano was a "leveler of distinctions." Player piano manufacturers agreed, declaring that they had forged a new way to pursue "a revolutionary musical democracy in America."[13] Yet when one studies the claim that the automated piano's ability to provide a repeatable musical experience was "democratizing," one may debate the degree to which this technology democratized music across all levels of society. The Aeolian Company's own Duo-Art Pianola, first introduced in 1913, was not built "for the people" but for the wealthy. By virtue of a 1909 agreement with Steinway & Sons, Aeolian was able to install the Duo-Art Pianola electrically-powered "reproducing system" in their elegant grands, which could cost up to five thousand dollars in those days. The music rolls that were widely advertised and produced for the Duo-Art, which were cut with a row of special holes on both sides that "automatically" controlled the expression—further de-skilling the technique of player pianism—reflected the preferred tastes of that class: Paderewski, Hofmann, Grainger, and other European classical pianists. The absence of African American music rolls for the Duo-Art is notable. The Aeolian Company offered only one roll by a black musician that would play on this high-end system, and that was Eubie Blake's "Negro Spirituals."

The older player pianos, however, which were often replaced by the electrically pumped reproducing piano, were sold secondhand and down-market, and certainly widened the market for black music. A similar situation was found at Ampico, which issued only two rolls of black pianists: Eubie Blake's "Charleston Rag" and J. Rosamonde Johnson's "Negro Spirituals." Artists who recorded for QRS Music Rolls, however, could have their rolls played on any of the Story & Clark line of player pianos available, which placed them in a position to develop a more accessible, class-neutral catalog of music. QRS aimed for and reached a wide audience, employing James P. Johnson, Fats Waller, Blind Boone, Eubie Blake, and others to assist J. Lawrence Cook in developing their "race" catalog.

In passing we should note that Fats learned how to play the piano on an older, foot-pumped player piano for which African American-inspired music was most widely available. As opposed to the more expensive electrically-powered reproducing pianos with automatically controlled tempo, the older foot-pumped players provided a less-economically-advantaged class with the training needed to play it manually. Had this educational function of the player piano ever been considered by modern music teachers? I was fortunate to receive an invitation from QRS Music Technology to be their guest at the National Association of Music Merchants (NAMM) annual convention in Anaheim, California. QRS's subsidiary, Story & Clark Pianos, had scheduled Scott "The Piano Guy" Houston, host of the widely popular PBS pledge show *Play Piano in a Flash!* as a guest speaker. I went to seek his opinion about the educational potential of the player piano.

The NAMM Expo is a major international trade show where manufacturers have exhibits allowing dealers to get "hands on" demonstrations of their merchandise—whether instruments, sheet music, amplifiers, or quirky inventions that fall between the standard categories. A four-day event in January, the expo draws tens of thousands of people exploring some 8,000 booths and sound rooms. Once there, I came across a crowd gathered around what sounded like a band playing. To my surprise, I discovered that they were being entertained by an automated ensemble composed of an electric guitar, drum set, and player piano belting out Credence Clearwater Revival's "Bad Moon Rising." It was an exhibition by "Automated Live Music Systems," and a sign on the amplifier announced that the company had won a silver medal at the Seoul International Invention Fair in 2004. I observed the amused crowd, most of them taking pictures of the spectacle and grooving on the music, eyes fixed on the entertainment. "Yeah!" yelled a young woman with nose ring and purple streaks in her hair, "Who needs that drummer anymore! Good riddance!"

The piano gallery was located in a third-floor ballroom. The first exhibit inside the doors was Story & Clark Pianos. Spread over 1,200 square feet were about two dozen new grand, baby grand, and upright pianos, both conventional instruments and others equipped with their modern "Pianomation" system that I had previously seen at my uncle's house. An upright player was located in a special exhibition space. Wired to a plasma TV, it was playing the music of Norah Jones synchronized to the screen video of her playing "live" in New Orleans. The camera occasionally showed a close-up of her hands on the keyboard. The player piano's keys moved in synchrony with the video performance. It was a more unusual experience than seeing "Rachmaninoff" play. The video's accompanying of the player piano would have made any philosopher think twice about what constitutes the essence of listening to a "live" performance.

A number of other pianos on display had different technologies that facilitated learning to play the instrument. Headsets could be plugged into one that silenced the sound of the hammers hitting the strings, allowing for practice that would allow one's neighbors to enjoy their peace. Another upright player piano had a plasma TV that emerged from the cabinet. The video playing on this screen was that of Scott Houston offering a mini-lesson on the "Tips and Cheap Tricks" of piano technique. While I was watching him on TV, Terry Dolan, a QRS representative, introduced me to "The Piano Guy" himself. Scott claims that he can teach anyone to play the piano in a matter of hours, not years. If the fact that he has raised over fourteen million dollars for public TV since 2003 is any indication (among the highest-grossing pledge specials in public television's broadcasting history), then there may well be a large public eager to take a shortcut to becoming pianists.

I explained to him that I was researching the history of the player piano and was interested in ways that it was, and might continue to be, an educational aid. I inquired whether he had ever thought about using it as part of his tool kit.

> "Imagine if this piano which is attached to a TV and playing your video was set up so that as you were explaining the principles of pianism the player piano could demonstrate what you are talking about, then the student could imitate it. Would that be helpful?"
>
> "We're already doing it," he answered. "Video sync'd along to the QRS recordings is all we are doing. It is smoking hot for educational experiences. You know, whether having a teacher sit beside you or having the player piano demonstrate the actions for you—the end user experience is the same."
>
> "Do you think the public will buy it for its educational value?" I asked.
>
> "Many manufacturers of player pianos pitch it as 'Let's drink some wine and watch my player piano.' This is missing the boat. The killer application of the player piano is not entertainment but education. How cool would it be on my show if I have a guest on and we record what he is demonstrating both on video and on the piano and send both, synchronized, to the viewers. But you are right, it is getting a critical mass

of these out there. There's probably only fifty of these new systems sold. A lot of my viewers watch but have no intention of playing. It's the *New Yankee Workshop* syndrome. They watch a guy do all the work but don't run out to buy all the equipment."

"I've had some discussions with musicians about what the player piano captures and whether individuality can be recorded," I said. "It seems that it can be faithful to the reproduction of the piece, but reproduction is different from performance. The player piano is sort of like a methodical student."

"When learning to play the piano," said Scott, "music teachers give you an A+ if you robotically reproduce the music. You are rewarded for being robotic—exactly reproducing the dynamics. But once learned, you put your emotions into it. Playing the piano becomes an exercise in creativity. That's where it becomes individual. Ask a painter to paint the same pot of flowers three times and you won't get the exact same picture. If you want it *exactly*, then go to a photocopier."

"Or take a picture," I said. "Stick to video."

"You are right, reproducing is not the same as performing, but both have their own space. Music is what happens at that moment. If you want to keep making it, you need to allow for time to go on. If you want to be nostalgic, record it."

The ability to play and immediately hear and watch how you just played was now part of modern player piano technology. Scott and I sat at a piano equipped with a Compact Flash device. This contains a memory chip that records each strike of a key—a computerized version of the "note on, note off" recording principle developed by Melville Clark nearly a hundred years previously. Scott instructed me on how to play a few notes. Then I pushed the playback button on the memory box and the piano replayed exactly what I had just performed. It was an extraordinary experience. I gained a whole new appreciation of Rachmaninoff's stunned cry that "I have just heard myself play!"

Scott was intrigued about the idea that the player piano had an educational function in the past. I told him that I had first learned about this dimension of it when I read that Fats Waller had imitated its key's motion.

"Really!" he replied. "I'll have to bring that up at my next seminar. It goes some way to demonstrate the power of learning to play by following simple example."

"And he is not the only one," I added.

Since encountering the Fats Waller story, I had been investigating the biographies of other pianists to see if the player piano helped anyone else. I was surprised by the findings.

In his autobiography, Duke Ellington recalled the first time he saw a player piano at a friend's house when he was young, and listened to a roll by James P. Johnson. "This was, of course, an entirely new avenue of adventure for me, and I went back there every day and listened. Percy slowed the mechanism down so that I could see which keys on the piano were going down as I digested Johnson's wonderful sounds. I played with it until I had his 'Carolina Shout' down pat, and then Percy would go out on the town with me and show me off."[14]

The American pianist Joe "Stride" Turner, another disciple of James P. Johnson, who spent most of his career helping to spread jazz music across Europe, was asked how he learned to play "Carolina Shout" and "Harlem Strut" in the 1910s. "Was it by sheet music or by ear?" asked the interviewer. "I was known as a child prodigy," replied Turner, "and I copied the piano rolls; we had a player piano in the house."[15]

Blues singer Ethel Waters toured with Fletcher Henderson, with whom she argued about the way he was playing the accompaniments, refusing to give her what she called the "damn-it-to-hell bass."

> "When we reached Chicago I got some piano rolls that Jimmy Johnson had made and pounded out each passage to Henderson. To prove to me he could do it, Fletch began to practice. He got so perfect, listening to James P. Johnson play on the player piano, that he could press down the keys as the rolls played, never missing a note."[16]

Vincent Persichetti, composer and music instructor at Juilliard, whose students included Thelonious Monk, Philip Glass, and Hall Overton, answered the first question of an interview where he was asked, "What do you remember of your childhood?" by saying: "In the beginning, God created a Cunningham player piano. I was two and played Verdi, Schumann, and Nevin piano rolls, hanging onto the music rack as I tried to reach the pedal mechanism with my feet."[17]

Mary Lou Williams, the "First Lady of the Jazz Keyboard," who was born in 1910 and started playing when she was three, was spellbound as a youth by Scott Joplin, Jack Howard, Fats Waller, James P. Johnson, and Jelly Roll Morton. Asked whether she had had any formal instruction in the piano, she said she hadn't. "My mother wouldn't allow a teacher near me," she said. "I used to listen to the self-player piano a lot. My stepfather, Fletcher Burley, paid $1,000 for a player piano for our home. . . . It was on this instrument that I learned to play a few classical tunes, by pressing my fingers down with the keys."[18]

The educational trend continued through generations. In the 1940s, the jazz pianist Tommy Flanagan, like "other pianists of his generation," according to his biographer, "learned his way around the ivories on the family player piano, by pumping the pedals and watching the patterns dance across the keys. From the ages of five through ten, this was his main method of self-instruction."[19] The player piano even helped to guide others in a musical career in ways that didn't necessarily concentrate on learning to play the piano. The Andrew Sisters found early musical inspiration in the player piano. A neighbor recalled that "Patty, who was about two years old and still in diapers, jiggled up and down in time to the music from the player piano Mrs. Andrews was playing. Patty had pretty good rhythm at that age."

Patty's sister LaVerne recalled that she and her sister enjoyed the player piano. "Patty and I knew how to put the rollers on. We'd share the little tiny seat, and each of us put both of our feet on the pedals and pumped away, and then we'd sing with the music."[20] Even Frank Sinatra said that he first got the idea to make money from singing when he was eleven at his parents' bar, which had a player piano. "Occasionally, one of the men in the bar would pick me up and put me on the piano. I'd sing along with the music on the roll. One day I got a nickel. I said, 'This is the racket.'"[21] Even institutions were interested in the educational value provided by player pianos. Companies proudly advertised that their players were being purchased by music departments at universities such as Harvard and UCLA. In

England, the Aeolian Company sold players to Rugby, Harrow, the Royal College of Music, and the University of London.

A boon to the respectability of the industry came from the Royal Academy of Music in London, which in 1925 wrote to the *Musical Times* about the educational use of the player piano. An advisory committee was formed to investigate the issue and decided that "educationalists have not made full use of the facilities that exist for training the pupils of schools and the adult students of colleges in the knowledge and appreciation of music by means of the use of the player piano, including recently recorded rolls by great artists."[22] Their recommendation was that more institutions should establish collections for academic study.

While it took nearly three decades and the sale of hundreds of thousands of player pianos for serious public consideration to develop about the educational value of the player piano, its effects on making pianists out of pianolists were already well appreciated by the likes of Fats Waller. It was with great pride, therefore, that Fats took to the recording seat at QRS Music to cut his own piano rolls. What he suddenly discovered, however, was an ironic twist to the way one interacts with the marking piano when recording. One could *not play* in the normal way. Having studied the action of the player piano in order to replicate the performance and acquire the skills of a pianist, Fats learned that when one was recording for piano rolls, it was necessary to learn to play like a player piano, almost like a machine.

The stride and ragtime that James P. Johnson and Fats Waller played, and that J. Lawrence Cook edited and arranged for the production of music rolls, had features designed especially for the player piano that were not part of a live performance. This was because for the first time in history both the artist and the arranger were working in a studio that had the ability to manipulate the way the music would be recorded and replayed rather than printed as sheet music. When James P. Johnson brought Fats Waller into the recording studio at QRS Music Rolls, Fats had never seen anything like it. The marking piano at which he and James would play looked like it was on a complicated life-support system, with a thick bundle of rubber hoses connecting it to a machine with a large drum of paper woven through it for registering thousands of marks. "Dad was fascinated by the process," recalled Fats's son, Maurice.[23] But it was very different from playing in a club.

When an artist sat down for the first time at a machine that was designed to record every action one's fingers make in order for the public to replay that piece at their leisure, the artist's fingers had a tendency to stiffen up. In the words of Art Tatum, another jazz artist who recorded for QRS, "the moment I sit down there I'm scared to death."[24] Eventually the recording department set up a piano in a separate room and a pianist would come in during the morning and loosen up on that and then in the afternoon would enter the recording room and say, "I'm ready when you are." However, even then, the process was more involved than simply playing a song.

For all the respect and admiration that talents like James and Fats, among dozens of other pianists, had earned for their improvisations and skilled stride techniques, their turns at the marking piano were long, laborious processes. Player pianists needed to "slow down their thinking." Fats would spend the whole day working on a roll, according to Lawrence. "They have these natural players and improvisers," said Lawrence, but "sometimes the stuff they do, something is missing." The pianist had to develop a new ear and style, not for improvisation, but for playing so that despite repeated listening, one gets the impression of improvisation but improvisation done with technical perfection. "And that is the best stuff; you can always tell," said Lawrence. "But any of the better stuff they do, guys worked on that. Fats and all. And Jimmy and all. You had to. You don't just sit down and play."[25]

During the recording session, Lawrence sat and listened to the tempo and duration of the performance. As the composer and musician Eugene Chadbourne wrote in the *All Music Guide*, "An important aspect of Cook's job was to figure out the exact recipe of pianists such as Fats Waller or Jelly Roll Morton, players whose virtuoso extemporization left many other arrangers scratching their heads, if not banging them against the piano bench."[26] Yet despite working closely with the artist during the recording session, the real talent Lawrence had was making it sound natural when coming off the roll. After marking up long stretches of the piano roll, it was necessary, if somewhat improvident in the eyes of devotees, for Lawrence then to edit down the piece, often using only about a third of what was played for the master roll. "I preserved as much as I possibly could of his actual stuff," he said, but there were limits to the length of a roll and there were also demands for precision.

The necessity of editing, which helped the audience hear "natural" play, was illustrated years later when Eubie Blake returned to QRS Music to record some rolls in the early 1970s. An employee who worked for QRS at that time remembered listening to one of Blake's master rolls. Suddenly there was an inexplicable silence, "absolutely noteless, in the middle of the recording. It lasted for just 8 bars—but one would have thought that perhaps the AC plug to the recording piano had been pulled." However, a simultaneous audio recording made the day of Blake's session provided the reason. In the middle of the hiatus, "Eubie had stopped playing and just sat there snapping his fingers, singing at the top of his voice, and tapping his feet for the 8 bars."[27] While apparently natural sounding in the end, it also illustrated something else that was lost in the recording process. There was soul play running through Blake's veins which could not be captured by the rolls.

One editing trick was introduced when a composition contained repeated choruses that sound identical throughout the roll. When asked if each chorus was actually played that way twice, Lawrence confessed. "Anything that's identical is repeated mechanically. . . . For example, you would put on the editing sheet: 'fourth chorus—first eight measures of chorus number one. Pick this up at the eight measure and do four.'"[28] The editor also removed any extra notes that crept in during the recording. "You go to make a run, and your hand hits something else, stretching it," explained Lawrence. It happened all the time, so the carbon marks on the roll would be erased, or the hole that was punched was taped over.

At the same time, Lawrence would use his own artistic license and add a few notes to put his own distinctive touch—his musical "signature"—on the roll. Of all the rolls Lawrence would arrange during his career, which spanned five decades, he could always tell which rolls were his, "because I can recognize my stuff."[29] The pianists didn't mind his interventions at all; it made them sound more distinguished. "Everyone was happy with the recording session," said Maurice Waller, "and Dad was so proud of his work that he kept a copy of the roll in his pocket."[30]

The public was happy to believe that through the magic of the rolls they were listening to a "live," and perfect, piece of music. It was apparent proof of the extraordinary talent of modern musicians—of the almost machinelike precision of their performance. In fact, for the artists, the player piano presented a personal challenge to their own capabilities. One music critic writing in the *Yale Review* in 1920 commented, "As human fingers cannot compete with a machine in mere accuracy of speed, they must be employed in something else," which he suggested should be more practice![31]

Learning tricks from the player piano is just what some artists did. One feature associated with piano rolls was the two-handed break, requiring a command of the keyboard that James incorporated in his live playing. The critics raved. "Listen to Jimmy Johnson today—and watch his fingers," one commentator wrote. "Abandon and rubato there are, in abundance; but every finger at every note knows just where it is going. The blending of the improvisatory spirit with the precision of the virtuoso makes for a delicious uncertainty that at no moment slips out of control."[32] Precision and accuracy thus became virtues that were shared by both virtuosi and machines.

In the later 1910s, people could for the first time approach "this modern miracle, the player, and draw from its hidden sources the sweetest harmonies ever conceived by mortal man," in the words of John McTammany. By "means of the player alone, they can reproduce with unerring accuracy and refined taste the marvelous works of the greatest masters, yes, and the themes of the various compositions, with unerring technic and ever-increasing appreciation."[33] The technological triumph was later touted by advocates of industry and enterprise.

In the process of preparing the myriad holes of a piano roll, "Every detail is measured," explained *Scientific American* magazine in 1927, the same year they first reported on the practical demonstration of television. Also certain effects, "heretofore regarded almost as manifestations of the soul of the artist, are being analyzed for mechanical reproduction through the record music roll."[34] Through celebrated "laboratory techniques," not only the spirit but the skillful precision of virtuosi pianists was painstakingly captured in the machine. The secret they sprung was that *even more* was accomplished.

It was revealed that human errors could be eliminated through the precision of mechanical reproduction. "We sometimes hear a performance which sounds perfect," the article went on. "Apparently there is not a flaw existing in the playing. Records of such performances when analyzed sometimes reveal unbelievable faults." However, through the attention of the technicians, "wrong notes which were accidentally struck by the pianist" were eliminated. The player piano was better than human; it never made mistakes.

Ironically, the first music critics to appreciate the player piano did not perceive its mechanical ingenuity. "The fact that artistic expression instead of machine-like precision has been its aim is what has caused its possibilities as a musical instrument to appeal to me," stated Gustav Kobbé in 1912. Instead of grinding out music, the player piano allowed its operator to experience "the expression, the real interpretation" of the piece because, as it stated right on the roll's box with the artist's signature, "The line on this roll indicates the tempo according to my interpretation." "Practically," said Kobbé, "I have been taught how to play it by the great artist." The roll, he concluded, "has been 'metrostyled' by the virtuoso himself."[35]

Companies needed to find a way to stress the human element in the production of music or risk losing a market that was familiar with conventional musical performance. By 1926, QRS Music Rolls was selling a staggering 6.7 million rolls a year. They had just purchased the United States Music Company, which, ten years earlier, had been outselling them with J. Lawrence Cook's homemade master rolls; this added another 2 million rolls a year to their market domination.[36] QRS had advertised that their rolls "are better" since they were *not* produced mechanically but created through live play. While this was strictly not true, what mattered—but what remained invisible—was the fact that the production of rolls *did* nevertheless require a great deal of artistic skill. It was a new era in music with new specialties of which the public at large remained ignorant. There was as yet no cultural understanding of how the production of music could be different from a club performance except for the absence of the pianist.

With increased attention to the capabilities of the player piano, salesmen soon had to confront customers' confusion about how a "mechanical" instrument could possibly produce genuine music. An Ampico sales handbook for their employees provided a standardized answer. "All musical instruments are 'mechanical' in the sense you use the word," they were to reply. "The piano itself, for example, might be viewed as simply a physical assemblage of keys, strings, hammers, and so on. . . . It is [a] wonderfully ingenious, yet simple, instrument for bringing back to the keys the touch of the master's fingers." The salesmen were then directed to let the player piano "speak for itself by playing some of the recordings."[37]

Those who remained indignant, alleging that mechanical music was somehow debased, were challenged by the claim that those who engaged the player piano's mechanized routines were not doing anything very different from the manner by which virtuosi learned to play through practice. In the haste to condemn the technology—and commercialization—such critics ignored the fact that skilled pianists were themselves machinelike. "It is a matter of wonder," wrote the British musicologist Ernest Newlandsmith in his 1904 tract *The Temple of Art*, "that anyone can be found to speak against mechanical piano-players, when they remember that they are only mechanical to the extent that a pianist has to be."[38] This was also the message offered by George Bernard Shaw in 1911 when he introduced a concert of pianola music at the Camera Club in London, where he drew a parallel with a different kind of criticism. Like the player piano, photography is "an art which is disparaged by those who believe that when a lens is in a box it is mechanical, but not when it is in a man's head. . . . Here also it is said to be mechanical to use a lever in a box, but not mechanical when the lever is to be found in the human hand."[39]

Many musicians who learn to play an instrument recognize how much acquiring skill involves the "internalization" of machinelike acts. "Anyone who has witnessed or been a beginning pianist or guitarist learning a chord production notices substantial awkwardness," wrote the modern jazz musician David Sudnow. "As my hands began to form constellations, . . . a consistency developed in seeing not its note-for-noteness, but the pattern of its location as a configuration emerging out of the broader visual field of the terrain."[40] Anyone who thought there was a dehumanizing aspect to the player piano had only to be told that Fats Waller and other great musicians learned to play from imitating it.

So what was lost or gained—denied or possessed—in producing music on player piano rolls? In hindsight, it was invaluable for aficionados and students of ragtime, stride piano, and jazz to have music arranged in the 1910s and 1920s in order for them to analyze these compositions. While studying the technique of original ragtime artists in the "ragtime revival" of the 1950s, Dr. Hubert Pruett, one of the foremost collectors of ragtime on piano rolls, wondered whether it was the performance or arrangement that mattered most to his study of jazz. "The value of ragtime to jazz," he concluded, "is not a technical one, but rather consists of *an attitude toward compositional structure*." To the original composers, including J. Lawrence Cook, James P. Johnson, and Fats Waller, such attitudes were manifest in their concern to preserve their pioneering techniques—their unique melodic forms—in the arrangements found in their music rolls.[41]

However, some critics insisted that because such skills were transferred to a machine there was a greater risk that those without exceptional talent would lose the chance to learn to play the piano in the conventional way. The effects of mechanization would lead to the dissociation of music with aesthetic contemplation. In 1906 John Philip Sousa, conductor of the famous marching band, argued that interest in musical composition was being replaced with passive listening, leading to the gradual silencing of the town band, amateur performer, and pianist, "until there will be left only the mechanical device and the professional executants."[42] The ease with which player piano manufacturers sold their instruments and rolls suggested that consumers were more interested in "performance without practice" than in laborious music appreciation. According to philosophers of mass culture, this preference was symptomatic of the commercialization of leisure.

Chapter 10

Music for the Masses?

A RETHINKING OF what responding to music meant began to occur as the public became more familiar with the capabilities of the player piano. Consider the 1920 concert at Carnegie Hall organized by the American Piano Company. Five eminent pianists, Artur Rubinstein, Leopold Godowsky, Benno Moiseiwitsch, Leo Ornstein, and Mischa Levitzki, alternated their performance with renditions from an Ampico player piano. During the final number when Levitzki was playing Liszt's "Hungarian Rhapsody," he suddenly raised his hands while the piano continued to play. As the composition reached its crescendo, Levitzki plunged back into the live performance, at which point the audience erupted in a salvo of applause.[1]

In 1927, the well-known British music critic Ernest Newman attended a concert in London where Aeolian's Duo-Art system was played alongside the performance of the great French pianist Alfred Cortot. During the concert, Newman shut his eyes and attempted to distinguish between the piano roll and "the real thing." "Now and again I would say to myself: 'This is Cortot' or 'This is Duo-Art,' but on opening my eyes I found myself as often wrong as right."[2] The audiences were amazed that the pianist could take command of the performance and perform like the machine. It inverted the original marketing celebration of the player piano. Instead of humanizing the machine by appealing to its virtuoso qualities, now a pianist's talent was measured by how closely it approximated the machine's rendition of the music. The machine began to set the standard. Whereas at one time the public was impressed by the mere appearance of it playing "by itself"—hailing it as a triumph of technological ingenuity—the more familiar the public became with the player piano, the more consistent were their expectations of what music should sound like. This in itself was a noted feature of player pianism. When writing about the Dynaline developed by Story & Clark to regulate the playback of its player piano rolls, the Chicago *Indicator* in 1908 stressed the fact that, owing to the "manufacturing system" built into the pianos, "tone and touch may be developed, just as certain styles of architecture and certain schemes of color have been developed, so that they appeal agreeably to the artistic sense of every normally constituted person. We might call this process 'Standardization.'"[3]

To make the experience of owning a player piano more appealing to a broader audience, the owners needed to do as little work as possible to make the music sound consistently good. Throughout the 1910s and particularly in the 1920s, the marketing strategies moved from selling the player piano as something one engaged with to become an entertainer to a truly popular piece of entertainment. Where once the mainstay of the industry was its claim that family, friends, and neighbors "may approach this modern miracle, the player, and draw from its hidden sources the sweetest harmonies ever conceived by mortal man," such enthusiastic claims became less frequent when some manufacturers began to promote "high-class electric" players.[4] In claiming that no one actually ever could properly "play" the player—it "never has been well played by the people and never will be satisfactory to them as long as they have to work it themselves"—the industry's solution seemed obvious: reduce the act to flipping a switch. "Now," argued one dealer in a trade announcement from 1917, "a player piano that they can play by the mere turning of a switch, we have something that can be called popular."[5]

While some claimed that mechanical musical instruments "democratized" music, others saw "popularity" as tantamount to mediocrity. "The talking machine and player-piano, among other devices, have been of inestimable assistance to mediocrity, by enabling it to assert, directly and in unmistakable manner, its own preferences in music." This is what happens when the masses have means to musical reproduction. No longer will the imperial court set the tone, nor the highest-paid virtuosi. "The favored and select who, once upon a time, passed such judgments on an admired artist, have been multiplied beyond counting, divided still though they may be on the merits of this or that popular 'record' or 'film.' Popularity is mediocrity's all-powerful lure."[6] Accessibility might have been a leveler of distinctions, but who wanted that?

Perhaps what was particularly disturbing to the ears of critics was that a machine, rather than a person, was the new mediator of aesthetic expression. The machine was what was being valued, not a person. However, this criticism begged another question, the answer to which might help to quell the allegations about the emergence of machine-age mediocrity: Was the player piano a machine or a musical instrument? Did it facilitate freedom of expression or limit the boundaries of aesthetic appreciation? According to some composers and writers, the devices were not merely mechanical because of the artistic engagement afforded the player pianist.

In 1925, the British music critic Sydney Grew declared that "fifteen years ago the player-piano arrived at perfection." He said that because great pianists such as Grieg and Paderewski had "identified themselves" with player piano manufacturers and had enthusiastically recorded rolls, "hardly a European musician of note has failed to recognize that it was an instrument of music, not a machine."[7] What was it that such luminary pianists found virtuous about the player piano? It was precisely that it captured their music for repeated listening by future generations.

This point prompted a correspondent to the *Musical Times* to write a word in favor of mechanized music. "I am getting tired of the constant girding at 'our mechanized age,'" he wrote in 1929. "It is a very pleasant age, and the machines are going to make it a great deal pleasanter." His point was that there were masterpieces of music available to listen to, and machines made it possible to listen to them as many times as one desired. Being a progressive technophile, he had just purchased a gramophone and over the past months had listened to "Brahms's Quintet in F minor, thirty-five times; Schubert's Trio in B flat, Op. 99, twenty-five times; Tchaikovsky's 'Pathétique' Symphony, twenty times—and so on." To attack the way that machines have become part of modern-day aesthetic appreciation was, to his mind, as senseless as it was for "the weavers of Bolton to break the machines in the 18th century." "Let us make the most and the best of our 'civilization-made machines' and not talk so much about our 'machine-made civilization,'" he pleaded.[8]

The reference to the gramophone signaled the arrival of a diversified technological soundscape. It was not obvious at the time that the "talking machine" technology would flourish the way it did. The same spirit of technophilia that originally captivated the public's interest in the player piano, and that later prompted the letter from the above correspondent, bred a new culture of music appreciation that had its roots in player pianism. Even Compton Mackenzie, cofounder of the British magazine the *Gramophone*, wrote in 1924 that "I think we gramophonists are a bit too tolerant, you know. I feel that since I devoted some of my time to the player-piano I have certainly become more exacting in my judgments of sound boxes. The piano is a fine bracer of one's ears after too entire an absorption in the world of gramophone sound."[9]

As the aural historian Emily Thompson has shown, throughout the 1920s the gramophone was improving in fidelity and gaining a larger market share, posing increasing competition to the player piano.[10] An article in the *Musical Times* in 1921 foreshadowed the competition. For years, there had been "a mere piling-up of superlatives" designed to impress the critics of the quality of the gramophone. Yet, wrote Ulric Daubeny, they had "too many obvious shortcomings to stand in the remotest likelihood of superseding *original performance*." Not so with the latest gramophone, a prototype of which the author had previewed. "The inventor of the new machine claims, and we think justly, that, given his machine and a pianoforte in the same room, a listener outside the door could scarcely distinguish from which source the sounds came." The drawback was that as yet the machine was not ready for the market, and it would, for a time, "remain a rich man's machine."[11] While this would change for the gramophone and other emerging technologies, it was much more difficult for the prices of player pianos to drop enough so that a wide public could keep purchasing them—especially after October 1929.

The Great Depression and increasing competition from rival technologies starved the automatic music market. Numerous manufacturers dropped out of business. Many AMICAns and other devotees of

player piano history have wondered why, or how, such a phenome-
nally successful industry could have the bottom fall out from under it
so quickly. While the broader perspective which spans a decade or
two would no doubt see both social and technological issues at work
in this shift of fortune, some microperspectives can help identify certain forces of change. The British musicologist Julian Dyer points to
sales statistics from the U.S. Census Bureau that show that player
piano sales, and indeed all (non-player) piano sales, started a decline
throughout the 1920s. In 1923, 347,000 pianos were sold, along with
194,000 player pianos. In 1927, those figures dropped 51% to
130,000 and 95,000, respectively. A recent Harvard Business School
analysis of these statistics explained the decline in demand in part as
the result of the "counter attraction offered by automobiles and moving pictures for recreation; the trend toward apartment living in the
cities; and the development of the phonograph and radio."[12] So the
social factors that contributed to the demise of the player piano generally link it to a market that may have reached its saturation point and
a shift in the public's interest in entertainment.

The emergence of certain technologies that rivaled the player
piano as providers of entertainment is relevant too. The collector,
restorer, and prolific author of works on mechanical musical instruments Arthur Reblitz recognized that the beginning of the demise of
the market for player pianos happened before the stock market collapse in 1929. However, he also draws attention to a specific event in
1926: the introduction of the electronically amplified radio and the
beginnings of quality radio programming. "Small crystal radios had
been popular for years before this," he noted in a discussion forum in
Mechanical Music Digest, "but the introduction of the amplified
radio made it practical for broadcasting companies to spend money
on interesting programming because it could be enjoyed simultaneously by more than one person per radio set."[13]

Alert to the public's changing preferences in musical entertainment, some player piano manufacturers used the new technologies to
diversify their product lines. As early as 1921, QRS Music Rolls
began manufacturing parts for Chicago Radio Laboratory, a small
outfit that built five radios a year from a garage in a suburb north of
Chicago. Two years later it was renamed Zenith Corporation. At that
time, QRS's president, Thomas Pletcher, was appointed vice president

of Zenith. With the music roll business flourishing, this was a remarkably foresighted action for QRS to take. It is another irony of history that the radio would later be considered to have had a direct impact on player piano sales and would eventually eclipse them in the market.[14]

Radio, the phonograph, and—in the 1930s—the jukebox, which contained as many as twenty-five records at a time for play in public places, bolstering the record industry, all worked against the popularity of the player piano. In 1936, *Time* magazine reported on the huge drop in piano sales between 1925 and 1935, noting that piano makers, once the "aristocrats of the music industry," were now seen to be as "impoverished as the aristocracy of Tsarist Russia."[15]

Ironically, in 1937 the president of the National Piano Manufacturers Association of America, Lothrop Perkins Bull, declared that the radio was "creating a renaissance in the public love for good music which may bring with it 'the Golden Age' of the piano."[16] Bull was an interested party to events in the piano industry, not only as president of NPMAA but as a businessman. Having married a descendant of Hampton Story, Bull became president of Story & Clark pianos and was trying in every way to resurrect their once powerful brand of player pianos.

One strategy, spearheaded by Bull's business associate, Melville Clark, nephew of the inventor of the Apollo, who handled sales of Story & Clark player pianos in upstate New York, was to enroll the support of "the Tune Detective," Sigmund Spaeth. Known "to millions" through his publicity materials as "a humanizer and simplifier of music for the layman," Spaeth was paid three hundred dollars for a public lecture in 1938 to promote their pianos. He stressed the previously successful point that player pianos were educational and accessible to the populace.[17] Story & Clark managed to stay afloat, if somewhat listing, throughout the turbulent 1930s. Meanwhile their sister company, QRS Music Rolls, was struggling in its own right.

Like the rest of the player piano industry, QRS Music had fallen on hard times. Despite the continued success of QRS throughout the 1920s, Pletcher gradually had less interest in the primary focus of the company and was willing to take risks to sell unrelated products, such as neon signs, home movie cameras, phonographs, and musical toys. When the stock market crashed in 1929, Pletcher lost an estimated four million dollars of personal wealth and left the company in ruins.

So appalled by Pletcher's business practices was Ernest Clark, son of the company's founder, Melville Clark (and owner of the Clark Orchestra Roll Company), that he later wrote about the "terrible waste, and wanton destruction of machines that prevailed under the Pletcher-Page management. I can easily see where the masters [of rolls] may have gone to—the boiler room where the fire is the hottest."[18]

In 1931, a veteran employee of the now-bankrupt company, Max Kortlander, purchased it, drawing on the fortune he made in 1919 with his hit song "Tell Me." He had continued to produce a number of popular rolls for QRS throughout the 1920s. When he acquired the company, Kortlander renamed it Imperial Industrial Corp. The offices were on the third floor of a rambling brick factory in the Bronx. Committed to the company, and acting more as a munificent musician than acute businessman, Kortlander maintained about twenty-five employees, including J. Lawrence Cook, who supplemented his income by working as a clerk at a post office near Grand Central Station and by offering piano lessons. The company could no longer pay artists to come in and record rolls for them, so Lawrence concentrated on producing rolls that imitated the performing styles of jazz improvisers by carefully listening to phonograph records and transcribing what he heard into musical scores. He would then play each piece on the perforating machine, becoming the recording artist and arranger.[19]

In 1941, Lawrence had marked his twentieth anniversary with QRS. When roll cutting was slow, he would spend some time with his wife, daughter, and son, whom he named Jean Lawrence Cook. He also managed to take advantage of some spare time to finish a creative writing course at the local community college and began writing a regular column called "Professional Piano Pointers" in the "Pedagogics" section of the *International Musician*, the official publication of the American Federation of Musicians. In one of his early contributions published in May 1941, Lawrence wrote about changing styles in playing the piano and the pianist's technique, the "mechanical aspect" of pianism that, when it is well developed, "one is but faintly aware of its existence as such." Just as he had worked to make his own presence as technician—arranger and editor of piano rolls— invisible, so the mechanical technique of playing the piano could become invisible to the audience. The work that went into acquiring this skill becomes hidden, and the audience simply hears the polished performance. Lawrence's thoughts about style and technique provide some insight not only into his understanding of the pianist's art and craft but how he used that knowledge to improve the way he manipulated piano roll arrangements to make them sound natural.

Lawrence was a lifelong student of music. As he explained, "player roll work necessitates endless research and analysis of all types and styles of popular piano playing."[20] By scrutinizing the nuances of others, which he meticulously strove to imitate when arranging music rolls, he became versed in all kinds of styles. He drew on this experience to advise his students. The typical student might have come to see him, explaining that they had "picked up some ideas here and there" and "figured out [the basics of playing the piano] myself from studying piano rolls and phonograph records." As a teacher—and roll arranger—Lawrence saw nothing wrong with this. "I recommend direct imitation at the start," he said. "As a matter of fact, some students may at first be so lacking in creative ability and even in adaptation that no other course will be feasible."[21] Eventually, when technical aspects of covering the keys were mastered, then one or two tricks could be perfected for certain types of chords or resolutions that would add "the real signature of your style," he said. It was Lawrence's ability to identify the tricks that great pianists employed and to develop a few of his own for the arrangement of rolls that made him a singular imitator of style and a successful recording artist and editor.

In his early years at QRS Music Rolls, Lawrence took every opportunity to study different dimensions of musical composition, structure, and harmonic principles. Referring to the latter, Lawrence recalled that his colleagues heckled him when he embarked on a course of studying harmony. "What are you doing," they said, "preparing to become highbrow? What do you expect to get out of the study of 'legitimate' harmony that will benefit you in this line of work?" However, harmony, he was convinced, was the "orthography, grammar, and rhetoric of music," and his understanding of harmonization was what allowed him to succeed "in a sort of 'survival of the fittest' role." His commitment was to the music, rather than to just the technology used to reproduce it. As he explained,

> "No one can deny that radio, the depression and what not had a great deal to do with the virtual extinction of the player piano, but

your writer has always contended and still contends that the limited qualifications of the majority of the so-called recording artists—their utter ignorance of the rudiments of harmony—had much to do with it. Their copious tremolos relentlessly plagued the ears of innocent law abiding citizens. Their reckless voicing, their elementary and often total lack of a sense of balance irked the sensibilities of the really musical mind. Their frequent attempts to use as many of the eighty-eight notes as the pneumatic power of their player pianos would allow, played havoc with the hammers and strings of pianos that could not possibly stand the strain.[22]

Lawrence's explanation of how QRS managed to stay in business was revealing of his opinions not only about his capabilities as an arranger but of the general commitment of the company to artistic principles. This commitment is what set QRS Music apart from the rest of the music industry: it was owned and managed by musicians, not by businessmen.

Despite the risks taken, in the early 1940s an unexpected boon to the player piano business came as a result of the actions of one James Caesar Petrillo, president of the American Federation of Musicians, the nation's largest musicians' union. In 1941, Petrillo began banning the recording of music for phonograph, jukebox, or radio. Player piano rolls, however, were exempted.

In the 1930s, the American Federation of Musicians had used its membership base of some 140,000 musicians to negotiate collective bargaining agreements with radio broadcasters, thereby creating a stranglehold on radio chains and record producers. As recording technologies progressed and financial hardship hit America and Europe, the union strove to preserve the jobs of musicians who played for silent movies, negotiating minimum wages and securing relief for unemployed musicians through the U.S. Government's Works Projects Administration. For the first time, mechanical musical devices—particularly jukeboxes—began to jeopardize the livelihood of musicians. As the historian Paul Oliver put it in his *Story of the Blues*, "Juke-boxes began to replace live musicians everywhere."[23]

Petrillo was a notoriously tough union boss. After his election as president in 1940, he focused his attention on obtaining better royalties for musicians from record companies. Meeting much hostility, Petrillo decreed a ban on all commercial recording by union members between 1942 and 1944 and again in 1948. He announced that all union musicians were forbidden from making records for jukeboxes or performing for radio shows, leading *Time* magazine to report on the threat this posed to the coin-operated phonograph business and to small radio stations.[24] "During the past several months there has been such a sharp increase in the demand for player rolls that we have had to abandon all teaching activities," Lawrence happily informed the readers of his column in the *International Musician*.[25] Thus, player piano rolls had the first of their revivals since their peak sales twenty years earlier. "Of the scores of roll companies that were in operation throughout the world twenty years ago," wrote Lawrence in 1942, "only a single one has carried on and is still doing good business today. The present writer is the head recording artist of that company."[26] In 1943, QRS was manufacturing about half a million rolls a year, with major sales of certain titles, including "Let Me Call You Sweetheart," "The Star Spangled Banner," and "The Beer Barrel Polka." While this resurgence kept old player piano companies such as Story & Clark and QRS in business, the contemporary cultural climate had changed. The music they produced was no longer a novelty, but its revival occurred during a period when phonographs and jukeboxes had proliferated. The technological, entrepreneurial, and musical advantages that the player piano business enjoyed in the first decades of the twentieth century were countered by the philosophies of those who had reservations about "machine-made civilization" and had criticisms of the entertainment industry.

In agreeing with Max Weber that the piano had been transformed from a musical instrument into a piece of bourgeois furniture, the German critic Theodore Adorno declared that "the whole jazz business" had sacrificed the meaning of the "actual performance" at the altar of commercialization.[27] Not only had the labor—the musician and technicians—disappeared, but in the process of making furniture out of musical instruments, the meaning of the music—the core of the musician's identity—had disappeared and the catalogs of best-selling titles of music rolls had become fetishized.[28] Through a series of articles written about the sociology of music in the 1940s and 1950s, Adorno worried that the act of listening to reproductions (he cited the phonographic record) would be accepted as culturally equivalent to listening to live performances and fostering the belief that one possessed musical skill. He used "the negative power of jazz and blues" as proof of the alienation of the masses from themselves and from the European, bourgeois appreciation of classical music that he held as a paradigmatic cultural aesthetic.[29]

In the mid-twentieth century, when industrial capitalism was seen as one element in a dystopic society, some writers warned that human ingenuity would be rendered useless in an age of mechanistic morality. For example, Kurt Vonnegut's first novel, *Player Piano*, told of young PhDs who used mechanical gadgetry to steal the "essence" of a skilled machinist named Rudy Hertz to streamline industrial production and eliminate the need for more Rudy Hertzes in the future. Hertz wound up in a saloon putting nickels in a machine to play songs on a player piano, Vonnegut's symbol of a society in which human activities, even in the arts, had been mechanized and stripped of all human feeling. The piano, the narrator tells us, delivered "exactly five cents of joy."[30] Similarly, William Gaddis, in his posthumous novella *Agape Agape*, described the player piano as a prototype of digital music that represented the catastrophic convergence of mechanization and humanism that created the oxymoronic "entertainment industry." The player piano thus became the symbol of the commercialization of culture that supposedly dehumanized music. At the same time, the mechanical principles by which it operated were themselves hidden by the suggestion that the machine possessed "soul," and that from it the works of virtuosi emanated.

Part of the success of the piano roll industry lay in the imaginations of the editors and arrangers who composed their own work or adapted the music brought to them by their friends, such as Fats Waller working with J. Lawrence Cook. Waller did not care that his compositions were arranged by Lawrence for music rolls and given a fictitious identity, published under pseudonyms to make it appear that the list of employed musicians was longer than it really was. He was far more concerned with the attention that audiences gave him when he performed live.

One day, when Waller was broke and worn out after a bout of heavy drinking and playing, he had a chat with Max Kortlander. "He said he would like to do what you're doing," Kortlander told Lawrence, "putting stuff down on the master paper like you're doing. I told him I'd give him a regular job." Waller was slipped an advance on pay and was supposed to show up a few days later to begin work. He never showed up. "It was much to the benefit of not only Fats but the music loving public," said Lawrence. "Because if he had come, he would have been buried there, just like I was."[31]

Selling rolls for the player piano—the instrument that taught Waller how to play—kept him going until his big break. After he missed his appointment at QRS, he attended a party thrown by George Gershwin where Waller played the piano and sang. A representative from Victor Records happened to have been there and was duly impressed. "You won't believe this," Waller said to Lawrence, "but I got a recording date with Victor next week." Soon the world, and history, would recognize the unmistakable entertainer that Thomas "Fats" Waller was. Lawrence remained "buried" in the recording rooms at QRS Music Rolls, hidden behind pseudonyms and the marking piano until he retired in the late 1960s. In 1949, Lawrence had his first hit song, "The Old Piano Roll Blues," which he sold to Abbey Records, which got it on the radio. It reached number seventeen on the charts. "But it was my misfortune to have been with a bunch of thieves who gypped me out of everything due me, so here I am," Lawrence later recalled.[32]

His talent in the recording department of the world's largest manufacturer of piano rolls helped to transform the music industry, gave life to a new kind of music, and helped others to become famous. However, he never regretted the path his life had taken. When, in his seventies, he was asked what he did, he replied, "I call myself a player-pianist," and chuckled. "If they want to get sophisticated I tell 'em I'm a composer or arranger."[33]

Unlike Waller or James P. Johnson, J. Lawrence Cook—the arranger and composer of over twenty thousand piano rolls throughout his career—remains largely invisible to history, though he left a legacy of a unique slice of Americana for aficionados. "Any time you talk about player pianos or the rolls, my name pops up," he said.[34] To make it seem as if there had been more people behind the scenes recording music, Lawrence created fictitious names. However, few people who enjoy music rolls have any knowledge of those artists hidden within the technology. It is ironic that the orphan who named himself also assumed the identity of a number of fictitious pianists. If one learns where to look, one can find their traces hidden in music rolls past. They seem to be invisible, but we can still hear them by listening to the sounds of history.

Epilogue

S EVIDENCED through company records, product lines, sales, media notice, catalogues of piano rolls, and historical artifacts, the player piano was remarkably popular in the first half of the twentieth century. Not only was it an innovative mechanical wonder but the music recordings produced for it introduced a new kind of entertainment and marked the birth of a mechanical musical industry. What makes the history of this musical technology so unique is that the automatic musical instrument was symbolic of, and was celebrated according to, different ideologies of American ingenuity and progress.

On one hand it represented mechanical genius. The player piano's intricate construction, fine craftsmanship, and mass production embodied the early twentieth-century disposition for industrial prowess. Inventors and engineers took something as highly individualized and skillful as the ability to play a musical instrument and mechanized it. This captured the public's imagination and mesmerized audiences. Almost anyone can associate with the difficulties of learning to play the piano. People understood that attributes such as talent were more developed in some over others, and that "natural ability" was something intangible, some sort of tacit command over the keyboard that was incommunicable but highly regarded. Yet suddenly these machines were made to imitate human performance. Somehow the skill of playing the piano was transferred to a complex configuration of wires, rubber hoses, bellows, levers, and rolls of perforated paper encased within a conventional-looking piano. In some cases a mere flip of a switch animated the instrument, while in foot-pumped models a novice was able to interact with the machine while appearing to perform like a virtuoso.

The player piano changed the concept of a live performance. It also served the interests of one philosophy of musical appreciation that privileged familiarity with music over the ability to play. The music historian Timothy Day, in his thorough account of *A Century of Recorded Music*, draws attention to the views of Waldo Selden Pratt, a professor from the Hartford Theological Seminary in Connecticut who at the end of the nineteenth century lectured to the Musical Association in London on the topic of musical appreciation. Pratt conveyed his interest in "the musical culture of the huge masses of people who will never be musicians in any technical sense, and in the creation of a popular sentiment about music that shall securely link it with the abiding interests of intellectual and spiritual life."[1] This sentiment was echoed soon after by commentators writing about the promise of the player piano as a promoter of a musical democracy. It is an affirmation of this potential that young musicians, particularly in African American communities who had no resources to pay for personal instruction, could imitate the motions of a player piano and share in "the creation of popular sentiment about music." It is also an irony that that same opportunity provided the foundation for these musicians to redefine music styles according to their own tastes, which further democratized the production of music.

But later a critique of mechanization and mass production emerged. The loss of privilege seemed to rankle certain high-brow or religious guardians of the European classics who did not like seeing "live" music—particularly dance music like ragtime or stride—played in ballrooms, saloons, or even concert halls. The manifestations of the "entertainment industry" were labeled dehumanizing. When the player piano began to be dismissed in the musical trade press as mechanical gadgetry with no real "touch" or ability to truthfully convey the nuances of a performance, manufacturers took this as a challenge to the limits of their technology, and an opportunity to make advances over their competition.

The player piano business reinvented itself. Whereas previously it was precisely its mechanical construction that attracted admiration and formed the core of its identity, now it was important to render its mechanics invisible. The marketing literature and sales pitches stressed how very humanlike the instrument was. While the player piano had long been associated with the human touch—possessing the qualities of "the master's fingers"—it was time to humanize the machine even more. One way of doing this was to let the instrument "speak" for itself. Ampico devised a window display for music stores that featured a grand piano with an unwound roll draped over its keys that told its own history. "I am the AMPICO," it declared. "I re-enact the playing of the world's greatest pianists and bring their musical magic into your home."[2] An advertisement the company ran in newspapers announcing forthcoming concerts drew attention to the "human piano" that was featured in the performance.[3]

For companies that once primarily celebrated the technological innovations of their machines, they now also stressed the humanism that it embodied. When the *Musical Courier* wrote about Aeolian's Metrostyle device, which aided player pianists in their renditions when playing the rolls, it noted that it now considered "piano-playing taken out of the realm of automatism and placed at one step into the very highest rung of the ladder of individualism."[4]

The irony was that in order for the player piano to sound human, the labor-intensive work of arranging and editing the rolls to make it sound that way was itself rendered invisible. Only when flaws in the piano rolls emerge to introduce an off note are listeners reminded of the limitations and imperfections of human production. The player piano played in an interstitial space between machine reproduction and human performance, but in so doing it diverted attention away from the conditions of its own existence. It came to represent the epitome of both a machine and a perfect human performance. This itself was an expression of a musical ideology. As the great Austrian pianist Artur Schnabel is supposed to have said: "Great music . . . is music that's better than it can be played."[5] The player piano produced great music.

One thing the player piano could not do was miniaturize itself. The player piano industry was built around the primacy of the piano as a piece of furniture and something exactly like the standard piano people could actually play. However, the main competition in the marketplace for musical machines came from smaller pieces of furniture, such as the gramophone, the radio, and the jukebox. Known as "coin-operating phonographs" or a variant before the term "jukebox" came into common parlance in the 1940s, this particular kind of musical machine was born in San Francisco in the 1890s when the Pacific Phonograph Company placed one in the Palais Royal Saloon.

According to jukebox historian Kerry Segrave, if it were not for the existence of player pianos, the early jukebox might very well have been far more successful. Quoting *Billboard* magazine writer Walter Hurd's observation that "the coin-operated piano had its big day during that period" between 1900 and 1925, Segrave has little to say about coin-operated phonographs until the 1940s when two technological developments and a society emerging from the Great Depression create a condition favorable to its rise: the radio had created a tremendous interest in a wide variety of song selection, and the amplifier allowed for jukebox records to be enjoyed more socially (previously, one had to stand next to the machine wearing a stethoscope). As one journalist wrote in 1937: "Without the fast and high development of the radio the modern phonograph would never have come into being. It did not have the necessary sound qualities which amplification made possible. The industry borrowed technical advances which had taken place in the radio industry."[6]

At the same time as financial constraints limited the growth of the player piano industry in the post-Depression era, the advantages of the radio and jukebox were incorporated into the business plan of an industry intent on keeping music flowing to the masses. *Variety* magazine reported that "the most profitable business in coin music was the 'music machine' [jukebox] with small overhead, practically no upkeep, no advertising costs, and no losses." It added that "pianos, once the big moment in the coin-operated music business, have now gone the way of the zither concert and the town pump."[7] But, as we have seen, while the player piano industry did indeed languish during the 1930s and 1940s, it also saw a revival during the 1950s and 1960s. Other than the world of collectors and aficionados such as the AMICAns who emerged in the 1960s, those features of the player piano that originally attracted the interest of musicians and audiences rekindled interest in the automated instrument, namely the uniqueness of its style of performance.

At the International Music Festival in Los Angeles in 1962, conductor Franz Waxman raised his baton and the orchestra sailed into the opening bars of Stravinsky's piano concerto. When he gave a nod for the first piano passage, the audience "did 2,000 double takes," according to a report in *Time* magazine.[8] A player piano had been introduced in place of where the great pianist would have sat. "The absent Igor had made a piano roll of the concerto's first movement in 1925, was in Europe at the time of this pianistic hanky-panky and missed hearing Stravinsky playing Stravinsky." In the 1960s the player piano was coming back into its own. QRS Music had a new account and had helped Macy's in Manhattan to stock a twenty-five-hundred-roll library from which the store sold about two hundred rolls a week, compared with ten rolls a week only two years previously. "Lone survivor of the once more than 50 U.S. roll makers, Q.R.S. sees brighter days ahead," continued the report in *Time* magazine. At this time, roll-recording was linked to new computer technology, which once again gave it a cutting-edge feel. "Its artist-in-residence, J. Lawrence Cook, turns out the rolls by playing on a special piano rigged to a device like an IBM machine, which punches the proper holes in a master role. Then the master roll is placed on the production perforator, which can punch out more than 30 finished roles at a time."[9] Also back in business was Aeolian Music Rolls of Glendale, California, which was producing another fifteen hundred rolls a day for the swelling market.

Like a blast from the past, groups gathered around player pianos in cabarets and coffee houses across the country. "When we have a banquet or bachelor party," said the owner of Barney's Market Club in Chicago, "they don't play cards after dinner like they used to; they congregate around the piano, throw their arms around each other's shoulders, drink their beer, puff their cigars, and rip off the good old songs." The piano in the parlor also came back to life. "Many buyers are women who recall the pleasure of pumping one as a child and want to share the fun with their own kids."[10]

Perhaps at the dawning of the digital age and the maturing of the first generation of TV viewers, the interaction between human novice and expert machine was once again an appealing form of entertainment. For musical scholars and collectors of Americana, the fragile rolls and the period piano helped them to recreate the music of history. Studying the movements of a musical machine was as close as they could get to studying the gestures of the musicians themselves. However much was revealed about the performers by studying traces of their performance on archived rolls, for others the appealing feature of player pianos was found in their ability to do things that humans cannot. This is what fascinated one of the most well-known composers *for* player piano music: Conlon Nancarrow.

Born in Texarkana, Arkansas, in 1912, Nancarrow failed miserably at his piano lessons when he was a boy but decided to devote his life to the piano anyway. When he was seventeen he had a "total revelation" about musical composition when he heard Stravinsky play *Rite of Spring* at a concert. His first composition, *Prelude*, was published in *New Music Edition* before he went off to Spain to join the Abraham Lincoln Brigade to fight the spread of fascism. In 1938 his composition was reviewed by well-known critic and composer Aaron Copland in *Modern Music*, where he wrote that Nancarrow's work shows "a remarkable surety in an unknown composer, plus a degree of invention and imagination that immediately gives him a place among our talented younger men."[11]

His compositions were challenging. In the words of one admirer, they "make high demands on the performer."[12] Nonetheless, after his return from Spain, in 1941 a septet he composed was to be performed in New York. Unfortunately the musicians repeatedly missed practice, and on performance night each kept playing out of place. "Everything was lost," lamented Nancarrow, "it was a real disaster." After this experience he decided to get rid of human performers altogether, and he dedicated the rest of his career to composing for the player piano.

He had come across the book *New Musical Resources* by the musical theorist and pioneer pianist Henry Cowell, whose proposals to introduce simultaneously multiple rhythmic patterns influenced the American avant-garde. For Nancarrow, it had "the most influence of anything I've ever read in music."[13] While Nancarrow would say, "I just write a piece of music. It just happens that a lot of them are unplayable," he nevertheless desired to hear his compositions and to not be hindered by the limitations of a human performer. In 1947, he met J. Lawrence Cook at QRS and learned how to use a hand punching machine to produce piano rolls. By this time Nancarrow had emigrated to Mexico, where he returned and began work composing forty-nine *Studies for Player Piano*. In July 1962, just weeks after the Los Angeles audience was stunned by the player piano's rendition of

Stravinsky at the International Music Festival, Nancarrow organized a two-player-piano concert in Sala Ponce in the Palacio de Bellas Artes in Mexico City. Only a few friends showed up. Nancarrow received a MacArthur "genius award" Fellowship in 1982, by which time his compositions had been recorded by the German Wergo label. Occasionally throughout the 1980s and 1990s, live player piano performances were organized to present his work. He died in 1997.

It took some time, but the work of another avant-garde performer who was inspired by the player piano also found a new audience. This brings us to a special exhibit at the National Gallery of Art in Washington, D.C., in 2006, where George Antheil's *Le Ballet Mécanique* was performed using Story & Clark player pianos. The origins of the composition stem back to the 1910s and 20s during the heyday of player pianism and the rise of experimental mechanical music. Musical "modernity" at that time was defined through one's engagement with avant-garde compositions that reflected the cacophony of the metropolitan soundscape. Such music was said to bear "all the marks of a nerve-strung, strident, mechanized civilization."[14] Charles Ives's 1906 composition, "Central Park in the Dark," placed mechanical music in the middle of urban noise by having player pianos underscore the sounds of street cars, fire engines, shouts, and songs. Bohemian "separatists" embraced both mechanical and African American music in rejection of elitist, if also racist, discrimination. One example is the reception that the American pianist George Antheil received when he moved to Paris in 1920.

Antheil's friends included James Joyce, Gertrude Stein, Pablo Picasso, and Ezra Pound, who were intrigued with how he had adapted his piano and had "invented new mechanisms of this particular age," resulting in a style of music new to them. In a piece called *Mechanisms*, he was said to have captured "the rhythm of modern America with a strange combination of esthetic beauty and sheer cacophony." When he returned to New York in 1927 he performed *Le Ballet Mécanique* at Carnegie Hall, where his score included "six pianos, one pianola or mechanical player piano [reduced from an original plan to have sixteen player pianos], bass drums, xylophones, whistles, rattles, electric bells, sewing machine motors, an airplane propeller, and two large pieces of tin"—an aural equivalent to Picasso's canvass. While one shocked woman exclaimed that the noise of the subway "seems sweet after that," others who embraced the artistic expression of the urban soundscape thought that the "threatening machinery had become strangely humanized."[15]

Antheil composed *Le Ballet Mécanique* in 1924 as a film score. According to Paul D. Lehrman, music lecturer at Tufts University and expert in musical instrument digital interface (MIDI) and computer music, the French Dadaist painter Fernand Léger, photographer Man Ray, and an American cinematographer named Dudley Murphy created a film of that name for which Antheil's music was to be the accompaniment.[16] In 2001, Anthology Film Archives began "a worldwide crusade" to reintroduce the film with life performances of Antheil's score. They recruited Lehrman to revive the music in collaboration with Eric Singer of the League of Electronic Musical Urban Robots. This led to the performance at the National Gallery of Art in 2006, which hosted "Dada," the first major museum exhibition in the United States to explore in-depth the influential avant-garde art movement.[17]

I arrived during a spring afternoon taking note of the cherry blossoms, hoards of school groups, and the lack of parking spaces. The exhibit was in the east building, the modern part of the National Gallery. It has a lofty vestibule flooded with natural light with balconies on various levels and suspended walkways that cut through the open space, casting bold shadows. Letters repeating the word d-a-d-a d-a-d-a d-a-d-a were stuck to the pink granite steps leading visitors to the exhibition. On the upper mezzanine in front of a large banner with red and white letters announcing "DADA" were sixteen black baby grand player pianos. They lined a wall of windows which overlooked a queue of tourist buses parked along Constitution Avenue.

It was difficult to imagine the sight of sixteen pianos in one large space without thinking that it would resemble a showroom, but their arrangement made it appear like a concert stage. It was clear that they were part of an exhibition, so no one would dare touch them. I had the impression that most visitors thought that the mere presence of sixteen player pianos was itself a Dada expression. Was it not very Dada-like that pianos which can play by themselves were gathered in a great quantity to sit there silently? It was a spectacle worthy of Marcel Duchamp.

Through the adjacent door was the gallery that presented the rest of the exhibit. There was a film showing documentary footage of the battles and carnage of World War I. The movies were silent. Museum patrons quietly shuffled from one display to another. With little notice, the hour of one o'clock in the afternoon arrived and suddenly, rapturously, the pianos began to play.

> "Here we go again," said one ticket agent to another, both young women.
> Visitors around the gallery stopped in their tracks and stared at the spectacle.
> "Tourists always react in a funny way," said the ticket agent. "It is very abrasive."

Sixteen QRS Pianomation-driven grand player pianos, three xylophones, four bass drums, a tam-tam, a siren, and three "airplane propellors" were all controlled using MIDI technology. It was a technological feat.

Paul Lehrman had contacted QRS Music president Tom Dolan with the proposition of partnering with the National Gallery of Art for the exhibition, and they were happy to get on board. It provided a unique opportunity for them to raise awareness about modern piano-based entertainment systems, though publicity materials from QRS were quick to point out that they specialized in producing "non abrasive" music by allowing owners to synchronize player piano performances with concert DVDs of popular artists such as Diana Krall, Norah Jones, and Billy Joel. But for the moment it was George Antheil's day. It was an opportunity for modern technology to resonate the sounds of history. Of course, many aficionados of Americana, such as many members of AMICA, prefer the real deal—the vintage instruments and the authentic rolls. But watching the newly manufactured pianos, rigged with the digital systems that allow them to play a century of artists' recordings, not only showed that the industry lives on but that it continues to evolve.

Today, the recording of music is a multinational industry worth billions of dollars. From its humble beginnings, which first impressed entertainers and observers alike with its ability to capture and repeat live performances, the player piano proves that it can still command a curious audience. And today it is just as true as it was in the beginning of this musical industry: the best way to get inside music's meaning is by active participation. From the very first to the very latest player piano, the magic is that anyone from novice to virtuoso can assume the seat of the performer and gain a new perspective on the meanings of the sounds of history.

Notes

Preface

1. Lisa Fagg's account of this story is posted at www.doctorjazz.co.uk/page11.html; kudos to the website's host, Mike Meddings, for gathering so much information on J. Lawrence Cook.

2. Kurt Vonnegut, *Player Piano* (New York: Dell, 1999), 32.

3. Tom Davin, "Conversations with James P. Johnson," in *Ragtime: Its History, Composers, and Music*, ed. John Edward Hasse, 166–77 (New York: Schirmer Books, 1985), 171.

4. Michael Chanan, *Repeated Takes: A Short History of Recording and its Effects on Music* (New York: Verso, 1995); Michael Chanan, *Musica Practica: The Social Practice of Western Music from Gregorian Chant to Postmodernism* (London: Verso, 1994).

5. Russell Sanjek, *From Print to Plastic: Publishing and Promoting America's Popular Music (1900–1980)* (New York: Institute for Studies in American Music, 1983).

6. Timothy Day, *A Century of Recorded Music: Listening to Musical History* (New Haven, CT: Yale University Press, 2000), 77–78; Jonathan Sterne, *The Audible Past: Cultural Origins of Sound Reproduction* (Durham, NC: Duke University Press, 2003), 204–205.

7. Harold Schonberg, *The Great Pianists from Mozart to the Present* (New York: Simon and Schuster, 1963). My study follows Bob Billings and

175

Ginny Billings, *The Billings Rollography* (Reno, NV: Rock Soup Press, 1990), who list hundreds of pianists who recorded for QRS Music as a guide to the QRS archives to investigate the diversity and details of collaboration.

8. Histories of the player piano center around memorabilia, such as cataloged in Arthur Ord-Hume, *Player Piano: The History of the Mechanical Piano and How to Repair It* (London: George Allen & Unwin, 1970); Harvey Roehl, *Player Piano Treasury* (Vestal, NY: Vestal Press, 1961); histories of the radio and phonograph, such as William Kenney, *Recorded Music in American Life: The Phonograph and Popular Memory 1890–1945* (Oxford: Oxford University Press, 1999); Erika Brady, *A Spiral Way: How the Phonograph Changed Ethnography* (Jackson: University Press of Mississippi, 1999); Roland Gelatt, *The Fabulous Phonograph, 1877–1977* (New York: Collier, 1977); and Susan Douglas, *Listening In: Radio and the American Imagination* (New York: Times Books, 1999), provide models for studying the relations between technology and entertainment, but the different nature of the technology and creative context of earlier player pianos further distinguish the proposed study.

9. David Suisman, "The Sound of Money: Music, Machines and Markets, 1890–1925" (PhD diss., Columbia University, 2002), 54.

10. Isaac Goldberg, *Tin Pan Alley: A Chronicle of American Popular Music* (New York: John Day, repr. 1961).

11. Suisman, "The Sound of Money," 59.

12. Trevor Pinch and Frank Trocco, *Analog Days: The Invention and Impact of the Moog Synthesizer* (Cambridge, MA: Harvard University Press, 2002); Timothy Taylor, *Strange Sounds: Music, Technology and Culture* (London: Routledge, 2002); Emily Thompson, *The Soundscape of Modernity: Architectural Acoustics and the Culture of Listening in America 1900–1933* (Cambridge, MA: MIT Press, 2002); Douglas Kahn, *Noise, Water, Meat: A History of Sound in the Arts* (Cambridge, MA: MIT Press, 1999)

13. There is much historiography to draw on for the context of advertising and consumption, and scholars including Roland Marchand, Lizabeth Cohen, and William Leach inform my study.

14. Richard Leppert, *The Sight of Sound: Music, Representation and the History of the Body* (Berkeley: University of California Press, 1993), chap. 4; Simon Frith, "The Industrialization of Popular Music," in *Popular Music and Communication*, ed. James Lull (New York: Sage, 1992).

15. "The Democracy of Music Achieved by Invention," *Current Literature* 42 (1907): 670–73; Yolanda Mero, "Musical Democracy vs. Pianism," *The Musician* 22 (1917): 494; see also Craig Roell, *The Piano in America 1890–1940* (Chapel Hill: University of North Carolina Press, 1989), 38–39, 96.

16. Mark Katz, *Capturing Sound: How Technology Has Changed Music* (Berkeley: University of California Press, 2004); Emily Thompson, "Machines, Music and the Quest for Fidelity: Marketing the Edison Phonograph in America, 1877–1925," *Musical Quarterly* 79 (1995): 131–73; Michael Saffle, ed., *Perspectives on American Music 1900–1950*, vol. 3 (New York: Garland, 2000).

Chapter 2

1. Jesse Lazear to Charlotte Sweitzer, July 20, 1890, University of Virginia Archives, Yellow Fever Collection.

2. George Whitney Jr., interview by John Martini, August 13, 2002, Tape 1, Side A, National Park Service.

3. George Whitney Jr., interview by John Martini, August 13, 2002, Tape 2, Side A, National Park Service.

4. Edward Zelinski, "About the Musee Mecanique Collection," www.museemechanique.org.

5. Ken Garcia, "Laughing Sal has tears in her eyes: Cliff House Arcade Mustn't Close Down," *San Francisco Chronicle*, March 12, 2002.

6. www.museemechanique.org/about.html.

7. See brief history and personal reminiscences of acquaintances to those discussed in the next few paragraphs in the pages of the Mechanical Musical Press, www.mechanicalmusicpress.com.

8. Arthur Reblitz, *The Golden Age of Automatic Musical Instruments* (Woodsville, NH: Mechanical Musical Press, 2001), 309.

9. Bob Moore, "Growing up in Roseland Park," www.mechanicalmusicpress.com/history/pianella/w32_2_p2.htm.

10. Tim Trager, "Mechanical Music at Theme Parks—Opportunities Lost," *Mechanical Music Digest*, January 12, 2001, letter 5, www.mmdigest.com/archives.

11. Stephen Kent Goodman, "Mechanical Music at Theme Parks," *Mechanical Music Digest*, January 13, 2001, letter 10, www.mmdigest.com/archives.

12. Marty Roenigk, "Mechanical Music on Display," *Mechanical Music Digest*, January 13, 2001, letter 7, www.mmdigest.com/archives.

13. See interview in Eureka Springs Online, 2004: www.eurekaspringsonline.com/interviews_marty_roenigk.htm.

Chapter 3

1. John McTammany, *The Technical History of the Player* (New York: Musical Courier Company, 1915), ii.

2. Simon Schaffer, "Babbage's Dancer," in *Cultural Babbage: Technology, Time and Invention*, ed. Francis Spufford and Jenny Uglow, 69 (London: Faber, 1996); see also Simon Schaffer, "Enlightened Automata," in *The Sciences in Enlightened Europe*, ed. William Clark, Jan Golinski, and Simon Schaffer, 126–65 (Chicago: University of Chicago Press, 1999).

3. Gaby Wood, *Living Dolls: A Magical History of the Quest for Mechanical Life* (London: Faber, 2002), Introduction; see also the website dedicated to the history of these dolls by Julie Porter, www.delectra.com/jporter/acMdaEng.html.

4. Description in Marion Melius, "Music by Electricity," *The World's Work* (1906): 7660–63.

5. Ferrucio Busoni, *Sketch of a New Esthetic in Music* (New York: Dover, 1962), 38.

6. Max Weber's "History of the Piano," in *The Rational and Social Foundations of Music*, ed. Don Martindale, Johannes Riedel, and Gertrude Neuwirth (Carbondale: Southern Illinois University Press, 1958), 124.

7. Reid quoted in Jervis Anderson, *This Was Harlem: A Cultural Portrait 1900–1950* (New York: Farrar, Straus, Giroux, 1981), 156.

8. Arthur Loesser, *Men, Women and Pianos: A Social History* (New York: Simon & Schuster, 1954), 549.

9. John Higham, "The Reorientation of American Culture in the 1890's," in *Writing American History* (Bloomington: University of Indiana Press, 1970), 73–102.

10. Neil Leonard, *Jazz: Myth and Religion* (Oxford: Oxford University Press, 1987), 4.

11. Walter Benjamin, "The Work of Art in the Age of Mechanical Reproduction" (1936), section 9, online at www.marxists.org/reference/subject/philosophy/works/ge/benjamin.htm.

12. Cyril Ehrlich, *The Piano: A History* (London: J.M. Dent, 1976), 136.

13. Quoted in McTammany, *Technical History*, iv.

14. Michael Montgomery, Trebor Tichenor, and John Edward Hasse, "Ragtime on Piano Rolls," in *Ragtime: Its History, Composers and Music*, ed. John Edward Hasse, 90–101 (New York: Schirmer Books, 1985), 90.

15. Quote from Trevor Pinch and Karin Bijsterveld, "'Should One Applaud?' Breaches and Boundaries in the Reception of New Technology in Music," *Technology and Culture* (2003): 542.

16. McTammany, *Technical History*, iii.

17. Loesser, *Men, Women and Pianos*, 581.

18. M.V. Molloy, "Mechanical Music Men," *Los Angeles Times*, May 1, 1988, 25.

19. Sally Dugan and David Dugan, *The Day the World Took Off: The Roots of the Industrial Revolution* (Basingstoke: Macmillan, 2000), 40–41.

20. Shirley Wilcox, "The Player Piano: Mechanical Evolution of the Automatic Keyboard," *Contemporary Keyboard* (May 1981): 17, mentions Morse.

21. This information is from Q. David Bowers, *Encyclopedia of Automatic Musical Instruments* (Vestal, NY: Vestal Press, 1972), 255.

22. Michel Nallino, in *Musiques Mecaniques Vivantes* 27 (1998).

23. While this information is produced in numerous places, I recommend visiting the revamped site of the Pianola Institute, which has a clear and more detailed history of all this: www.pianola.org.

24. General information on hundreds of piano companies can be surveyed at www.pianos.co.uk/info/pianos.

25. See Reginald Reynolds, "The Paderewski of the Player Piano" [pamphlet], (Great Britain: Player Piano Group, 1998), for contemporary description of playing the pianola.

26. Douglas Heffer, "The Coupleux Brothers and Aeolian of France," *Mechanical Music Digest*, no. 2, February 8, 2002, www.mmdigest.com/ archives. Heffer refers to an academic dissertation by Olivier Carpentier that provides greater detail.

27. Alfred Dolge, *Pianos and Their Makers*, vol. 2 (Vestal, NY: Vestal Press, 1913), 44–45.

28. Craig Roell, "Musical Instrument Manufacturing," *Encyclopedia of Chicago*, online at www.encyclopedia.chicagohistory.org/pages/864.html.

29. Jim Edwards and Wynette Edwards, *Chicago Entertainment Between the Wars, 1919–1939* (Chicago: Arcadia, 2003), 61.

30. Quoted in Craig Roell, *The Piano in America 1890–1940* (Chapel Hill, University of North Carolina Press, 1989), 40.

31. "This Man Invented the First Player-Piano," advertisement by Simplex Player Actions (a Theodore Brown company) in *The Indicator* (1914), Melville Clark Music Collection, Box 25, "Advertising," Syracuse University Library.

32. Statistics from Roell, *Piano in America*, 32.

33. Welte-Mignon advertisement, reprinted in Harvey Roehl, *Player Piano Treasury* (Vestal, NY: Vestal Press, 1961), 69.

34. Arthur Reblitz, *The Golden Age of Automatic Musical Instruments* (Woodsville, NH: Mechanical Musical Press, 2001), 204.

35. Advertisement, "The Aeolian Company Announces the New Pianola Piano, 'The First Complete Piano,'" University of Maryland, Howe Collection of Musical Instrument Literature (hereafter "Howe Collection"), Mechanical Musical Instruments, Series General Information, Box 1.

36. Story & Clark brochure, undated. Howe Collection, Piano, Series General Information, Box 22.

37. "Useful Career Closed by Death of Melville Clark," *Presto* (November 7, 1918), 9.

38. "The Genius of Melville Clark," *The Musical Age* (January 16, 1909): 245.

39. Melville Clark Piano Co., *Reasons Why the Melville Clark Apollo Player Piano Is the Standard Instrument of the World*, brochure describing new design features, n.d. (ca. 1910), Clark Music Company archive, Syracuse University, Box 25, Advertising.

40. "Holding the Mirror to Nature," n.d. (ca. 1910), Howe Collection, Mechanical Musical Instruments, Series General Information, Box 4.

41. Dolge, *Pianos,* 58.

42. McTammany, *Technical History,* 104.

Chapter 4

1. Jesse Hamlin, "There's Nothing Mechanical about It: Player Pianos Hammer the Heartstrings of Alamo Square," *San Francisco Chronicle*, October 7, 2004.

2. Jim Edwards and Wynette Edwards, *Chicago Entertainment Between the Wars, 1919–1939* (Chicago: Arcadia, 2003), 62.

3. All Reutlinger quotations from personal interview, 13 February 2006.

4. Werner Muensterberger and Vicki Austin-Smith, *Collecting: An Unruly Passion. Psychological Perspectives* (New York: Harcourt, 1995), 11 (emphasis in original).

5. Susan Kubian, "Nuts about Collecting: Food Magnate Attracts Cornucopia of Entertainment Machines," *Chicago Tribune*, August 30, 1992, Section 18, 8.

6. John Farrell, "The Future of Mechanical Music," *Mechanical Music Digest*, no. 1, March 1, 2004, www.mmdigest.com/archives.

7. Harvey Roehl, "Every Collector's Dream," *News Bulletin*, Musical Box Society International, vol. 10, no. 6 (1964): 1–2.

8. All quotations that follow are from Larry Givens, "Four Essays on Collecting," 1993, typed manuscript, Howe Collection, Mechanical Musical Instruments.

Chapter 5

1. Vincent Morgan, in correspondence with Brian Dolan, June 28, 2005; background info posted on *Mechanical Music Digest*, July 4, 2004, item 6, www.mmdigest.com/archives.

2. A few collections of ethnic rolls exist. Bob Berkman at QRS Music wrote a brief history of the ethnic rolls that they produced including Greek,

Ukrainian, Jewish, and other types that "tell the story of America's immigrant populations in surprising and engaging ways." Berkman, personal correspondence. More information at www.qrsmusic.com. The Ethnomusicology Archive at UCLA has a collection, while the Polish Museum in Chicago has player piano rolls created by Paderewski. See also Berkman's recently released "Jewish Music from Rare Piano Rolls": www.klezmerola.com/.

3. *Mechanical Music Digest*, July 12, 2004, item 4, www.mmdigest.com/archives.

4. Carroll Brent Chilton, *The De-Assification of Music: A Propagandist Magazine of One Number, Containing News of Importance to all Music Lovers, Especially to all Owners of Player Pianos* (1922), New York Public Library, Library for the Performing Arts.

5. Harvey Roehl, *Player Piano Treasury* (Vestal, NY: Vestal Press, 1961), 141.

6. Stanislaw Lem, *His Master's Voice* (Evanston: Northwestern University Press, 1999; originally published 1968), 145.

7. David Todd, *Stars and Telescopes* (Boston: Little, Brown & Co., 1899), quoted in Robbie Rhodes, "Solar Eclipse Telescope Controlled by Music Roll," *Mechanical Music Digest*, February 1, 2002, item 3, www.mmdigest.com/archives.

8. George Antheil, *Bad Boy of Music* (New York: Samuel French, 1990; originally published 1945), see also Tony Rothman, *Everything's Relative: And Other Fables from Science and Technology* (New York: Wiley, 2003), chap. 16, www.physics.princeton.edu/~trothman/relative_contents.html.

9. August 11, 1942, U.S. Patent 2,292,387; see Rothman, *Everything's Relative*, chap. 16.

10. Tom Standage, *The Victorian Internet* (New York: Berkley Trade, 1999).

11. Quoted in James R. Gaines, ed., *The Lives of the Piano* (New York: Holt, Rinehart and Winston, 1981), 25.

12. Benoit Mandelbrot, *The Misbehavior of Markets: A Fractal View of Risk, Ruin and Reward* (New York: Basic Books, 2004), 263.

13. John Kobler, *Capone* (Cambridge, MA: Da Capo Press, 2003), 81.

14. www.wiscasset.net/artcraft/studio.htm.

15. See Reginald Reynolds, "A Note on the Technique of Recording," *The Pianola Journal* 7 (1994), www.pianola.org/journal/journal_vol7-8.cfm.

Chapter 6

1. Jean Lawrence Cook, "Autobiography," reprinted in *The Billings Rollography*, vol. 5, ed. Ginny Billings and Bob Billings (Reno, NV: Rock Soup Press, 1994), 30.

2. Census data from ancestry.com. My thanks to Bob Hatch for digging out this information for me. See also Charles Keith, *A Review of McMinn County, TN, 1819–1968* (Athens, TN, 1969), for a brief overview.

3. Cook, "Autobiography," 32.

4. Cook, "Autobiography," 35.

5. Cook, "Autobiography," 40.

6. Cook, *Online Autobiography*, ed. Jean Lawrence Cook (son), retrieved from www.amica.org/amica_publications/past-bulletin-articles/past-bulletin-articl es-main.htm.

7. Cook, "Autobiography," 31.

8. Richard Lieberman, *Steinway and Sons* (New Haven, CT: Yale University Press, 1997), 181, writes, "In 1923, the player piano accounted for more than half of all pianos shipped in America," though contemporary reports suggest this may have occurred prior to 1923.

9. *New York Times*, February 9, 1918, 17.

10. Quoted in Reid Badger, *A Life in Ragtime: A Biography of James Reese Europe* (Oxford: Oxford University Press, 1995), 53.

11. Roland Gelatt, *The Fabulous Phonograph 1877–1977* (New York: Macmillan, 1954), 189.

12. Gelatt, *Fabulous Phonograph*, 190.

13. Standard Music Roll Co., *Ten Points of Superiority of the Electra Music Rolls*, brochure with Bell's signed testimonial. Howe Collection, Mechanical Musical Instruments (emphasis in original).

14. "The Blasius Piano is the Tone Standard of the World," Blasius and Sons Trade Card, Howe Collection, Mechanical Musical Instruments, Series Oversized, Box 1.

15. David Suisman, personal correspondence with author; see also his "The Sound of Money: Music, Machines and Markets, 1890–1925" (PhD diss., Columbia University, 2002).

16. David Nice, *Prokofiev: From Russia to the West, 1891-1935* (New Haven, CT: Yale University Press, 2003), 157.

17. The Aeolian Company, *The Metrostyle* (1903), Howe Collection, Mechanical Musical Instruments, Series Roll Catalogues, Box 1.

18. Bruce Haring, *Beyond the Charts: The MP3 and the Digital Revolution* (Los Angeles: Off the Charts, 2000), 23.

19. Robert Kimball and Alfred Simon, *The Gershwins* (New York: Atheneum, 1973), 12. Charles Browning, an orchestra musician, teacher, and piano roll artist who in the late 1910s cut thirty rolls per month for Wurlitzer, was paid five cents per foot and spent three hours recording five hundred feet of roll, according to his son, James Browning, "Whatever Happened to the Player Piano?" *Music Journal* 23 (1965): 42–43, though five hundred feet in three hours would be an amazing amount: J. Lawrence

Cook said in an interview that "it takes about three hours to make a fox trot of 30 feet," which is good for 2 1/2 minutes of dancing. *Billings Rollography*, 30.

20. Badger, *Life in Ragtime*, 53.

21. Jack Batterson, *Blind Boone: Missouri's Ragtime Pioneer* (Columbia: University of Missouri Press, 1998), 21–22; also Lynn Abbott and Doug Seroff, *Out of Sight: The Rise of African American Popular Music 1889–1895* (Jackson: University Press of Mississippi, 2003).

22. Melissa Fuell, *Blind Boone: His Early Life and His Achievements* (Kansas City, MO: Burton, 1915), 135.

23. Eileen Southern, *The Music of Black Americans: A History* (New York: W.W. Norton, 1997), 310.

24. Cook, *Online Autobiography*.

25. Tom Davin, "Conversations with James P. Johnson," in *Ragtime: Its History, Composers and Music*, ed. John Edward Hasse (New York: Schirmer Books, 1985), 171.

26. Hasse, *Ragtime*, 6.

27. Scott Brown, *James P. Johnson: A Case of Mistaken Identity. A James P. Johnson Discography 1917–1950* (New Brunswick, NJ: Rutgers University Press, 1986), 26.

28. Davin, "Conversations," 169.

29. *New York Times*, September 22, 1881, 11.

30. Davin, "Conversations," 172.

31. Brown, *James P. Johnson*, 25.

32. Brown, *James P. Johnson*, 86.

33. Schreyer, "Banjo," 58.

34. Brown, *James P. Johnson*, 70.

35. Davin, "Conversations," 170.

36. Gunther Schuller, "Rags, the Classics and Jazz," in *Ragtime: Its History, Composers and Music*, ed. John Edward Hasse, 79–89 (New York: Schirmer Books, 1985), 87.

37. Brown, *James P. Johnson*, 87.

38. Davin, "Conversations," 174.

39. Davin, *Conversations*, 173.

40. Dolge, *Pianos*, 9.

41. Brown, *James P. Johnson*, 83.

42. Brown, *James P. Johnson*, 60.

43. Brown, *James P. Johnson*, 120.

44. Badger, *Life in Ragtime*, 97.

45. Badger, *Life in Ragtime*, 122.

46. Brown, *James P. Johnson*, 60.

Chapter 7

1. Reid Badger, *A Life in Ragtime: A Biography of James Reese Europe* (Oxford: Oxford Univedrsity Press, 1995), 83.

2. Brown, *James P. Johnson: A Case of Mistaken Identity. A James P. Johnson Discography 1917–1950* (New Brunswick, NJ Rutgers University Press, 1986), 15.

3. Quoted in Neil Leonard, "The Reactions to Ragtime," in *Ragtime: Its History, Composers, and Music,* ed. John Edward Hasse, 102–113 (New York: Schirmer Books, 1985), 105.

4. Thomas Pletcher, *Apollo Player Piano: Confidential Selling Information* (1916), 13, Howe Collection, Mechanical Musical Instruments, Series General Information, Box 1.

5. Pletcher, *Apollo Player Piano,* 35.

6. Michael Montgomery, Trebor Tichenor, and John Edward Hasse, "Ragtime on Piano Rolls," 95.

7. Leo Oehmler, "Ragtime: A Pernicious Evil and Enemy of True Art," *Musical Observer* 11 (1914): 15; The rich literature on the reactions to jazz includes Edward Berlin, *Ragtime: A Musical and Cultural History* (www .backinprint.com, 2002); Neil Leonard, *Jazz and the White Americans* (Chicago: University of Chicago Press, 1962); Neil Leonard, *Jazz: Myth and Religion* (Oxford: Oxford University Press, 1987); Dena Epstein, *Sinful Tunes and Spirituals: Black Folk Music to the Civil War* (Urbana: University of Illinois Press, 1997).

8. Quoted in Robert Walser, ed., *Keeping Time: Readings in Jazz History* (Oxford: Oxford University Press, 1999), 35.

9. Leonard, "Reactions," 107.

10. Rhodri Hayward, "Demonology, Neurology, and Medicine in Edwardian Britain," *Bulletin of the History of Medicine* 78 (2004): 37–58.

11. Lawrence Levine, *Black Culture and Black Consciousness* (New York: Oxford University Press, 1977).

12. Houston Baker, *Modernism and the Harlem Renaissance* (Chicago: University of Chicago Press, 1987), 101.

13. Paul Carter, *The Twenties in America* (New York: Thomas Crowell, 1971), 24.

14. Carter, *The Twenties in America,* 25.

15. "To the Musician with a Head of His Own," undated bulletin in Syracuse University, Melville Clark Papers, Box 25, Advertising.

16. Craig Roell, *The Piano in America 1890–1940* (Chapel Hill: University of North Carolina Press, 1989), 34.

17. Charles Nanry, "Jazz and Modernism: Twin-Born Children of the Age of Invention," in *Annual Review of Jazz Studies,* ed. Dan Morganstern, (1982), 146.

18. Harvey Roehl, *Player Piano Treasury*, 2nd ed. (Vestal, NY: Vestal Press, 1973), 42.

19. See advertisements in Roehl, *Player Piano Treasury* (1961), 24, 42.

20. Quoted in Roell, *Piano in America*, 158.

21. "Chopin 1810–1849," Program by the Music Research Foundation, December 8–10, 1949, in the Melville Clark Papers, Syracuse University, Special Collections, Series I, Box 149, Clark Letters.

22. Bob Baker, "Other Uses for Player Pianos," *Mechanical Music Digest*, February 4, 2002, no. 3.

23. John Tuttle, "Other Uses for Player Pianos," *Mechanical Music Digest*, February 5, 2002, no. 4.

24. Lt. C. R. Eagle to Aeolian, 15 July 1919, Howe Collection, Mechanical Musical Instruments, Series General Information, Box 1.

25. Howe Collection, Mechanical Musical Instruments, Series General Information, Box 1.

26. John F. Kasson, *Amusing the Millions: Coney Island at the Turn of the Century* (New York: Hill & Wang, 1978).

27. John McTammany, *The Technical History of the Player* (New York: Musical Courier Company, 1915), vi.

28. Roehl, *Player Piano Treasury*, 69.

29. Howe Collection, Series Advertisements, Box 1.

30. Howe Collection, Mechanical Musical Instruments, Series General Information, Box 1.

31. Loesser, *Men, Women and Pianos*, 560.

32. Loesser, *Men, Women, and Pianos*, 583.

33. "P.A.," *Musical Times*, 1 January 1924, 52.

34. Roehl, *Player Piano Treasury* (1961), 69.

35. "A Word to the Cultured Woman," Melville Clark Piano Company, ca. 1920, Syracuse University, Melville Clark Collection, Box 25, Advertising Cuts and Flyers.

36. Roehl, *Player Piano Treasury* (1961), 32, 39.

37. Gustav Kobbé, *The Pianolist: A Guide for Pianola Players* (New York: Moffat, Yard & Co., 1912), 5.

38. Kobbé, *The Pianolist*, 6.

39. There is much historiography to draw on for the context of advertising and consumption, and scholars including Roland Marchand, Lizabeth Cohen, and William Leach inform this analysis; more particularly, the merchandizing of music has been explored by David Suisman, "The Sound of Money: Music, Machines and Markets, 1890–1925" PhD diss., Columbia University, 2002).

40. "The Democracy of Music Achieved by Invention," 670–73; Yolanda Mero, "Musical Democracy vs. Pianism," *The Musician* 22 (1917); 494; see also Roell, *Piano in America*, 38–39, 96.

41. Roehl, *Player Piano Treasury* (1961), 51.

42. *New York Times*, February 9, 1918, 17.

43. J. P. McEvoy, *Slams of Life: With Malice for All, and Charity Toward None* (Chicago: P.F. Volland Co., 1919), 21.

44. *New York Times*, December 3, 1931, 26.

45. Richard Leppert, *The Sight of Sound: Music, Representation and the History of the Body* (Berkeley, University of California Press, 1993), chap. 4 (see preface, n. 13); Simon Frith, "The Industrialization of Popular Music," in *Popular Music and Communication*, ed. James Lull (New York: Sage, 1992).

46. Sydney Grew, "The Player-Piano," *Music and Letters* 6 (1925): 240.

Chapter 8

1. Jeff Barnhart website, www.jeffbarnhart.com/.

2. Gunther Schuller, "Rags, the Classics and Jazz," John Edward Hasse, 79–89 (New York: Schirmer Books), 87.

3. Henry Pleasants, *The Agony of Modern Music* (New York: Simon and Schuster, 1955), 176.

4. *Musical Courier*, February 11, 1903.

5. Chickering advertisement, undated, circa 1920. Syracuse University, Melville Clark Music Archive, Box 25, Advertising.

6. Mark Mitchell, *Vladimir de Pachmann: A Piano Virtuoso's Life and Art* (Bloomington: Indiana University Press, 2002), 111.

7. Pachmann to W.C. Heaton, August 1, 1925, reproduced in an advertisement in the Melville Clark Music Collection, Box 26, Syracuse University.

8. Augustus Manns, *Reprint of Correspondence in 'Daily Mail' on Music by Machinery* (London, 1903), booklet in Howe Collection, Mechanical Musical Instruments, General Information, Box 4.

9. Reginald Reynolds, "The Paderewski of the Player Piano" [pamphlet], (Great Britain: Player Piano Group) 4.

10. Reynolds, *Paderewski* in *Ragtime: Its History, Composer and Music*, ed. 5.

11. Reginald Reynolds, "A Note on the Technique of Recording," *The Pianola Journal* 7 (1994): www.pianola.org/journal/journal_vol. 7–8.cfm.

12. The Mozart and Haydn stories are recounted in Arthur W.J.G. Ord-Hume, "Cogs and Crotchets: A View of Mechanical Music," *Early Music*, April 1983, 167–71, quote on p. 170.

13. Russell Roth, "The Ragtime Revival: A Critique," *American Quarterly* 2 (1950), 331–332.

14. Artis Wodehouse, "Tracing Gershwin's Piano Rolls," in *The Gershwin Style: New Looks at the Music of George Gershwin*, ed. Wayne Schneider, 209–223 (Oxford: Oxford University Press, 1999), 210.

15. Wodehouse, "Tracing Gershwin's Piano Rolls," 212.

16. www.artiswodehouse.com/.

17. "The Esthetics of Contemporary Music," *Musical Quarterly* 15 (1929): 265, quoted in Trevor Pinch and Karin Bijsterveld, "'Should One Applaud?' Breaches and Boundaries in the Reception of New Technology in Music," *Technology and Culture (2003): 541.*

18. *Quoted in Pinch and Bijsterveld, "'Should One Applaud?'" 541.*

19. *Pinch and Bijsterveld, "'Should One Applaud?'"*

20. Mike Montgomery, "Cook Interview," reprinted in Ginny and Bob Billings, *The Billings Rollography*, vol. 5 (Reno, NV: Rock Soup Press, 1994), 41.

21. The role of arrangers who become in part the "invisible entertainers" of this story are not dissimilar to the "invisible technicians" who form part of the network of actors involved in the production of scientific knowledge as described by Steven Shapin in *A Social History of Truth: Civility and Science in Seventeenth-Century England* (Chicago: University of Chicago Press, 1994), chapter 8.

22. *Billings Rollography*, vol. 3, 12.

23. "Death of Melville Clark," Useful Career Closed by Presto (November 7, 1918), 9 (see chap. 3, n. 37).

24. The legend appeared in a small notice in a 1926 trade journal; see Berkman, "History," 4; Berkman points out that QRS might originally have stood for "Quality Roll Supply" or "Quick Roll Service."

25. Melville Clark Piano Company (Wurlitzer) archives, Northern Illinois University: www.dig.lib.niu.edu/dekalb/hist-piano.html; "Death of Melville Clark," 9–10 (see chap. 3, n. 37).

26. The figure is from a Kortlander biography: www.doctorjazz2.free serve.co.uk/maxkort.html#intromax, where it states: "His 1919 fox trot 'Tell Me' sold for $100,000, the highest lump sum paid for any popular song up to that time."

27. LeRoy Barnett, "Let the Good Times Roll," *Michigan History Magazine* March/April 2000, 13.

28. Montgomery, "Interview," 24; this and the following dialogue between Lawrence and Kortlander come from this source.

Chapter 9

1. Arthur Badrock, "The (Second) English Parlophone Race Series," *Talking Machine Review* 89 (Spring 1995): 2779–81; Helge Thygesen, *Black*

Swan: The Record Label of the Harlem Renaissance (Radnor, PA: VJM, 1996).

2. Mike Montgomery, "Cook Interview," reprinted in Ginny and Bob Billings, *The Billings Rollography*, vol. 5 (Reno, NV: Rock Soup Press, 1994), 43.

3. See the discussion of the difference between Johnson's "Carolina Shout" as recorded by him in 1918 and the QRS version released in May 1921 in Scott Brown, *James P. Johnson: A Case of Mistaken Identity. A James P. Johnson Discography 1917–1950* (New Brunswick, NJ: Rutgers University Press), 132–33. Lawrence's quote in *Billings Rollography*, vol. 5, 141.

4. Maurice Waller and Anthony Calabrese, *Fats Waller* (New York: Schirmer Books, 1977), 27.

5. Waller and Calabrese, *Fats Waller*, 27; Alyn Shipton, *Fats Waller: The Cheerful Little Earful* (London: Continuum, 2002), 10.

6. Waller and Calabrese, *Fats Waller*, 27.

7. Waller and Calabrese, *Fats Waller*, 29.

8. Shipton, *Fats Waller*, 21.

9. Reproduced in advertisement, Howe Collection, Piano, Series Advertisements, Box 1.

10. Robert Haven Schauffler, "The Mission of Mechanical Music," *The Century* 89 (1914): 297.

11. The Aeolian Company, *The Weight of Evidence* (New York: Author, 1914), 1.

12. Howe Collection, Mechanical Musical Instruments, Series General Information, Box 1.

13. "The Democracy of Music Achieved by Invention," 670–73; Mero, "Musical Democracy vs. Pianism," 494; see also Craig Roell, *The Piano in America 1890–1940* (Chapel Hill, University of North Carolina Press, 1989), 38–39, 96.

14. Duke Ellington, *Music Is My Mistress* (Cambridge, MA: Da Capo Press, 1988), 34.

15. James Renel Burden, "Conversation with Joe Turner: Last of the Stride Pianists," *The Black Perspective in Music* 9 (1981): 185.

16. Ethel Waters and Charles Samuels, *His Eye Is on the Sparrow* (Westport, CT: Greenwood Press, 1978), 147.

17. Rudy Shackelford, "Conversations with Vincent Persichetti," *Perspectives of New Music* 20 (1981): 104.

18. D. Antoinette Handy, "Conversations with Mary Lou Williams," *The Black Perspective in Music* 8 (1980): 198-99; also Linda Dahl, *Morning Glory: A Biography of Mary Lou Williams* (Berkeley: University of California Press, 2001): 26–27.

19. Robert Doerschuk, *The Giants of Jazz Piano* (San Francisco: Backbeat Books, 2001), 103.

20. H. Arlo Nimmo, *The Andrews Sisters: A Biography and Career Record* (Jefferson, NC: McFarland & Co, 2004), 13, 20.

21. Sinatra, in a 1986 lecture he gave at Yale University, quoted in John Lahr, *Show and Tell: New Yorker Profiles* (Berkeley: University of California Press, 2002), 56.

22. "The Educational Use of the Player-Piano," *The Musical Times* 66 (March 1, 1925): 253.

23. Waller and Calabrese, *Fats Waller*, 46.

24. Montgomery, "Interview," 58.

25. Montgomery, "Interview," 58.

26. Eugene Chadbourne, biography of J. Lawrence Cook, *All Music Guide*, at www.artistsdirect.com.

27. Ken List, "Recording Eubie Blake at QRS," *Mechanical Music Digest* March 21, 1998, no. 12.

28. Montgomery, "Interview," 60.

29. Waller and Calabrese, *Fats Waller*, 46.

30. Montgomery, "Interview," 59.

31. Arthur Whiting, "The Mechanical Player," *Yale Review* 8 (1920): 1.

32. Quoted in Brown, *James P. Johnson*, 130.

33. John McTammany, *The Technical History of the Player* (New York: Musical Courier Company, 1915), vi.

34. "Recording the Soul of Piano Playing," *Scientific American* (November 1927).

35. Gustav Kobbé, *The Pianolist: A Guide for Pianola Players* (New York: Moffat, Yard & Co., 1912), 14, 23, 29.

36. "QRS Interests Purchase U.S. Music Co." (November 6, 1926), reprinted in Harvey Roehl, *Player Piano Treasury* (Vestal, NY: Vestal Press 1961), 170.

37. Larry Givens, *Re-Enacting the Artist* (Vestal, NY: Vestal Press, 1970), 130–31.

38. Ernest Newlandsmith, *The Temple of Art: A Plea for the Higher Realisation of the Artistic Vocation*, 1st ed. (London: Longmans, 1904), 40.

39. Shaw quoted in Colin Osman, "The Camera and the Pianola," *The Pianola* 5 (1993): 1.

40. David Sudnow, *The Way of the Hand: The Organization of Improvised Conduct* (London: Routledge, 1978), quoted in Harry Collins, *Artificial Experts: Social Knowledge and Intelligent Machines* (Cambridge, MA: MIT Press, 1990), 76.

41. Roth, "The Ragtime Revival," 332 (emphasis in original).

42. John Philip Sousa, "Menace of Mechanical Music," *Appleton's Magazine* 8 (1906): 280.

Chapter 10

1. Arthur Loesser, *Men, Women and Pianos: A Social History* (New York: Simon & Schuster, 1954), p. 585.

2. Ernest Newman, *The Piano-Player and Its Music* (London: Grant Richards, 1920), 15.

3. Chicago *Indicator*, January 11, 1908, Howe Collection, Piano, Series General Information, Box 22.

4. William Geppert, quoted in John McTammany, *The Technical History of the Player* (New York: Musical Courier Company, 1915), vi.

5. Roehl, *Player Piano Treasury* (1961), 47.

6. Carl Engel, "The Miraculous Appeal of Mediocrity," *The Musical Quarterly* 5 (1919): 453–62, 461.

7. Sydney Grew, "The Player-Piano," *Music and Letters* 6 (1925): 236.

8. *The Musical Times* 70 (July 1, 1929): 637.

9. Grew, "Player-Piano," 239.

10. Thompson, "Machines, Music and the Quest for Fidelity."

11. Ulric Daubeny, "The Gramophone—Present and Future," *The Musical Times* 62 (1921): 477 (emphasis in original).

12. Julian Dyer, "Demise of American Piano Company," *Mechanical Music Digest*, April 12, 2001, no. 5.

13. *Mechanical Music Digest* (March 4, 2001), no. 2.

14. Harold Cones and John Bryant, *Zenith Radios: The Early Years 1919–1935* (Atglen, PA: Schiffer Publishing, 1997). I'd like to thank Bob Berkman at QRS for directing my attention to this.

15. In 1925, piano sales were around 320,000 units. They dipped to as low as 27,000 units in 1932, but climbed to 65,000 in 1935.

16. *New York Times*, July 27, 1937, 23.

17. Sigmund Spaeth to Miss Laug (Melville Clark Music Co.), November 14, 1938, with publicity material in Syracuse University Library, Melville Clark Collection, Series I, Box 149.

18. E. G. Clark to Imperial Industrial Corp., January 7, 1939, Howe Collection, Mechanical Musical Instruments, General Information, Box 4.

19. "Roll On, Imperial," *Time*, February 15, 1943.

20. *International Musician* 40, no. 6 (1941): 25–26.

21. *International Musician* 38, no. 11 (1941): 25.

22. *International Musician* 40, no. 9 (1942): 21.

23. Paul Oliver, *The Story of the Blues* (Northeastern University Press, 1998), 140.

24. "Caesar Dixit," *Time*, June 22, 1942.

25. *International Musician* 40, no. 6 (1941): 25–26.

26. *International Musician* 40, no. 9 (1942): 21.

27. Theodore Adorno, "The Curves of the Needle," in *Essays on Music*, ed. Richard Leppert, trans. Susan Gillespie (Berkeley: University of California Press, 2002), 273 for Weber; Adorno, "On the Fetish-Character in Music," 295–96.

28. Theodore Gracyk, "Adorno, Jazz and the Aesthetics of Popular Music," *Musical Quarterly* 76 (1992): 532–33; Max Paddison, "The Critique Criticized: Adorno and Popular Music," in *Popular Music 2: Theory and Method*, ed. Richard Middleton and David Horn, (Cambridge: Cambridge University Press, 1982), 201–18.

29. Herbert Marcuse, *The Aesthetic Dimension* (New York: Beacon, 1979); see also Eric Hobsbawm, *The Jazz Scene* (London: Pantheon, 1993 [reprint from 1959]). Peter Martin, *Sounds and Society: Themes in the Sociology of Music* (Manchester: Manchester University Press, 1995), chap. 3; Martin Jay, *Adorno* (Cambridge, MA: Harvard University Press, 1984).

30. Kurt Vonnegut, *Player Piano* (New York: Dell, 1952), 28; Leonard Mustazza, "The Machine Within: Mechanization, Human Discontent, and the Genre of Vonnegut's 'Player Piano,'" *Papers on Language and Literature* 25 (1989): 104–5; Naomi Ritter, *Art as Spectacle: Images of the Entertainer since Romanticism* (Columbia: University of Missouri Press, 1989), 44–47; Douglas Kahn, *Noise, Water, Meat: A History of Sound in the Arts* (Cambridge, MA: MIT Press, 1999), for discussion of the connections between artists, engineers and instruments.

31. Mike Montgomery, "Cook Interview," reprinted in Ginny and Bob Billings, *The Billings Rollography*, vol. 5 (Reno, NY: Rock Soup Press, 1994), 45.

32. Letter from J. Lawrence Cook dated 6 July 1953, reproduced online at www.mmdigest.com/MMMedia/fatswaller1.html.

33. *Buffalo Courier-Express*, June 27, 1975, reprinted in *Billings Rollography*, vol. 5, 141.

34. *Billings Rollography*, vol. 5, 143.

Epilogue

1. Timothy Day, *A Century of Recorded Music: Listening to Musical History* (New Haven, CT: Yale University Press, 2000), 77 (see preface, n. 6).

2. Larry Givens, *Re-Enacting the Artist* (Vestal, NY: Vestal Press), 3.

3. Syracuse University Library, Melville Clark Collection, Box 25.

4. *Musical Courier*, February 11, 1903.

5. Day, *Century of Recorded Music*, 229.

6. Quoted in Kerry Segrave, *Jukeboxes: An American Social History* (Jefferson, NC: McFarland & Co., 2002), 41.

7. Segrave, *Jukeboxes*, 46.

8. "No Hands," *Time*, June 22, 1962.

9. "No Hands".

10. "No Hands".

11. Jürgen Hocker, "My Soul is in the Machine: Conlon Nancarrow—Composer for Player Piano, Precursor of Computer Music," in *'I Sing the Body Electric': Music and Technology in the 20th Century*, ed. Hans-Joachim Braun, 84–96 (Hofheim, Germany: Wolke Verlag, 2000), 86.

12. Hocker, "My Soul is in the Machine".

13. Quoted in Kyle Gann, *The Music of Conlon Nancarrow* (Cambridge: Cambridge University Press, 1995), 43; see also Peter Garland, *Americas: Essays on American Music and Culture, 1973–1980* (Santa Fe: Soundings Press, 1982).

14. Emily Thompson, *The Soundscape of Modernity: Architectural Acoustics and the Culture of Listening in America 1900–1933* (Cambridge, MA: MIT Press, 2002, 131 (see chap. 1, n. 12).

15. Trevor Pinch and Karin Bijsterveld, "Sound Studies: New Technologies and Music," *Social Studies of Science* 34 (2004): 635–48.

16. Paul D. Lehrman, "Moving Pictures," *Sound on Sound*, September 2002, www.soundonsound.com/sos/sep02/articles/balletmecanique.asp.

17. For more information see www.antheil.org.

Selected Bibliography

Abbott, Lynn, and Doug Seroff. *Out of Sight: The Rise of African American Popular Music 1889–1895*. Jackson: University Press of Mississippi, 2002.

Adorno, Theodor W. *Essays on Music*, ed. Richard Leppert, trans. Susan Gillespie. Berkeley: University of California Press, 2002.

Badger, Reid. *A Life in Ragtime: A Biography of James Reese Europe*. Oxford: Oxford University Press, 1995.

Badrock, Arthur. "The (Second) English Parlophone Race Series." *Talking Machine Review* 89 (Spring 1995): 2779–81.

Baker, Houston. *Modernism and the Harlem Renaissance*. Chicago: University of Chicago Press, 1987.

Braun, Hans Joachim, ed. *"I Sing the Body Electric": Music and Technology in the 20th Century*. Hofheim, Germany: Wolke Verlag, 2000.

Brown, Scott. *James P. Johnson: A Case of Mistaken Identity; A James P. Johnson Discography 1917–1950*. New Brunswick: Rutgers University Press, 1986.

Burden, James Renel. "Conversation with Joe Turner: 'Last of the Stride Pianists.'" *The Black Perspective in Music* 9 (1981): 183–92.

Collins, Harry. *Artificial Experts: Social Knowledge and Intelligent Machines*. Cambridge, MA: MIT Press, 1990.

Cook, Jean Lawrence. "Autobiography," reprinted in *The Billings Rollography*, vol. 5, by Ginny Billings and Bob Billings, 27–40. Reno, NV: Rock Soup Press, 1994.

Davin, Tom. "Conversations with James P. Johnson," *The Jazz Review* (1959), reprinted in *Ragtime: Its History, Composers, and Music*, ed. John Edward Hasse, 166–77. New York: Schirmer Books, 1985.

Day, Timothy. *A Century of Recorded Music: Listening to Musical History.* New Haven and London: Yale University Press, 2000.

Dolge, Alfred. *Pianos and Their Makers*, vol. 2. Vestal, NY: Vestal Press, 1913.

Gann, Kyle. *The Music of Conlon Nancarrow.* Cambridge: Cambridge University Press, 1995.

Givens, Larry. *Re-Enacting the Artist: A Story of the Ampico Reproducing Piano.* Vestal, NY: Vestal Press, 1970.

Gracyk, Theodore, "Adorno, Jazz and the Aesthetics of Popular Music," *Musical Quarterly* 76 (1992), 532–33.

Grew, Sydney. "The Player-Piano," *Music and Letters* 6 (1925): 236–47.

Hasse, John Edward, ed. *Ragtime: Its History, Composers, and Music.* New York: Schirmer Books, 1985.

Hocker, Jürgen. "My Soul is in the Machine: Conlon Nancarrow—Composer for Player Piano, Precursor of Computer Music," in *"I Sing the Body Electric": Music and Technology in the 20th Century*, ed. Hans-Joachim Braun, 84–96. Hofheim, Germany: Wolke Verlag, 2000.

Jay, Martin. *Adorno.* Cambridge, MA: Harvard University Press, 1984.

Jordan, John. *Machine-Age Ideology: Social Engineering and American Liberalism 1911–1939.* Chapel Hill: University of North Carolina Press, 1994.

Kahn, Douglas. *Noise, Water, Meat: A History of Sound in the Arts.* Cambridge, MA: MIT Press, 1999.

Kasson, John. *Amusing the Millions: Coney Island at the Turn of the Century.* New York: Hill & Wang, 1978.

Katx, Mark. *Capturing Sound: How Technology Has Changed Music.* Berkeley: University of California Press, 2004.

Kobbé, Gustav. *The Pianolist: A Guide for Pianola Players.* New York: Moffat, Yard & Co., 1912.

Leonard, Neil. *Jazz: Myth and Religion.* Oxford: Oxford University Press, 1987.

———. "The Reactions to Ragtime," in *Ragtime: Its History, Composers, and Music*, ed. John Edward Hasse, 102–13. New York: Schirmer Books, 1985.

Levine, Lawrence. *Black Culture and Black Consciousness.* New York: Oxford University Press, 1977.

Loesser, Arthur. *Men, Women and Pianos: A Social History.* New York: Simon & Schuster, 1954.

Martin, Peter. *Sounds and Society: Themes in the Sociology of Music*. Manchester: Manchester University Press, 1995.

McTammany, John. *The Technical History of the Player*. New York: Musical Courier Company, 1915.

Montgomery, Michael, Trebor Tichenor, and John Edward Hasse, "Ragtime on Piano Rolls," in *Ragtime: Its History, Composers and Music*, ed. John Edward Hasse, 90–101. New York: Schirmer Books, 1985.

Montgomery, Mike. "Cook Interview," reprinted in *The Billings Rollography*, vol. 5, by Ginny Billings and Bob Billings, 41–69. Reno, NV: Rock Soup Press, 1994.

Mustazza, Leonard. "The Machine Within: Mechanization, Human Discontent, and the Genre of Vonnegut's 'Player Piano,'" *Papers on Language and Literature* 25 (1989): 99–110.

Nanry, Charles. "Jazz and Modernism: Twin-Born Children of the Age of Invention," *Annual Review of Jazz Studies* 1 (1982): 146–54.

Newman, Ernest. *The Piano-Player and Its Music*. London: Grant Richards, 1920.

Osman, Colin. "The Camera and the Pianola," *The Pianola* 5 (1993): 1.

Paddison, Max. "The Critique Criticized: Adorno and Popular Music," in *Popular Music 2: Theory and Method*, ed. Richard Middleton and David Horn, 201–18. Cambridge: Cambridge University Press, 1982.

Pinch, Trevor, and Karin Bijsterveld, "Sound Studies: New Technologies and Music," *Social Studies of Science* 34 (2004): 635–48.

Pinch, Trevor, and Frank Trocco. *Analog Days: The Invention and Impact of the Moog Synthesizer*. Cambridge, MA: Harvard University Press, 2002.

Reblitz, Arthur. *The Golden Age of Automatic Musical Instruments*. Woodsville, NH: Mechanical Musical Press, 2001.

Ritter, Naomi. *Art as Spectacle: Images of the Entertainer since Romanticism*. Columbia: University of Missouri Press, 1989.

Roehl, Harvey. *Player Piano Treasury*, 2nd ed. Vestal, NY: Vestal Press, 1973.

Roth, Russell. "The Ragtime Revival: A Critique," *American Quarterly* 2 (1950): 329–39.

Schuller, Gunther. "Rags, the Classics and Jazz," in *Ragtime: Its History, Composers, and Music*, ed. John Edward Hasse. New York: Schirmer Books, 1985.

Segrave, Kerry. *Jukeboxes: An American Social History*. Jefferson, NC: McFarland & Co., 2002.

Shipton, Alyn. *Fats Waller: The Cheerful Little Earful*. London: Continuum, 2002.

Sousa, John Philip. "Menace of Mechanical Music," *Appleton's Magazine* 8 (1906): 278–84.

Sudnow, David. *The Way of the Hand: The Organization of Improvised Conduct*. London: Routledge, 1978.

Thompson, Emily. *The Soundscape of Modernity: Architectural Acoustics and the Culture of Listening in America 1900–1933*. Cambridge, MA: MIT Press, 2002.

Thygesen, Helge. *Black Swan: The Record Label of the Harlem Renaissance*. Radnor, PA: VJM, 1996.

Vonnegut, Kurt. *Player Piano*. New York: Dell, 1952.

Wodehouse, Artis. "Tracing Gershwin's Piano Rolls," in *The Gershwin Style: New Looks at the Music of George Gershwin*, ed. Wayne Schneider, 209–23. Oxford: Oxford University Press, 1999.

Index

"42nd Street" song, 79
88-note players, 49–50
AAIMM (Association des Amis des Instruments et de la Musique Mécanique), 36
accessibility, 19–23, 139, 155, 158
Adorno, Theodore, 162–63
Aeolian Company. *See also* Pianola; "42nd Street" song, 79; Duo-Art player system, 118; French headquarters of, 36; history of, 42–44, 46–48; and idea of musical democracy, 139–40; James P. Johnson's recordings for, 100–1, 135; machines as standards, 153154; marketing campaign of, 109–13; Metrostyle feature, 122, 167; Reginald Reynolds' promotion of player pianos, 125; renewed popularity of player pianos in 1960s, 169; role of arrangers in sound of rolls, 129–30; sales to universities, 146; superiority of piano roll music, 92–94
Aeolian Hall, 100

Aeriol, 46
African American music. *See also specific artists by name*; adoption of European method, 98; and avant-garde performances, 171; concerns over popularity of, 103–8; and freedom of interpretation, 122; importance of piano to, 33; importance of player pianos to ragtime music, 94–95, 100–102; ragtime styles, 99; recreation of by white musicians, 127–18; studying through use of player piano, 137–18; widened market for, 140
Agape Agape, 163
Agony of Modern Music, The, 121
Allan, Maud, 112
American Federation of Musicians, 94, 161
American Piano Company. *See* Ampico
AMICA (Automated Musical Instrument Collector's Association): French equivalent of, 36; meetings

of, 58–63; memorabilia, 9–10;
modern versus vintage players, 173;
overview, 7; role of Richard Reutlinger in founding of, 55
Ampico (American Piano Company):
1920 Carnegie Hall concert, 153;
advertising by, 113, 123; grand
player piano, 59–61; humanization
of player pianos by, 167; market for
African American music, 140;
Rachmaninoff recordings for,
69–70; sales handbook of, 150
"analytical engine", 74
Andrew Sisters, 145
Angelus, 43
Antheil, George, 75, 77, 171–73
Apollo Concert Grand Piano Player,
50–51
Apollo Marking Piano, 51, 84–85
Apollo player piano: advertising for
women, 113; overview, 1, 5;
salesmen, 104; unique design of,
50–51
archives, 10, 29
Arden, Victor, 130, 132
Armstrong, Louis, 16
Artcraft Music Rolls, 79
"Artempo" label, 101, 135
Association des Amis des Instruments
et de la Musique Mécanique
(AAIMM), 36
Automata: during Age of Enlighten-
ment, 31; Le Théâtre des Auto-
mates exhibit, 38–41; in mass
entertainment, 33; in Musée Méca-
nique, 15, 18; from Playland, 11; in
private collections, 25
Automated Musical Instrument
Collector's Association. see
AMICA
Automatic Music Paper Company, 42
Autopiano Company, 109

Babbage, Charles, 73–74
Baker, Bob, 109
Baker, Houston, 106

Baldwin company, 44
band organs, 9, 22–24, 29, 68
Barbary Coast: An Informal History of
the San Francisco Underworld,
The, 12
Barnhart, Anne, 117, 120
Barnhart, Jeff, 117–19
barrel organs, 126
Bartels, Carl, 96
Basin Park Hotel, Arkansas, 28
Bell, Alexander Graham, 92
Benjamin, Walter, 33, 176
Bennett, Tony, 3
Bennett & White, 101
Bent, George, 45
Berkman, Bob, 80–85
Bijsterveld, Karin, 129
Blake, Eubie, 95–96, 99, 128, 148
Blasius & Sons, 92
Bockisch, Karl, 46
Boone, John, 95, 99, 101, 140
Boy Scouts of America, 110
Brooks, Russell, 136–17
Brooks, Shelton, 100
Brown, Theodore, 46
Bruder Fairground Organs, 62
Bull, Lothrop Perkins, 158
Burley, Fletcher, 145
Busoni, Ferruccio, 32, 122, 125, 176

Cable Company, 44
Cahill, Thaddeus, 32
camera obscura, 12
Campbell, S. Brun, 127
Carnegie Hall, 153
Carola Inner Player piano, 44
Carter, Paul, 106
Castle, Irene, 112
Cecilian player, 124
"Celebrity Series" of piano rolls, 82
Century of Recorded Music, A, 166
Chadbourne, Eugene, 147
Chaminade, 93
Chicago Radio Laboratory, 157
Chickering & Sons, 123
Chickering player piano, 67, 123

Chilton, Carroll Brent, 73
Clark, Ernest, 159
Clark, Melville, 48–51, 78, 108–9, 130–31. *See also* Melville Clark Piano Company; QRS Music Technologies
Clark & Co., 49
Clark Music Company, 108. *See also* Melville Clark Piano Company
Clark Orchestra Roll Company, 159
Clark's Trading Post, New Hampshire, 24
classic cars, 64
Clef Club, 94, 101
Cliff House, San Francisco: maintenance of machines, 18–19; overview, 8–12, 15, 24, 57; recreation of Americana, 21
Coinola coin-operated piano, 56
"coin-operating phonographs", 168
collecting, psychology of, 62–64, 66–67
Compact Flash devices, 143
Coney Island, 11, 24–25, 97
Confidential Selling Information, 104–5
Cook, J. Lawrence: attitude toward compositional structure, 152; beginning of career with QRS, 132–34; development of QRS race music department, 137, 140; early life of, 87–91; Fats Waller as student of, 136–37; focus on work of James P. Johnson, 135–36; friendship with Eubie Blake, 95; later career of, 159–64; player piano roll arrangements by, 129–30; recording process, 146–48; renewed popularity of player pianos in 1960s, 169; roll editing process, 83–86
Cook, Jacob Lincoln, 88
Cook, Jean Lawrence, 159
Coots, Danny, 117, 119–20
Copland, Aaron, 170
copyrights, 93–94

Cortot, Alfred, 153
Coupleux brothers, 43
Cowell, Henry, 170
craftsmanship, 16–17, 25, 36, 165
Credence Clearwater Revival, 141
Cremona photoplayer, 24
Crescent Hotel and Spa, Arkansas, 27
Crucifix, The, 87
Cunningham player piano, 145

Daubeny, Ulric, 156
Day, Timothy, 166
De Pachmann, Vladimir, 124
De Vaucanson, Jacques, 40
"De-Assification of Music, The" pamphlet, 73
"degeneration theory", 105
democratization of music, 153–64
Deutsches Museum, Munich, 17
"difference engine", 74
digitization of player pianos, 2–4, 141–42, 173
Disney, Walt, 21–22
Disneyland, 11, 21–23, 26, 28–29
Dolan, Richard, 1–5
Dolan, Terry, 142–43
Dolge, Alfred, 51–53, 130
drafting-board technique, 51
Drake's Dancing Class, 99
Drehobl Bros. Art Glass, 16
Du Bois, W.E.B., 101
Duo-Art player system, 100, 118, 125, 140, 153
Dyer, Julian, 157
Dynaline system, 51

Edison, Thomas, 16, 92–93
educational value of mechanical music: in modern times, 141–44; overview, 138–41; pianists helped by, 144–48
Edward, Prince of Wales, 78
electrocardiograms, 78
Ellington, Duke, 144
"Entertainer, The", 121
ethnic music, 72

Ets-Hokin, Jeremy, 11
Etude, The, 95
Euphona pianos, 44
Eureka Springs, Arkansas, 27
Europe, James Reese, 94, 98, 101
"Every Collector's Dream" story,
    65–66
expression player pianos, 47

Fisherman's Wharf, San Francisco, 14
Flanagan, Tommy, 145
"Four Essays on Collecting", 66
Fourneaux, Jean Louis, 39, 41–43

Gaddis, William, 163
Gage, B. M., 110
Garcia, Ken, 13
Gavioli fairground organ, 24
Gavioli organ factory, 36
Geppert, William, 31, 111
Gershwin, George: keyboard ability of,
    128; "Rialto Ripples" piano rag,
    63; roll recording by, 94
Gershwin Plays Gershwin CD, 128
Giannini, Bruto, 98, 100
Givens, Larry, 8, 22, 66–68
Gotham & Attucks, 99–100
"Graduola" lever, 92
gramophones, 155–56, 168
grand player pianos, 50–51
Great Depression, 11, 20, 156, 168
Grew, Sydney, 155
Gulbransen-Dickinson company, 44

Haines, Francine, 91
Haines Normal and Industrial Insti-
    tute, Georgia, 90–91, 95
Harlem, New York, 33, 100, 106, 110,
    136, 138
harmoniums, 42
Harney, Ben, 99
Hatch, Robert A., 35–36, 39–40
Hathaway, Terry, 21
Haydn, Joseph, 126
health effects of music, 107–9
Hell's Kitchen, New York, 86, 97, 101

Henderson, Douglas, 79
Henderson, Fletcher, 144
His Master's Voice, 74–75
"Holding the Mirror to Nature"
    brochure, 51–52
Horowitz, Vladimir, 83, 85
Houston, Scott, 141–43
Hughes, Langston, 102
Hupfeld Phonoliszt Violinas, 24
Hurd, Walter, 168

inner player pianos, 46
internal player pianos, 46
International Music Festival, 169
Ives, Charles, 171
Ivory & Gold, 117

J. P. Seeburg KT (Seeburg Eagle) nick-
    elodeon, 16–18
J. T. Wamelink & Son, 112
Jackson, Alva, Dr., 27
Jacquard, Joseph Marie, 40
Jacquard loom, 40–41, 74, 78
Jacquet-Droz, Henri-Louis, 32
Jacquet-Droz, Pierre, 32
Janzen, Franz, 96
Jazz: and commercialization, 162–63;
    educational value of mechanical
    music, 144–45; and modernism,
    105–8; preserving artist's intentions
    through recording, 120–22; trans-
    lation to medium of player piano,
    94–95; value of ragtime to, 151–52
Jazz Age, 106
Johnson, Aston, 125
Johnson, J. Rosamond, 101
Johnson, James P.: attitude toward
    compositional structure, 152;
    career with Aeolian Company,
    100–101; early life of, 96–100; as
    idol of J. Lawrence Cook, 135;
    influence on other pianists, 144; as
    mentor of Fats Waller, 136–37;
    opinion of Gershwin's ability, 128
Joplin, Scott, 99–101, 121, 127, 145
Jouets et Automates Francais, 36

jukeboxes, 20, 56, 67, 158, 161–62, 168
Jungles Casino, The, 99

Klugh, Paul, 44
Knott's Berry Farm, California, 21, 23–24
Kobbé, Gustav, 114, 139–40, 150
Kortlander, Max, 132–34, 137, 159, 163

Laffing Sal, 14–15
Lamarr, Hedy, 75, 77
Laney, Lucy Craft, 91
Las Vegas, 1–5, 36
Lawton, Marlene, 63
Le Ballet Mécanique, 77, 171–72
Le Praxinoscope, 15
Leabarjan perforator, 96
League of Electronic Musical Urban Robots, 172
Lease, John, 96
Léger, Fernand, 172
Lehrman, Paul D., 172
Lem, Stanislaw, 74–75
Levine, Lawrence, 106
Levitzki, Mischa, 153
Liberace, 2, 82–83, 85
Lion King, The, 3
Loesser, Arthur, 111–12
Lomax, Alan, 127

M. Welte & Sons
Deutsches Museum collection, 17
innovations by, 45–47
Welte Philharmonic Salon Model 4, 27
Mackenzie, Compton, 156
Macy's, 169
Maelzel, Johann, 32
Mandelbrot, Benoit, 78
Manns, Augustus, 124
Maple & Co., 124
Marchal, Claude, 36
McEvoy, J. P., 115
McTammany, John: acknowledgement of Clark's innovations, 51; first

player piano design by, 42–43;
marketing of player pianos, 111;
overview, 31, 34; player piano as technological triumph, 149
mechanical birds, 29
Mechanical Music Digest, 22–23, 72, 75, 79, 109, 157
Mechanical Orguinette Company, 42
Mechanimals, 25
Mechantiques, 27, 29
Medding, Mike, 91
Melville Clark Piano Company, 50–51, 106–8, 111, 130–31. See also Story & Clark pianos
memorabilia, 9–10
Mermod Frères German cylinder music box, 29
metronomes, 32
Metrostyle, 48, 50, 93, 122, 167
MIDI (musical instrument digital interface), 172–73
Miles, Floyd, 27
Miles Musical Museum, 27–28
Mills Novelty Company, 12
Mills Violano Virtuoso, 24, 28, 56, 119
Mister Jelly Roll, 127
Modernism and the Harlem Renaissance, 106
Monroe Organ Reed Company, 42
Moog synthesizer, 129
Moore, Bob, 22–23
Morgan, Vincent, 71–72
Morse, Justinian, 41
Morse, Samuel, 77–78
Morton, Ferdinand "Jelly Roll", 91, 98–99
Moszkowski, Moritz, 93
Mozart, Wolfgang Amadeus, 126
Muensterberger, Werner, 62
Mullins, Mazie, 136
Murphy, Dudley, 172
Musée de la Musique Mécanique, Paris, 38–40, 42
Musée des Arts et Métiers, Paris, 38

Musée Mécanique, San Francisco:
deterioration of music rolls, 79;
efforts to save, 12–14; maintenance
of machines, 18–21; new home of,
14–17; overview, 8, 57
music boxes: AAIMM interest in,
36–37; at Disneyland, 21; at Mechantiques, 29; at Musée Mécanique,
8–9, 12–13; pin-barrel, 123;
storage of, 23
"Music for Your Moods" booklet
series, 108
Music Research Foundation, 108
"Music Row", 45
musical instrument digital interface
(MIDI), 172–73
Mutoscope "motion picture" machine,
20

NAMM (National Association of
Music Merchants), 141
Nancarrow, Conlon, 170–71
Nationaal Museum van Speelklok tot
Pierement, 126
National Association of Music
Merchants (NAMM), 141
National Association of Piano Manu-
facturers of America, 45
National Gallery of Art, 172
National Piano Manufacturers Associ-
ation of America, 158
National Player Piano, 19
"Negro Heaven" song, 79
Nevada City, Montana, 24
New Pianola, 46
New York Public Library, 128
Newlandsmith, Ernest, 151
Newman, Ernest, 153
Nickelodeons: finding, 65; KT special,
16–18; lack of appreciation for, 23;
in mass entertainment, 33; modern
cost of, 20–21; warning signs on,
56; "Nostalgic Series" of piano
rolls, 83

O'Banion, Dean, 79
Ohman, Phil, 130, 132

orchestrions: 1916 Seeburg G, 56; at
Crescent Hotel, 28; at Knott's Berry
Farm, 21; overview, 8–9; popu-
larity of, 37; replacement of by
jukeboxes, 67; in Reutlinger collec-
tion, 119; Seeburg Eagle, 16–17; at
St. Louis World's Fair, 45; Trager
collection of, 23–25; at Victorian
Palace, 62
Ord-Hume, Arthur W.J.G., 127

Pacific Phonograph Company, 168
Paderewski, Ignacy Jan, 93–94,
124–25
Pain, Robert, 46
"parlor houses", 12
Pascal, Blaise, 38
Peerless player piano, 66
perforating machines, 96
Persichetti, Vincent, 144–45
Petrillo, James Caesar, 161–62
Phantom of the Opera, 3
phonographs, 29, 51, 92–93, 107,
123, 158–62
photoplayers, 24, 56, 58, 87, 122
Pianista, 35, 39, 41–42, 46
Pianista Automatique, 41
piano mécanique, 9
piano pneumatique, 41–42
Pianola: as brand name, 31; educa-
tional value of, 139–40; marketing
of, 108–14; and perpetuation of
interpretations, 122; popularity of,
43–47
Pianolin, 65
Pianolist, The, 114
pianolists, 47–48
Pianomation system, 141
Pier 45, San Francisco, 14
Pijper, Willem, 129
Pinch, Trevor, 129
player banjo machines, 24
Player Piano, 163
"Player Piano Upstairs, The", 115
player-grands, 50–51
Playland, San Francisco, 11, 15, 21

Pleasants, Henry, 121
Pletcher, Thomas, 104–5, 131–32, 157–59
Pope Leo XIII, 111
Popper, Hugo, 46
Porter, Dorothy, 10, 12–13, 59–60, 69
Pratt, Waldo Selden, 166
preservation, 19–25
Pruett, Hubert, Dr., 151–52
psychology of collecting, 62–64, 66–67
"push-up players", 39, 42–43, 45–47, 50, 124

QRS Music Technologies: *Confidential Selling Information* booklet, 104; and cultural change, 157–62; "Dada" exhibit, 172; development of race music department, 137, 140; first African American recordings by, 95; history of, 130–32; J. Lawrence Cook's work for, 132–35; lyric rolls by, 72–74; modern player piano technology, 142–43; modern roll production, 79–83; piano rolls sold at Disneyland, 22; recording and editing process, 84–86; renewed popularity of player pianos in 1960s, 169; retrofitted pianos, 3; success of, 150

"race labels", 135, 140
Rachmaninoff, Sergi, 69–72, 98, 141, 143
radio, 157–158, 160–62, 168
ragtime: changed attitudes toward, 93; development of, 97–101; and ethnicity in recordings, 127–28; features designed for player pianos, 146–47; freedom of interpretation, 117–22; lyric rolls, 73; in mass entertainment, 33; overview, 1, 3; popularity of and player pianos, 94–95, 97; as source of controversy, 103–7; value of to jazz, 151–52

Raney, Albert Clifford, 21–23, 26, 29
Raney, Ruby, 21
Ray, Man, 172
Raynaud, Emile, 15
Reblitz, Arthur, 29, 62, 157, 176
Rebuilding the Player Piano, 8, 22, 66
Reid, Ira, 33
Remick & Co., 94
"rent parties", 33
reproducing pianos, 45–47
retrofitted pianos, 2–4, 141–42
Reutlinger, Richard, 55–62, 117–19, 122–23
Reynolds, Reginald, 124–25
Rhodes, Robbie, 75
Riverview Amusement Park, Chicago, 24
Roberts, Luckey, 99, 128
Roehl, Harvey, 65–66
Roehl, Marion, 65
Roell, Craig, 45
Roenigk, Elise, 27–28
Roenigk, Martin, 26–28, 176
roll editing, 84–85
roll-perforating machines, 80–81
Roosevelt, Theodore, 56, 109
Roseland Park, Canandaigua, New York, 22
Roth, Russell, 127
Rouillé, Philippe, 36, 42
Royal Academy of Music, 146
royalties, 93–94

Salon Carousels, 62
San Gabriel River Freeway, 21
Sanfilippo, Jasper, 62–63
Schauffler, Robert Haven, 138–39
Schnabel, Artur, 167
Schuller, Gunther, 98, 121
Seeburg, 28, 56, 67
Seeburg Eagle nickelodeon, 16–18
Seeburg orchestrion, 23, 28, 56, 62, 67
Seeburg player piano, 12, 21
Segrave, Kerry, 168
Serinette music box, 37
Seytre, Claude-Felix, 41

Shaw, George Bernard, 151
Sherman Clay, 18
Sinatra, Frank, 145
Singer, Eric, 172
Sissle, Noble, 95
Snowhill Institute, Alabama, 90
Souls of Black Folk, The, 101
Spaeth, Sigmund, 92, 158
Standard Music Roll Company, 92, 94
Standard Pneumatic Action Company, 108, 113
Starr Piano Company, 113
Steinway piano, 33, 100, 111, 118, 120
Story, Hampton, 49, 131, 158
Story & Camp, 49
Story & Clark Pianos: beginnings of, 49; and cultural change, 162; Dyna-line, 154; financial difficulties during 1930s, 158; production process, 130–31; QRS music rolls for, 140; retrofitted pianos, 2; use of pianos in education institutions, 111
Straight, Charlie, 73
Stravinsky, Igor, 93–94, 169, 171
stride, 100–101, 106, 146–47, 151, 166
Sudnow, David, 151
Suisman, David, 93
Sullivan, Bill, 22
Sullivan, Emmet, 27

Tangley roll-operated Calliaphone, 24
Tatum, Art, 147
telescopic cameras, 75–76
Thomas, Theodore, 104
Thompson, Emily, 156
Tick, Ramsi, 80, 82, 84
Tin Pan Alley, New York, 45, 86, 92, 100
Titan Hot 7, 117
Titanic (movie), 3
Titanic (ship), 27
torpedo guidance systems, 77
tracker bars, 47–48

Trager, Tim, 10–11, 23–26, 29, 62, 176
Tremaine, Henry, 42
Tremaine, William, 42
Triquet, Henri, 38
"Turkish chess player", 32
Turner, Joe, 144
Tuttle, John, 109

"Universal Music Reader", 73

Van Dyke, Henry, Dr., 105
vaudeville theater, 33, 55, 95, 99
Vestal Press, 65–66
Victor Records, 164
Victor Talking Machine Company, 44, 92
Violin-Virtuosos, 38
Virginia City, Montana, 7, 24, 55
Vonnegut, Kurt, 163
Votey, Edwin, 43

Wabash Avenue, Chicago, 45
Waller, Lillie Mae, 136
Waller, Maurice, 146
Waller, Thomas "Fats": development of QRS race music department, 137; early life of, 136–37; educational value of mechanical music, 140; recording process, 146–47; rise to fame of, 163–64
Walt Disney Corporation, 11, 14, 19, 21–23, 26
Walt Disney World, 22–23
Waters, Ethel, 144
Waxman, Franz, 169
Weber, Max, 33, 110, 162, 176
Weber Piano Company, 110
Weight of Evidence, The, 139
Welte, Edwin, 46
Welte Philharmonic Salon Model 4, 27
Welte-Mignon reproducing piano, 45–47, 93, 123–124
Wendling, Pete, 57
Werner player piano, 24
West, James, 110

"What is rhythm?" educational cate-
    chism, 106–107
Whitney, George, Sr., 11–12, 15
Wilcox & White Co., 45
Williams, Mary Lou, 145
Wodehouse, Artis, 128
women, marketing to, 111–14
"Word to the Cultured Woman, A",
    113
World War I, 109–10
Wurlitzer, 22–24, 29, 56, 66, 68, 131
Wurlitzer 125 military band organ, 68

Wurlitzer orchestrion, 62
Wurlitzer photoplayer, 24, 56, 58
Wurlitzer Pianino, 66
Wurlitzer-style 32 Concert PianOrch-
    estra, 21–24, 26, 29
W.W. Kimball company, 44

Young, Francis, 47

Zelinski, Dan, 15–21
Zelinski, Edward, 11–12, 16, 18,
    20–21, 176
Zenith Corporation, 157–58